Katherine .
Schneider
Grantham

CHANGING
H·A·B·I·T·S

CHANGING
H·A·B·I·T·S

A Memoir of
the Society of the
Sacred Heart

VVHarrison

DOUBLEDAY

New York   London   Toronto   Sydney   Auckland

All the photos herein are reprinted by permission of the Archives of the Society of the Sacred Heart, St. Louis, Missouri, except the following: the photos of Mother Marie Thérèse de Lescure and of the two nuns in transition habits are reprinted by permission of Stone Ridge Country Day School Archives, Bethesda, Maryland; the photo of the students at Hope Rural School is reprinted by permission of Robert Glick/People Weekly © 1986 Time Inc. All rights reserved.

Quotation from "Treasure of Love" by Joe Shapiro and Lou Stallman © 1956 Unichappell Music, Inc., Rightsong Music Inc. (Renewed). All Rights Reserved. Used by Permission.

Published by Doubleday, a division of Bantam Doubleday Dell Publishing Group, Inc., 666 Fifth Avenue, New York, New York 10103

"Doubleday" and the portrayal of an anchor with a dolphin are trademarks of Doubleday, a division of Bantam Doubleday Dell Publishing Group, Inc.

DISPLAY TYPOGRAPHY AND BINDING DESIGN BY CAROL MALCOLM

Library of Congress Cataloging-in-Publication Data

Harrison, V. V., 1942–
Changing habits : a memoir of the Society of the Sacred Heart /
V.V. Harrison.
p.   cm.
Includes index.
ISBN 0-385-24849-0
1. Society of the Sacred Heart—History.   2. Harrison, V.V.,
1942–   . I. Title.
BX4436.H37   1988b   88-25632
271'.93—dc19   CIP

November 1988
First Edition
BG

To my mother,
VIRGINIA WATTS HARRISON,
and to the memory of my father,
CYRIL R. HARRISON

When the battle rages fiercest
Round the standard of our King,
Let us closer press unto Him
Louder, clearer, let us sing.

Jesus be our King and Leader
Grant us in Thy toils a part,
Are we not Thy chosen soldiers
Children of Thy Sacred Heart.

— *Children of the Sacred Heart*
Traditional Sacred Heart Hymn

A·C·K·N·O·W·L·E·D·G·M·E·N·T·S

There are many people whose support, encouragement, and generosity made this book possible. My editor, Nan A. Talese, offered the opportunity, provided the guidance, and lent her practiced eye and wise insight to every page. Gail Buchicchio and Signe Warner Watson were invaluable in their separate but essential roles. Sister Anne Dyer was there from the beginning and was a constant source of inspiration. To Professor A. E. Claeyssens, Sister Marie Louise Carmody, Sister Mary Elizabeth Tobin, Grace Schrafft, and my friends in Washington whose faith and friendship never wavered, I owe a tremendous debt of gratitude. Barbara Flanagan added her exceptional talents as manuscript editor. My sister, Lee Harrison Child, and my nieces, Downing, Courtenay, and Anna, provided the irreplaceable ingredient of unconditional love. Thanks are also due to the numerous people who spoke with me and shared their memories of and observations about the Sacred Heart experience.

C·O·N·T·E·N·T·S

CHANGING
H·A·B·I·T·S

P·R·O·L·O·G·U·E

AT ONE TIME the scene was played out in Sacred Heart convents and schools all over the world. White faces bowed, framed by starched fluting, smooth alabaster hands cradled prayer books, pale lips moved in unison, turning cold Latin phrases into sweet a cappella music: nuns singing their morning Office at dawn.

"Deus in adjutorum intende," the familiar chant began, continuing until the stained-glass chapel windows brightened with sunlight.

At 7:15, when morning Office ended, the children in the boarding school marched into chapel, genuflected, and moved silently into dark, wooden pews. The nuns who had remained in the school to assist in the children's morning ritual bobbed their heads respectfully as they passed Reverend Mother and slid gracefully into their choir stalls along the chapel walls to await the beginning of Mass.

"In nomine Patris, et Filii, et Spiritus Sancti." The priest began the Mass, his silk chasuble in the color of the season — white for holidays, purple for Lent, and pink for Laetare Sunday — covering his black soutane and clerical collar. Some of the children made the Sign of the Cross haphazardly; others, following the nuns' lead, carefully hit the middle of the forehead, center of the chest, and the farthest point of each shoulder.

At communion time, the nuns led the children to the altar rail. Veils pulled forward to shield their faces, cuffs of their habits turned down to cover folded hands, they knelt in black solidarity like birds on a telephone wire, suspended from all human activity save prayer.

The children knelt to receive the host with varying degrees of reverence. Then they rose and squeaked back into their seats, their stomachs grumbling as breakfast smells drifted in from the kitchen.

The nuns remained kneeling, oblivious to all distractions. Some buried their faces in their hands in private supplication, others lifted their eyes to the tabernacle and moved their lips in open adoration.

They seemed the personification of perfection, those "brides of Christ." On their knees or on duty in the classrooms, they exuded a special brand of holiness, tranquillity, and dignity; but more, they represented to the children in the convent schools, with whom they shared their daily lives, an unwavering example of God's thought, word, and deed. They were tangible evidence of the Word made flesh, and the children were ever mindful, although not always appreciative, of how they dwelt among them.

In the nuns' refectory, where the nuns ate their meals cloistered from the rest of the world, silence was enforced except in the case of the nun who read a spiritual passage aloud during the meal. While Reverend Mother and her assistants took their places at the head of the table, the other nuns stood, hands folded waist high, waiting to be seated for the small meal that would take fifteen minutes to consume. When breakfast was over, the superior proceeded out of the refectory to begin Little Words, a time when permissions were granted or denied to the nuns who asked for them: a late sleep, an opportunity to stay up after night prayers, a request to write a letter or do extra penance. Requests for permissions were a familiar and important routine for the nuns, who had willingly submitted to the peculiar demands of religious life. It was not an easy life, nor was it meant to be. It was one that few understood and even fewer experienced, but for those who did, an indelible impression was left, one that haunted some and inspired others.

Today, as evening settles over Stone Ridge Country Day School of the Sacred Heart in Bethesda, Maryland, the nuns ready themselves for Liturgy. The doors of the chapel are closed, for tonight Liturgy will be held on the sun porch.

Their day's work completed, a dozen or so women mingle in the spacious glassed-in porch awaiting the priest. When he arrives wearing a navy blue blazer and open-collar shirt, they greet him by his first name, Joe.

The nuns are dressed in slacks, skirts, colorful turtlenecks, and sweaters. Some wear tasseled loafers with knee socks. As they chat amicably with Joe, they look more like an advertisement for L. L. Bean than a religious community.

Within a few minutes the conversation begins to wind down and Joe moves toward the couch at the far end of the room. He removes his jacket to reveal short sleeves and reaches for the priestly stole, kissing it before placing it around his neck. In front of him, on a low glass tabletop, is a chalice made of clay, a large platter, a small pitcher of water, and a bowl. One of the nuns lights two white candles on a side table as the other nuns begin to take their places on chairs and sofas around the room. A nun in a gray flannel skirt and high-heeled shoes pulls a record from its cover. Liturgy is about to begin.

They sit in silence listening to a folk song about God, Joe with bowed head and eyes shut, the others in a variety of prayerful poses, comfortably at ease with the mini-Mass they describe as "more relevant to the times."

When it's communion time on the sun porch, a nun gets up to begin passing the platter of consecrated wafers, then the chalice, around the room. The nuns remain seated as they each pick up a wafer from the platter as if it were an hors d'oeuvre and then wash it down with a swig of wine.

Before the final blessing they all rise and recite the Lord's Prayer. Liturgy ends with the nuns calling out in loud, effusive voices, "Thanks, Joe," the priest nodding his head to acknowledge their appreciation.

Dinner is announced promptly, and Joe takes his place in the buffet line, moving with the nuns past baskets of fresh bread and bowls of green salad that will accompany the main course, quiche.

They sit at tables of eight in the dimly lit dining room, which bears little resemblance to the refectory it once was. The photographs of severe-looking superiors have been taken down, the rule of silence is gone, so too the spiritual reading and the improvisatory sign language that accompanied mealtime in the cloister.

The Stone Ridge community today is representative of the new, liberated religious life that has recently been sanctioned by the Catholic Church and embraced by the Society of the Sacred Heart. The women from the chapels of yesterday have traded their austere, cloistered, monastic life for a contemporary one. They do not have husbands or children, but they do contend with most of life's other pleasures and pains. No longer bound to the Spartan, sometimes brutal restrictions of convent life, they have choices and freedoms never dreamed possible twenty years ago.

In the swing of change since the Second Vatican Council in the early 1960s, many of the old, well-known traditions that were identified with the Society of the Sacred Heart, its schools, and its way of life for more than one hundred and sixty years have vanished. In the transition, many beloved Sacred Heart nuns who balked at trading their wimples for turtlenecks, their contemplative life for an apostolic one, also vanished from the Society.

The period of adjustment following the changes and experimentation called for by Vatican II forced women who had unconditionally given themselves to God to engage in intense reevaluation and soul-searching. Many found themselves at a crossroads far more challenging and confusing than the one they faced initially in deciding to join the Society. To remain in the Society in the new, open, untried environment of modernity was for many even more difficult than following the rigorous medieval obligations of the past. For what had previously been imposed and unquestioningly accepted suddenly became a personal choice. Those who had not internalized the discipline of the cloistered life found themselves in real distress and conflict when the restrictions and safeguards of their religious lives were lifted.

What happened to the Mothers of the Sacred Heart is indicative of what happened to the Catholic Church and to this country in the mid-1960s. It was a period of major upheaval, personal uncertainty, and general turmoil.

Changing Habits is the story of how the absolute strictures of one religious order dissolved and dramatically affected a worldwide community of seven thousand nuns on five continents as well as the many generations of women whose lives those nuns had touched deeply.

The Long Approach

1

I WAS BAPTIZED a Catholic because my father was baptized one. My mother was a Protestant, and like many others who entered mixed marriages in the early 1940s, she willingly conceded the religious training of their children to her Catholic mate. Although they were both northerners, my parents chose to live in South Carolina, where in the early fifties less than one percent of the population was Catholic. As a result my sister and I grew up in a religious environment that was isolated and independent from all our other childhood experiences. It was the single area in our lives in which our mother did not participate and which our friends did not share.

In Camden, South Carolina, the Catholic church was by far the smallest, both in structure and in membership. Built by a woman of means for her Irish servants in the mid-1920s, the church occupied a piece of prime real estate on a wide, tree-lined street in a residential section of town. Its red tile roof, white stucco exterior, and Spanish design made it unique in a community rich in Confederate history and marked by colonial architecture. The bell in the tower atop the church rang out on Lyttleton Street just before Mass every Sunday and came to symbolize for me an hour of torture and, later, guilt.

Each time my father drove by the church, known as Our Lady of Perpetual Help, he doffed his soft brown hat out of respect for the Blessed Sacrament, which resided inside. This gesture of humility and reverence embarrassed me whenever I witnessed it, whether riding with him alone in the car or with a group of my friends in the back seat. Always I hoped he would choose a route that bypassed the church or forget to wear his hat. He seldom did either. My father was a gentleman of the old school and a strict conformist about his religion. Although his manner was easygoing and boyish, there was nothing frivolous about his faith.

When I questioned him on the origins of the hat-tipping habit, he explained that as a boy who loved horses growing up in New York City, he had watched in awe as skilled firemen with hands full of reins drove horse-drawn engines full speed down Fifth Avenue. On reaching Fiftieth Street they reflexively switched all the reins to one hand and tipped their caps in front of St. Patrick's Cathedral.

"That really impressed me," he said.

It impressed me too, but I could not help wishing he had left the custom in New York and not brought it with him to South Carolina, where Catholicism stood out like a Yankee accent. If the truth be known, I wished he had left his religion there too. But my father was unashamed of his devotion to the Church and my embarrassment was not going to prevent him from acknowledging it.

The first time I attended Mass with him, my eyes could barely see over the pew in front of us. In those days the parish was too small for a Sunday school or any other children's activities. There were no mite boxes, no Christmas pageants, no choir. Our Lady of Perpetual Help was a no-frills church that seemed aptly named. When I knelt on the hard, unpadded kneeler I had to strain to see the white-haired priest in colorful vestments moving briskly up and down the white marble stairs. Above the altar was a sparkling mosaic of Our Lady of Perpetual Help with butterflies fluttering around her head. At the side altars, chipped plaster statues of Mary holding the Baby Jesus and of Joseph holding a lily faced the double set of polished benches fashioned out of darkened pine. There were two cast-iron tables holding small red jars with flickering votive candles near the altar rail and a small confessional behind a grilled partition. I took particular interest in the strange copper-plated devices screwed to the back of each pew, designed to hold collection envelopes and men's hats. The priest was followed about the altar by two small boys dressed in mini-vestments. The boys brought things to the priest and then took them away for no apparent reason. The words they said were strange and mystifying. I had only a vague idea of what was taking place as the priest raised first a gold cup and then a large white circular object while bells rang out and people bowed their heads.

My father seemed completely at ease with the curious celebration and attempted to whisper explanations in my ear as the Mass moved on at an interminable, slow-motion pace.

The confusion and curiosity I experienced during my first encounter with the odd drama wore off quickly, especially when I learned from my father that going to Mass was not a one-shot deal like going to the circus but was an event I would be obliged to attend every Sunday for the rest of my life. Not long afterward I began to develop a real aversion to Sunday and its unsolicited obligation.

On Sunday mornings, our household woke to the aromas of pancakes, coffee, syrup, and sausages, and movement was slower and less frenetic than on the other days of the week. But I felt anger and outrage. I knew I would soon be forced to dress in clothes I detested, including a bonnet (women of all ages were still required to cover their heads in church), and forced to endure the silence and seriousness of Mass. Tantrums, tears, and threats often preceded my arrival at church. Few of my friends were forced to go to Sunday school every week, and when they were, they sat in sunny classrooms cutting out colorful pictures and listening to Bible stories; and they were rewarded with juice and cookies at the end. I, on the other hand, sat on a hard wooden bench, my red eyes fixed on the backs of unfamiliar heads, as bells rang out, collection baskets were passed, and people lined up to receive the small white host on their tongues while the priest murmured the words *"Corpus Christi."* My father said that the latter part was called communion and the little white host was the Body and Blood of Our Lord. He also told me that soon, when I had learned enough about being a Catholic, I would be able to receive communion like everyone else. Unlike most young Catholic girls of my era, who looked forward to dressing in white, clasping a prayer book, and smiling for their first communion photograph, I did not find the prospect at all appealing. It was a strange introduction to religion.

Attending Mass every Sunday after the first time was like watching an incomprehensible movie over and over again. I knew every line, every movement, what was coming next, but I did not understand the plot.

The sun streamed into the tiny church through stained-glass windows whose shapes, colors, and pictures I came to know as well as the photographs in my own scrapbook. Father Burke's flamboyant alto voice bounced off the terra-cotta walls into my small ears. He stood at the pulpit, his face turning red as both the church and his sermon heated up. My father listened attentively, his hands neatly folded in his lap, his legs uncrossed, his back pressed firmly against the pew. I squirmed beside him. Occasionally I pulled back the cuff of his soft white shirt to inspect his watch, wishing I was some-where, anywhere, else.

"And so, my dear friends, be about the Lord's work," Father Burke would shout as his hand slammed down on the open book in front of him. "Beat the devil at his own game, for if you don't he will surely claim you on the Day of Judgment."

Father Burke, as it turned out, was quite a character. A man of many charms, he was greatly beloved not only by his own flock but by the community at large — no small accomplishment for a Catho-lic priest in a small southern town. As a young man he had left home and joined the navy. It was rumored that he had once been connect-ed with the theater in New York and had been quite the man about town before he became a man of the cloth. He played the piano, liked good whiskey, and relished evenings with friends sharing a simple meal and singing Broadway tunes. In the afternoons, when weather permitted, we could see him pacing the lawn in front of the church, wearing his Roman collar and reading his breviary.

His small white house was on the church grounds. It was pristine without and very dark within. Cracked oil paintings of ships being tossed in high seas were hung on the paneled living room walls. Old books with strange titles and broken spines filled the bookcases. Two glass bottles with ship models inside sat on top of the mantel. Red and green lights fastened to the port and starboard sides of the doorway completed the nautical motif.

I visited the rectory several times with my father and sat on the cool leather sofa in the front room while my father talked with Father Burke in his office. I remember feeling strangely uncomfort-able in the house, perhaps because I knew that the man who lived there was so distinctly different from all the other men I knew. He wore strange clothes and had no family or regular job. And my father said that he never would. He seemed old to have a family, so that part didn't bother me as much as something else my father told me. He said that Father Burke had a special relationship to God, that he knew God in a very personal way. In my mind that was equivalent to being best friends with the tooth fairy or the Easter bunny, who were the only others I knew besides Santa Claus who were invisible and were imbued with mystical powers. This knowledge made me suspect that Father Burke knew a lot more about me than I would have liked, which was more or less confirmed each time I looked into his twinkling blue eyes.

"My little chickadee" was the way he addressed us children. I don't know if the other children got weak-kneed and dry-mouthed when he spoke to them, but I always did. My father treated him differently than he did other adults, more respectfully and more formally. His manner became stiff, his voice got lower and had a serious, somber edge to it when he said, "Yes, Father," or "No, Father," or "See you on Sunday, Father." I never asked why he treated the old priest with such deference or if he shared my eerie suspicion that Father Burke knew a lot more about us than he let on, but I was always glad when our visits ended.

As I grew, so too did the membership of Our Lady of Perpetual Help, especially after the Du Pont company moved to Camden. By the time my sister and I reached the ages of seven and eleven, religious instruction classes for children were instituted. These were held in the church hall, a dismal, depressing building behind the church, with little furniture and insufficient heat. The day we were informed of this additional obligation in our lives, my sister and I both cried. When we learned it was not Sunday school but Friday school we were going to be forced to attend, we screamed. This just seemed too much: another conspiracy to ruin our week. Now along with Mass on Sunday, no meat on Friday, and various other rules of the Church that our father enforced, we had to contend with religious instruction after school on the most anticipated day of the week. So Friday joined Sunday and together they became the most dreaded days in our lives.

The frozen fish we were served every Friday at home was always of the same consistency — white, slimy, and without a hint of flavor. Because it was bony, we had to eat it slowly and carefully, two words that were missing from my vocabulary and my eating habits. I complained bitterly to my mother, who sat at one end of the table and rang the silver bell to ask T.D., the cook, to bring in the ketchup bottle I pleaded for. My father sat at the other end of the table and informed me that eating fish once a week was "good discipline."

"Is it good discipline to choke to death?" I would exclaim, holding my hands around my throat.

"I don't want to be a Catholic anymore," I'd continue. "I want to be an Episcopal." "I want to be a Pistopal too," my sister would chime in. This would be followed by more well-meaning but ineffectual explanations from my father's end of the table and often ended with my dismissal to my room.

Until the introduction of Mass and Friday school into our lives, my sister and I fit snugly into our well-defined world of brown lace-ups and white socks. We went to a tiny private school started by northerners for their children which began at 8:45 in the morning and finished at 12:45 in the afternoon. Most of our friends at school were playmates from birth whose parents socialized with our parents and whose houses nearby provided the same security for us as our own. We had not had many opportunities to venture beyond the boundaries of our own neighborhood. We thought everyone lived the same way we did, wore the same outfits from Best & Company, went to dancing class on Wednesday nights, and rode horses in the afternoons. At Friday school we found out this was a myth.

The other children who attended religious instruction classes with us went to the Camden public school. The girls wore short-sleeved sweaters and full skirts and had home permanents. When they went inside the church they wore lace doilies on their heads while we sported a strange variety of hats pulled in haste from our mother's hatbox, making us look even more out of place than we felt. The Friday school boys wore paratrooper boots and flannel shirts and they knew games and jokes we didn't. Most came from families that said grace at meals and had holy water fonts in their bedrooms and plastic Jesuses on the dashboards of their cars. They knew stories about the lives of saints and words to hymns and prayers we had never heard. We felt painfully alone and out of place.

Each week two parochial school nuns drove thirty-two miles from Columbia, South Carolina, to Camden in a gray Plymouth sedan to instruct us in our religion. I think they were the first nuns any of the Friday school students had ever seen, and this gave us our first common bond; the second was the realization that none of us wanted to be there. The nuns were Sister Deneri, who was tall, thin, and young, and Sister Raphael, who was short, bespectacled, and old, with a hint of a mustache on her upper lip. Sister Deneri took the older group, of which I was a part, and Sister Raphael took the younger ones, which included my sister. I remember the look of horror on Sister Deneri's face when she learned that I had not yet made my first communion, for although my father was punctilious about upholding his own obligations to the Church, he had somehow managed to slip up on mine. Eleven was far past the age of reason, the accepted time for a Catholic child to kneel at the communion rail.

"Well, we must see about that right away," Sister Deneri said and went tripping off toward Father Burke's house.

Within a few months, after an accelerated course in catechism and the art of confession, I was ready to become a bona fide Catholic, although the "bona fide" was questionable.

School Days, Convent Ways

2

FOUR YEARS after my first encounter with nuns in Camden, at the age of fifteen I landed at Eden Hall, a Sacred Heart boarding school in Torresdale, Pennsylvania, on the outskirts of Philadelphia. (No one I have ever met, before, during, or since my school days there, has heard of Torresdale, and to this day I am not exactly sure where it is. For all I know, it could have been in the Twilight Zone. There were times when it certainly felt that way.) Because my route to Eden Hall was such a circuitous one, my father liked to think it was his brother in heaven, Joseph F. X. Harrison, S.J., who guided me there.

My first boarding school had been Garrison Forest, a traditional, nonsectarian girls' school in Maryland. I was dismissed after one year for a poor academic performance. Then I found myself boarding in Charleston, South Carolina, at Ashley Hall, where the atmosphere was as benign as the climate and the girls had long drawls and slim waists. They sauntered from class to class on rundown saddle shoes, breasts bulging underneath angora sweaters emblazoned with fraternity pins, wearing makeup, chewing gum, and harmonizing on songs from the hit parade.

"The treasure of love is easy to find. It's waiting for you if your hearrrrrrt isn't blind. . . ." But I wasn't looking for the treasure of love, I was seeking the hockey fields and tennis courts I had known at Garrison Forest. Of the former there were none, of the latter only one.

The transition was monumental. While Garrison Forest was rural and mildly Yankee, Ashley Hall was urban and distinctly southern. Just as I was learning to interpret Long Island lockjaw, decipher "boarding school print," and appreciate the value of a Brooks Brothers sweater, I was plunged into a southern-fried environment where powder and perfume were topics of debate and two boy-friends were preferable to one. At Garrison Forest the vernacular was based on a Waspy colloquialism. Mothers were called "Mum-my," places of residence "houses," and the single-word greeting was "Hi." At Ashley Hall mothers were "Mama," houses were "homes," and the greeting was "Hey." This was not a complete shock for I had been raised in the South, although in an unorthodox southern town where the ratio of northern to southern residents was uncommonly high. Because my parents were not true southerners, I had a high regard for Yankees, but I had the good sense to keep it to myself when the girls at Ashley Hall talked of carpetbaggers, waved Confederate flags, and sang "Dixie." As a displaced preppie, I found the adjustment difficult and longed to be among my friends in Maryland's Green Spring Valley, with whom I had begun a history. I resented the circumstances that had forced me way below the Ma-son-Dixon line to eat grits, spin 45s, and pretend I was in love with Pat Boone when I was really in love with James Dean. This, coupled with the knowledge that I alone had been responsible for ending my career at Garrison, made my entry into Ashley Hall joyless.

Still, things happened at Ashley Hall that significantly affected my life. One of these was my introduction to rock and roll music, which played on radios and hi-fi's day and night. Because my parents were a decade older than most, I thought Bing Crosby and Dinah Shore were still the king and queen of the music scene. At Ashley Hall I discovered the truth. Elvis Presley had stolen the crown and scepter and along with singers like Bill Haley and Buddy Holly had revolu-tionized the musical tastes of teenagers everywhere. In October 1956, along with many others in the school, I became a slave to rock and roll and a devoted reader of movie magazines like *Photoplay* and *Modern Screen*.

It was also at Ashley Hall that I stopped going to Mass on Sun-day. In the mid-fifties, South Carolina was still considered a mis-sionary district by the Catholic Church. The situation of Catholics in the larger community was reflected in the makeup of the student body at Ash-Can, the name I had given my new school shortly after my arrival. At Garrison Forest the number of Catholic girls had been small; at Ashley Hall there were four of us. So when the Protestants piled into buses on Sunday morning to ride to the churches of their choice, we four set off on foot, without supervision, to ours.

After a few weeks we began leaving Mass early. Soon we avoided it altogether in favor of a nearby drugstore where we mischievously whiled away the hour, smoking cigarettes, reading movie magazines, and sipping cherry Cokes. This routine went along without incident until Ash Wednesday, when we were given permission to skip morning classes to fulfill what we passed off as a "holy day of obligation" and instead were discovered in the drugstore by a teacher from Ashley Hall. She watched in horror as we dipped our thumbs into overflowing ashtrays and made smudge marks on our foreheads.

A phone call from the headmistress to my father prompted a visit from a young Catholic priest to the portals of Ashley Hall. After a lengthy, private chat and the discovery that he shared my admiration for James Dean (at the time I wore a gold medal around my neck, rapidly turning green, with a profile of the dead film star on one side and the words "Jimmy I love you" on the other), I agreed to resume going to Sunday Mass and to become more seriously committed to my religion. Part of that commitment was predicated on a deal I cut with the priest. He agreed to take me to see *East of Eden* and *Rebel Without a Cause* and I agreed to visit the drugstore only after the final blessing had been given from the altar. For the rest of the year I kept my part of the bargain, but the priest never lived up to his. In retaliation I went to see *The Bad Seed*, a movie banned by the Legion of Decency, and I lived in fear and guilt for months afterward.

By this time my father was having serious doubts about whether Ashley Hall was the right school for me. I shared his misgivings, but not for the same reasons. He must have thought it was a miracle at the hands of my uncle when he heard about Eden Hall.

After his brother's death in 1951, my father had become an even more ardent follower of Catholicism and often referred to my Uncle Joe in heaven as the guide who would make a difference in my sister's and my rather shaky Catholic upbringing. He was determined that we be not only practicing Catholics but believers.

And so, in June 1957, after Ashley Hall closed for the summer, I drove with my parents to the place called Torresdale and for the first time viewed the Convent of the Sacred Heart, Eden Hall. In some perverse way, I liked what I saw. For although I had never been near a Catholic school and my exposure to nuns had been limited to Friday school, what I observed that day appealed to me. I was not so much intimidated by the habit as curious to know why anyone would voluntarily get into one.

The summer brightness warmed the cold institutional setting as we walked the grounds of the campus, its vast lawns being manicured by men in denim overalls on small yellow tractors. Colorful flowerbeds framed the swards of green lawn, and the hulking oak trees, heavy with foliage, added tranquillity and stature to the large brownstone building with its sturdy casement windows. Eden Hall looked like a school of substance, and although it did not have the casual ambience of Garrison Forest or the southern comfort of Ashley Hall, it exuded stability and tradition and permanence.

It was not entirely curiosity or perversity that prompted me to decide to change schools for the third time, or the tennis courts and hockey fields I had missed at Ashley Hall, or even the fact that the school was located in the Northeast. It was a combination of all those things in addition to the prospect of three more years in Charleston, South Carolina, where my future seemed inexorably tied to the dreaded dreams of Tara, which I was not suited for and did not desire. The fact that I was probably equally unfit for life in a convent school briefly flashed through my mind as I caught one last glance, through the car window, of the monster fortress with crosses rising from its roof.

It was not hard to imagine Torresdale in its salad days as a town of wealth and sophistication: a vibrant place with expansive lawns, expensive cars in its driveways, and party music floating from its mansions. Perhaps it was because of the Depression or the war or natural attrition, but whatever the reason, at some time Torresdale had tarnished. Its well-heeled residents had left and never returned. Only their large, boarded-up houses overlooking the Delaware River gave proof that it had once been something more than another forgotten, broken, middle-class suburb. Yet because of its imperfections and nostalgic melancholy, Torresdale seemed the perfect locale for a convent boarding school owned and operated by the Society of the Sacred Heart.

When Eaton Hill, a sprawling 120-acre estate once owned by

Commodore John Barry, was purchased by the Society of the Sacred Heart in 1847 and added to the growing number of Sacred Heart schools throughout the world, the Society was less than fifty years old and Madeleine Sophie Barat, its foundress, was still alive. In its early days Eden Hall was not only a school but a working farm. Hayracks and cornfields stood next to playing fields, and in the spring students strained out of classroom windows to see the new calves. Some students came by boat, others by carriage, but they came in droves to be educated by the Madames of the Sacred Heart.

By the time I arrived, the property had been considerably reduced. Farm life had long since been abandoned and the Madames had become Mothers, but even without vegetable gardens and farm animals, Eden Hall appeared a self-contained world, far different from any school I had ever seen or known.

After naming their new school, the nuns had attached a brownstone addition to the original rose stucco mansion. Amid spires and crosses rising from various points of the mansard roof, a silver tower clock stood in singular splendor, striking off the hours in a low, doleful tone. A statue of St. Michael the Archangel, the school's patron saint, occupied a place of honor at one side of the gigantic stone structure, the only man besides the caretaker, Mr. Mooney, allowed to remain permanently on the property. Under his ivy-covered feet a plaque was inscribed: "Michael: Who is like God."

The campus, like life inside the school, varied with the seasons. In the winter it was gray, cold, and isolated, but in spring the sense of isolation melted away into a profusion of color, a joyous recognition of renewal combined with the welcome knowledge that the worst was over. A manmade lake was used for skating parties on the rare occasions when it froze, providing the students with an opportunity to see nuns on skates, moving considerably more gracefully than the penguins on ice they resembled.

In addition to the main building, there was a greenhouse that provided fresh flowers for the parlors and chapel, a lay teachers' cottage, four tennis courts, three hockey fields, a large gymnasium, and a cemetery for the nuns. There was also a house for the Mooney family and a parish school called St. Katherine's, where some members of the Eden Hall religious community taught. At the edge of the school property, an ancient railroad platform was visible. The railroad provided transportation to Philadelphia for Torresdale commuters — and an occasional runaway schoolgirl. It also provided an Eden Hall legend. It seems that during a severe blizzard in 1888 a Pennsylvania Railroad train was stranded by snowdrifts at the bottom of Eden Hall's property. The nuns mounted a rescue effort that saved the lives of hundreds of passengers and crew. Ever after, as a token of gratitude, the trains stopped for the students of Eden Hall. It was also rumored that because the nuns refused to sell the railroad a sufficient amount of property to straighten out a curve in the roadbed, every train was forced to slow down and blow its whistle as it approached the convent. Thus, train whistles and the constant sound of ringing school bells dominated school life.

A macadam strip, known as the Mac Walk, connected the school with the tiny train depot. At vacation time, accompanied by a flock of nuns and tilting from the weight of heavy suitcases, the boarding students marched to trains that would take them to Philadelphia and eventually home for the holidays. No scene is more vividly etched in my memory than that of the black-robed nuns setting a field of white handkerchiefs fluttering in the wind, waving good-bye, as the freedom train pulled out.

Of all the appendages to Eden Hall, none was more beautiful or impressive than the chapel. Central to Sacred Heart school life, the large Gothic chapel with its carved stone altar and yellowish Caen-stone exterior, unlike the buildings it was attached to, was an architectural triumph. It was designed to accommodate the religious, who occupied the single choir stalls along the walls and highbacked pews in back, and the students, who sat on polished wooden benches above unpadded wooden kneelers (leading to the condition "chapel knees," familiar to all Children of the Sacred Heart). Eden Hall's place of worship was awesome and inspiring.

The cornerstone was laid on October 30, 1849, and when construction was completed two years later, it became the first wholly consecrated chapel in the country. A stained-glass window near the altar bore the inscription "Erected by the Religious of the Sacred Heart in memory of Francis Drexel and Elizabeth Bouvier Drexel, his wife." The Stations of the Cross were a gift of Michael Bouvier, a distant relative of Jacqueline Bouvier Kennedy Onassis.

A cool silence radiated within the chapel's interior. Cuts of bright light streaked through the exquisite stained-glass windows, given in memory of prominent Philadelphia families, and fell on the gleaming mahogany floor. The smell of faded incense and fresh flowers lent it the authentic aroma of a House of God.

Three months after my decisive visit to Torresdale, on a memorable September morning, my mother and I wearily stepped from a sleeping car of the Silver Meteor, the train that carried us from Camden, South Carolina, to Thirtieth Street Station in Philadelphia. It was early and we were not expected for registration at Eden Hall until midafternoon. To pass the time and to distract us from the unexpressed apprehension connected with the event that lay ahead, we decided to see a movie.

A sophisticated woman of patrician, Protestant tastes, Mother looked somewhat out of place standing in line at a dilapidated movie house buying two tickets to an 11:00 A.M. film. She looked ready for lunch at the Acorn Club or a shopping spree at Wanamaker's, also on our agenda, but not for sitting in a sparsely filled movie theater watching Tony Curtis do battle with the Vikings.

The scene was equally incongruous as she attempted to make polite conversation with the nuns who greeted us on our arrival at the school. Although she had married a Catholic, Mother looked with suspicion on most Catholics and viewed my going to a Catholic boarding school, notwithstanding the reputation of the Sacred Heart nuns, as *déclassé*.

Neither my mother nor I was versed in the Sacred Heart tradition, and our lack of familiarity only increased our anxiety as we began our second tour of my new home. We walked through the massive main building, which looked a good deal more like a Charles Addams drawing than I remembered from my summer visit, among students, parents, and the ever-present ladies in black, acquiring class schedules, purchasing uniform shoes from a jolly man in a double-breasted maroon suit, and getting my dormitory assignment.

We attempted to locate my blond flip-top desk among a legion of others in the vast study hall, where a statue of Jesus, Sacred Heart exposed, hands extended, loomed above us. Neither of us took much consolation from the number of religious paintings, statues, and images that filled the corridors. It was definitely not Mother's crowd, and I was beginning to suspect it was not mine.

At the age of nine I had gone away to camp for two months in

New Hampshire without experiencing a day of homesickness. As an eighth grader I had arrived at Garrison Forest without parental escort, and although my parents drove me to Ashley Hall, I walked in alone. Now it was as if those separations had never happened. I stood close to my mother while a nun phoned for a taxi, anticipating something I knew was irreversible. As we waited together on the front porch, there was a mid-September coolness in the air and a rock in the pit of my stomach.

When the taxi pulled up, I felt my eyes burn, then flood, but I was too sad to be embarrassed. Mother kissed me and tried to say something encouraging, but we both knew there was nothing to say. I watched her move away from me, and when she got to the bottom of the steps I shamelessly cried out, "How could you do this to me?" When she closed the taxi door I began to sob.

My outburst caught the attention of a nun nearby, who came over and tried to give me a consoling hug, from which I recoiled. Then she took my hand and led me into one of the formal front parlors furnished in Victorian stiffness. We sat side by side on a prickly love seat as she reached into a mysterious part of her habit and brought forth a large white linen handkerchief.

"I know how you feel," she said, pressing the handkerchief into my hand, but I knew she didn't know. I had never felt such overwhelming loneliness before and was certain no one else had either.

"I know it seems very bleak to you now," she continued in a soft, low voice, as louder voices rang out from the hallway in shrieks of greeting. "I think if you give it a chance you will find you like it here," she said confidently, adding, "I can appreciate the difficulty in knowing no one in the school, but we are a family here and soon you will have friends and feel at home."

I continued weeping as she talked on about the sports and the spirit of "dear Eden," but when she stopped I resolved to tell her the truth. "I hate Catholics," I confessed, tears cascading down my cheeks, "and I probably hate nuns too."

My attempt to shock her failed. She gave me a faint smile, reached over, patted my knee, and replied firmly, "Well, we are going to keep you anyway." And I could tell she meant it.

Later I identified the nun with whom I shared that memorable moment as Reverend Mother Ashe. Head of the religious community at Eden Hall, she was by far the most imposing and intimidating nun at the school. After that initial encounter, I saw her only on formal occasions, but always I remembered the kindness in her stern face as she attempted to offer comfort and encouragement.

On my first night at Eden Hall I was introduced to my new schoolmates. I was not particularly concerned about their social status, but as a newly initiated slave to rock and roll and a skeptical Catholic, I thought I'd have a hard time relating to a group of girls with names like O'Brien, Monahan, and McCarthy who wore religious medals and responded to a chain of strange commands as if they were a pack of trained circus dogs. As the product of a mixed marriage where the father, not the mother, believed in the Virgin Mary and the mystery of transubstantiation, I knew that my brand of Catholicism was a lot different from theirs. I felt hopelessly lost and alone.

My roommate was a pretty, reticent Argentine. She spoke English with a clipped Spanish accent, and her piety was evidenced by the large Madonna medallion she wore around her neck on a heavy gold chain. For the third time in as many years I undressed with a stranger and engaged in the first awkward moments of conversation while we made up our beds. I welcomed the bell that signaled silence and lights out. In the darkness, trying to suppress my tears, I listened as my roommate whispered her prayers and the tower clock struck nine.

During my first week as a Child of the Sacred Heart, every encounter was strange and bewildering. At 6:30 A.M. a loud brass clangor rang out awakening me to the realities of my new world. A tall, bespectacled nun appeared in our doorway with a small vial of holy water.

"Sacred Heart of Jesus, Immaculate Heart of Mary," she intoned to each of us in turn. My roommate jumped from her bed, moved forward, and extended her fingers into the warm liquid. Blessing herself, she said, "I give you my heart." When the holy water was offered to me, my first impulse was to say "No, thank you," but I resisted the urge and reluctantly gave my heart too. With the nun still in attendance, we stripped our beds down to the mattress, folded the sheets, and donned bathrobes and slippers (no Child of the Sacred Heart was allowed out of her room with less than two layers of clothing) and scuffed down the corridor known as St. Madeleine Sophie to the lavatory. A line of mirrors reflected drowsy countenances hanging over sinks as morning ablutions were performed. A nun stood near the doorway to quash any form of mischief that might arise. Then we made a hasty retreat to the bedroom for bed making and dressing. The peeling off and putting on of the proper uniform was a thrice-daily occurrence at Eden Hall — morning, afternoon, and night — and was perhaps the only part of life at the Sacred Heart that went unobserved.

We all assembled in silence in the study hall downstairs to ready ourselves for Mass before breakfast. Radiators along the walls clanked and hissed, indicating that they too were slowly gearing up for the new school year. Students opened their desks, silently searching out missals and white chapel veils, made of stiff netting and anchored on our heads by clear plastic headbands.

Every minute of Sacred Heart school life was calculated to engender self-control and self-discipline. In her novel *Frost in May*, Antonia White wrote about her school days at Roehampton, a Sacred Heart school in England, where Vivien Leigh and Maureen O'Sullivan were schoolmates. The nuns worked, she said, "to turn out, not accomplished young women, nor agreeable wives, but soldiers of Christ, accustomed to hardship and ridicule and ingratitude." About the school she said, "In its cold, clear atmosphere everything had a sharper outline than in the comfortable, shapeless, scrambling life outside."

Customs, commands, and ceremony were linked to the order of the day, and wills were tested, bent, and sometimes broken. The nun in charge of discipline in Sacred Heart schools was called the "surveillant," and more than any other she was truly the most watchful Mother. With eyes like a hawk on both sides of her bonnet, she observed every action and reaction. During my first two years at Eden Hall the surveillant was Mother Frances Forden, and few who were watched by her during her thirteen-year stint there ever forgot her X-ray vision or drill sergeant tactics. She played favorites and had a penchant for pickiness, but she was also one of the most creative and charismatic nuns in the school.

It was Mother Forden who grabbed me out of line on my first morning as I marched to chapel with my schoolmates and informed me of the correct way to button the collar of my white, French-cuffed uniform blouse.

"We use all the buttons," she said, referring to the collar button, which I had left open. My mother, well acquainted with the world of fashion, adamantly opposed the practice of women closing any collar at the neck, characterizing it British at best and tacky at worst. She approved of the wool uniform jumper and white blouse, but she would have been appalled by the collar incident, her worst suspicions about nuns confirmed.

Again it was Mother Forden who summoned me into her office after Mass and shoved a thick, worn daily missal at me.

"You will need this," she said solemnly. "The one you have is only for Sundays, and here we go to Mass every day." I thanked her, embarrassed and angry that my father had not properly outfitted me with a Saint Andrew missal, the one most of my schoolmates appeared to carry.

Always it was Mother Forden, during those unforgettable first days, who instructed me, along with the other new girls, in the art of convent life, although none of the others appeared to be as lost or as unversed in the rituals of the Sacred Heart routine as I. On hearing that the "community" was coming around to inspect our rooms on the first weekend, I thought things must be awfully dull for the residents of Torresdale, only to learn that it was the community of nuns, not the citizenry, who would turn up at our dormitory. I felt like an alien dropped from another planet as I watched Mother Forden standing on a small wooden stool in study hall (adding an extra foot to her already imposing frame), lecturing, berating, instructing, seemingly never satisfied with our performance. She barked out orders and warnings with the impatience of a born dictator. It was her responsibility to get the school in shape and keep it there, to indoctrinate the new girls, and, as quickly as possible, to make us conform to school life. We were instructed in every aspect of Sacred Heart decorum and deportment, from the proper way to curtsy and genuflect to the manner in which we were expected to receive correction. Mother Forden pointed out that there was a purpose behind each rule and regulation, although she did not always disclose what that purpose was. Each rule was to be seriously regarded and unquestioningly obeyed. Life at the Sacred Heart was built around a set of universal traditions and regulations: holy water in the morning, Mass every day before breakfast, no lifting desk tops after study hall had begun, and always the rule of silence —

walking to and from classes silently in ranks, no radios in the dormitories on weekdays, and no speaking in the lavatories or in the hallways.

Even our clothing conformed to a prescribed Sacred Heart ideal. Our morning uniform consisted of a green plaid wool jumper, white French-cuffed blouse, and brown oxford shoes. In the afternoon, after classes, we dressed for gym in belted red tunics with white shirts and matching red bloomers. In the evenings for study hall and dinner, we wore a blue tweed jumper with black, low-heeled shoes. Our Sunday attire was a gray wool dress with scooped neck and three-quarter sleeves, finished off with red heels, and for feast days and special occasions, a white cotton short-sleeved dress and black heels.

The only articles of clothing that were allowed to be hung in the students' closets were the prescribed uniforms, which at Eden Hall did not include the school blazers. These were kept in a large closet near the study hall and were doled out only when the nuns deemed the chapel cold enough to warrant their use. Conversely, during the spring term, when the weather turned warm, no student could roll up her French cuffs without permission. The directives concerning these prohibitions and permissions were communicated through a sign on the blackboard written in the surveillant's flawless script.

Because the Society of the Sacred Heart was founded in France, many of the terms used in Sacred Heart schools retained their French names or associations. Each nun wrote R.S.C.J., for *Religieuse du Sacré Coeur de Jésus*, after her name, and the academic head of the school, or headmistress, was called the Mistress General. *Goûter* was an afternoon snack, *congés* were organized holidays spread throughout the school year, and feast wishes were tributes to Reverend Mother or a visiting religious dignitary. A feast wish was a special day that we carefully planned and eagerly anticipated — a day without classes, filled with games and contests. *Primes* was the weekly school assembly where Reverend Mother handed out blue Très Bien cards, brown Bien cards, and gray Assez Bien cards for very good, good, and satisfactory behavior. The French songs, such as *"Oui, je le crois"* ("Yes, I Believe"), French prayers, and a decidedly French formality made the restrained atmosphere at Eden Hall repressive and archaic.

Even more important than the Bien cards were ribbons, which

were awarded to students who achieved special merit: blue for the upper classes (grades eleven and twelve), green for middle classes (grades nine and ten), and pink for the lower classes (grades one through eight). All ribbons were voted on by the students, ratified by the religious, and awarded at a special ceremony at the beginning, middle, and end of the school year. Each recipient knelt in front of Reverend Mother as the coveted grosgrain sash was affixed over her right shoulder. To be a Ribbon was an honor sought by many but achieved by few.

Sports were another important, compulsory part of the school routine. Every Sacred Heart school was divided into two teams. Eden Hall's teams were the Reds and the Whites. Dressed in the uniform tunic and shirt, each student was required to appear on one of the athletic fields at the appropriate time to participate in an hour of physical activity that included field hockey in the fall, basketball in the winter, and tennis in the spring. There were intramural games every day, and varsity teams were given the honor of representing the school against other private schools in the area. At the end of the school year an entire day was given over to sports: Field day was a much anticipated occasion that provided an opportunity for individual students to compete against their peers in activities as diverse as softball throwing and pole vaulting. Prizes were awarded to the winners at a special ceremony where curtsies were offered to Reverend Mother in return for chevrons that were proudly pressed away in scrapbooks because they were never allowed to be sewn on any article of clothing.

We were taught the proper responses to a series of bells that called us from one class to another as well as to sports, to chapel, to meals, and to bed. The bell ringer, a student chosen monthly, always rang the bell in the same rhythm, and the message was always the same: time to end one activity and begin another. We learned to pull our chairs gently from the tables in the students' refectory without scraping the floor, we learned to sit with straight backs and uncrossed legs, we learned to speak in clear, well-modulated tones of voice and generally to behave in a manner befitting our station in life — which seemed to me much like Jane Eyre's. Mother Forden's constant message was that our conduct should reflect humility and gratitude at all times.

There was nothing arbitrary or unplanned about life at the Sacred

Heart. We had no choices, engaged in no debate, and were not part of a democracy. Communication was hampered by the many enforced silences; when talking was permitted, a nun always hovered nearby. We were never allowed to visit another bedroom on the dormitory floors except on Saturday afternoons, when time was allotted for baths, hair washing, letter writing, and phone calls. This was not just a strict school — this, I began to realize, was life closely aligned to that in a penal colony. I found it difficult to make friends or for that matter to find sufficient time to go to the bathroom. I moved from place to place on the Sacred Heart treadmill lonely, constipated, resentful, and bewildered.

Gradually Mother Forden's indoctrination began to take hold. After I learned the words to a few of the countless prayers and responses, knew which Mothers required a curtsy (although for a long time I found it hard to tell the nuns, and therefore their rank, apart), knew what a particular ringing bell meant, where I sat at mealtime, where my desk in study hall was, and what my classmates' names were without looking at their name tags — then my resistance began to crack. At times of recreation I joined in "general conversation" (discussions among the entire group, encouraged by the nuns to avoid cliques), amusing my schoolmates with stories about Garrison Forest and Ashley Hall — they had never met anyone who had gone to two Protestant boarding schools — but always I was desperate to fit my tales in before another bell rang. I joined in the eternal choruses of "Good morning, Mother," "Thank you, Mother," and "Mother, may I," which until Eden Hall had been a game I played with friends in my backyard.

The ubiquitous Mother Forden had informed us early on that whenever a Child of the Sacred Heart was scolded by a nun, the expected response was a simple "Thank you, Mother."

"What you are receiving is a gift," she pointed out, "no matter how humiliating or unjust it might seem at the time. To be corrected is to be helped, and when one receives help she is expected to express gratitude."

Eden Hall offered little that I could relate to. Even the singing, another integral part of Sacred Heart school life, left me bewildered. When I arrived I thought I knew the words to a lot of songs, but "Tantum Ergo" and "Panis Angelicus" were not in my repertoire; furthermore, they were sung in Latin. Much time and effort were

devoted to learning intricate liturgical music and Gregorian chant
that was used at Mass, Benediction, and other religious services.

Three times a week we sat at our desks in study hall while the
music director, Mr. Maskery, pounded the piano keys and we
pondered strange Latin phrases and square Gregorian notes in our
Pius X hymnbooks.

"Girls, girls," Mr. Maskery would shout after an aborted attempt
to lead us into a new piece, "let the music come from here," pointing
to the middle button of his tweed jacket, which would, with time,
like everything else, become a touchstone of familiarity. We would
begin again, and again, and yet again, until a bell would mercifully
ring out.

Downstairs in our refectory (we never said "dining room")
Mother Forden perched near a small table at the front of the room.
Their monastic rule prevented the nuns from eating with us children, but not from observing us. When everyone was at her assigned
place at the round wooden tables, a small bell rang and grace began.
"Bless us, Oh Lord, and these Thy gifts. . . ." A second tinkling
produced a chorus of "Good afternoon, Mother," and then we sat
down to await the third and final ring, which signaled the start of
conversation and the beginning of the meal.

"Thank you, Mother."

Instantly the room filled with voices and laughter, yet we all were
aware that if the noise level exceeded a certain decibel level, known
only to Mother Forden, the little silver bell would quickly return us
to silence. There was a certain cautious containment even in the joy
of mealtime, one of the few occasions when we were free to be
ourselves.

Every meal at Eden Hall was served from the shelves of carts
rolled in by ancient Irish maids with warts on their chins and mirac-
ulous medals around their necks. In pink pinafores they roamed the
refectory with varying degrees of efficiency, answering pleas for
more food with the resounding response "There ain't no more."

While Reverend Mother was the titular head of the school and the
religious community, the most important nun in the academic
ranks, the headmistress of the school, was the Mistress General.
Children of the Sacred Heart curtsied when we passed her as a sign
of respect, for as headmistress she was responsible for all student
permissions and all communication regarding student life. Every

outgoing letter, except to parents, was left in her office, unsealed, to be mailed. Hers was a demanding, round-the-clock job, and on every important issue her word was the last.

Each day the Mistress General came to the refectory at lunchtime with the coveted mail basket and her little black permissions book. She often appeared as the dishes were being cleared for dessert. In the chaos of clatter and chatter, the bell would ring and we all would automatically rise to greet her.

"Good afternoon, Mother."

"Good afternoon, children."

As the mail was passed out by members of the student government, the Mistress General roamed the refectory, writing in a small black book the names of those who wished to make phone calls to their parents or to visit the infirmary or to make any other special requests.

Eden Hall's Mistress General in my time was Mother Mary Elizabeth Tobin, a small, energetic woman who wore sturdy, thick-heeled black oxfords with her habit. Mother Tobin had risen quickly in the ranks of the Society of the Sacred Heart. As an administrator she was tops and as a nun she was among the most devout I ever knew. Unlike Mother Forden, who could be petulant, vindictive, and mercurial, Mother Tobin was patient, reserved, and astute. Her previous years as Mistress General at Stone Ridge, the Sacred Heart school in Maryland, had given her much practice in dealing with the multiplicity of problems that plague teenage girls at boarding school. Dubious from the start about my potential to become a true Child of the Sacred Heart, she nevertheless devoted much of her time and all of her wisdom to that end. I spent the most relaxed hours of my first weeks at Eden Hall sitting on a green hassock near her desk detailing my observations and complaints. She had given me permission to come whenever I felt the need, and during those early days and the weeks that followed, I came often. In the beginning, our conversation always followed the same pattern.

"Good evening, Mother," I would say while making a small curtsy.

"Good evening, dear," she'd respond, looking up from her desk work and removing her wire-rimmed glasses with one hand. "How are we tonight?"

"Not very well, Mother."

"I see. What seems to be the problem?"

"I hate it here."

"Yes, I think that has been well established. Still the same complaints?"

"I think so, Mother."

"Too much praying, not enough time to talk, and you miss your radio."

"Yes, Mother, that's about it. I can't concentrate without my radio."

"Well, I am sure it's difficult, dear, but I suspect you'll survive until the weekend. Have you made any friends?"

"No, Mother, I haven't found anyone in my class I like."

"Well, you will. Periods of adjustment are always hard, but in a few days I bet you will notice a big difference."

She'd motion toward the hassock, and I'd sit down as she swiveled her chair around to face me and begin the less formal part of our exchange. From the first time we talked, I liked Mother Tobin. She seemed so normal and well adjusted for a nun. Nothing I said seemed to disturb or shock her, and she laughed easily and often at my observations. For as much as I railed against the supervision and regimentation of the school rule, there was one element that intrigued me — the nuns. I could not believe that anyone mentally competent would voluntarily choose to live in a convent, shut away forever from all the pleasures of the world. So I began to ask Mother Tobin about her life before she entered the convent and about the mysterious thing called a vocation that had prompted her to make such a remarkable choice. She did not go into great detail, but to distract me from my misery, and perhaps to disprove my theory that all nuns must be masochists, she shared some stories about growing up in Albany, New York, going to Manhattanville College, and dancing at the Plaza. She said she became a nun because she realized she loved God more than she loved anyone else. She said that most nuns she knew were gifted, talented women who had much to offer the world but chose to give their lives to God "because once you know what you are meant to do it is very difficult not to do it."

"But how were you sure you were meant to do it?" I asked. She smiled and answered, "You will understand more when you have been here a little while longer," adding, "Whenever you have a question don't be afraid to ask. That is why I am here."

Then the bell for study hall would ring out and I would rise, curtsy, and find I actually felt better. Reassured that there was someone who seemed to understand my unhappiness but who remained convinced that it would pass gave me hope that it would. I knew I had an ally in Mother Tobin, and I knew something else. A vocation to religious life was a strange and mysterious phenomenon that I hoped was not contagious.

A favorite aphorism of the nuns at Eden Hall was "Youth is not meant for pleasure but for heroism." For me that heroism came slowly, if at all. But from the beginning I was determined to be strong and, if at all possible, to avoid disgrace. I made up my mind that if I survived, it would be because I wanted to, not because I was forced to.

When my parents called and gingerly asked how things were going, I told them that everything was fine. My mother inquired if a nun was standing behind me with a poker, but I assured her that I was speaking freely and truthfully, which is probably as close as I ever came to real heroism. In fact, there was no nun behind me, but the poker was there in the form of the responsibility I felt to my parents and to myself to live through the Sacred Heart experience and to learn from it.

One Heart and One Mind

3

◑ "SAINTED" WAS A TERM that Children of the Sacred Heart heard often in connection with the woman who founded the Society of the Sacred Heart and its worldwide network of schools. Indeed, Madeleine Sophie Barat is a saint, with three official posthumous miracles to her credit. She was canonized by the Catholic Church on May 24, 1925, in St. Peter's Basilica in Rome.

Like students in other academic institutions, Children of the Sacred Heart were forever being reminded of the great works and true devotion of their "beloved foundress." We sang songs about her, put on plays depicting her life, and continually prayed for her intercession in matters serious and small. Pictures and statues of her were prominently displayed in every Sacred Heart school, and the nuns spoke her name in the same solemn, reverent tone they used for the Holy Father.

Yet for all of our exposure to her name and accomplishments on earth and beyond, St. Madeleine Sophie remained a woman of mystery, half real, half fable, frozen in her saintliness in bronze and oil paint: a pious figure in the familiar white fluted bonnet, black cape, and silver cross. Her face, like that of an ancient ancestor, was one we recognized but were only marginally interested in.

As Children of the Sacred Heart, we were encouraged to have a special devotion to St. Madeleine Sophie because she was responsible for the spirit and tradition in our schools as well as for the strict, austere routine that governed our lives in places like Elmhurst, Forest Ridge, Duchesne, Kenwood, Noroton, and Eden Hall. Of course, some of us students held the opinion that for these acts alone she deserved to be strung up, not canonized.

At Eden Hall, at the end of a long, dark corridor named in her honor, a wooden statue of St. Madeleine Sophie, larger than life, stood under a dim light. The finely carved features draped in the traditional Sacred Heart habit gave the statue realistic, human qualities.

At least once during every school year, the St. Madeleine Sophie clone left its place of residence to participate unwittingly in an after-lights caper. Mischievous students would propel the statue to the door of an unsuspecting, and usually pious, schoolmate, and a firm knock would nearly always bring forth the desired reaction.

In researching her life years later, I found that Madeleine Sophie Barat was not only a woman of intelligence and accomplishment, but one with insight and humor who probably would have appreciated being used for a boarding school trick more than many of her modern daughters did. She lived a long, active life, shaped a religious community that extended around the globe, formulated a plan of studies that educated generations of Catholic women, and, until her death at age eighty-five, remained a strong, forceful woman of influence and vision.

It all started in France at the end of the eighteenth century, in an era of anticlericalism and Jansenism when Christian education was suppressed and the lives of all those connected with religion were threatened.

On December 12, 1779, in a French village called Joigny, the third child of Jacques and Marie Barat was born. They named her Madeleine Louise Sophie. Jacques Barat was a man of simple taste and limited education whose occupation reflected the countryside he lived in: He owned vineyards and made wine barrels.

The ancient Chinese curse commands, "May you live in interesting times." Madeleine Sophie Barat did more than live in them; she created them. Shaped by the destruction and desecration wrought by the French Revolution, she was called "a child of fire" because of the inferno that raged in the streets of Joigny on the night of her birth.

Eleven years younger than her brother, Louis, who was also her godfather, and twelve years her sister's junior, Sophie matured quickly. By age five she was already planning to be a nun, spending her playtime converting a doll's house into a Carmelite cell. Yet soon after she made her first communion, in the spring of 1789, the

National Assembly outlawed all religious congregations in France. Nuns and priests were released from their vows, monasteries and convents were closed, and France was plunged into violence and terror. In July the Bastille fell, and by October the royal family was imprisoned.

Louis Barat, who was studying to become a priest, returned home from his seminary in Sens to teach mathematics at a local college and assumed responsibility for his sister's education. A gifted and accomplished academician, Louis Barat held the enlightened view that women could and should be educated on a par with men. To test his conviction, he set up a broad classical curriculum for his little sister in their home, introducing her to academic subjects ranging from the traditional Latin, Greek, history, and literature to the more exotic study of botany, mathematics, and astronomy. Often he submitted Sophie to the same rigorous mathematical examinations he gave his male college students, and more than once his confidence in her was rewarded when she received the highest grade. The intellectual exposure she received through her brother's efforts was unique for its time, and although she sometimes railed against his strict surveillance and relentless discipline, in time her appreciation for learning overcame her resistance.

As she grew intellectually, she grew too in her love for God. "There was never a time when I did not want to belong to God," she later wrote. This religious sensibility was another bond she shared with her brother, and although Louis did not disapprove of his sister's early ambition to become a nun, he was determined to expose her to the wisdom of the ages, to develop in her a thoughtful, logical, inquisitive mind that he was certain would be of value no matter what vocation she ultimately chose to pursue.

By August 1792 the persecution and massacre of priests and nuns was all-encompassing and Louis was forced to relinquish his teaching duties at home and college and flee to Paris for safety. But his safety was short-lived, for in January 1793 Louis XVI went to the guillotine and in March of the same year Louis Barat was imprisoned in the infamous Conciergerie. The floor of his cell was stained with the blood of two hundred and eighty priests who had been murdered there six months earlier.

The Barat family remained safely in Joigny as Sophie pursued the studies her brother had mapped out for her before he left, and continued to help her mother with the household chores. By this time her older sister, Marie-Louise, had married, leaving thirteen-year-old Sophie alone with her parents. At her sister's wedding Sophie had proudly announced that this was to be the last wedding in her family. "Louis is a priest," she said, "and I intend to be a nun."

The Reign of Terror ended in the summer of 1794 when Robespierre went to the guillotine. Louis Barat was released from prison unharmed and returned to his parents' home, where he found that his younger sister had grown in age and wisdom and was more committed than ever to a religious life. She expressed to him her certainty about her vocation to serve God and her frustration at the difficulty in following her instincts while France continued to be without convents.

Louis returned to Paris and, after being ordained a priest in 1795, summoned Sophie from the small, provincial village of her birth to the city, where she could continue her studies in a more sophisticated and stimulating environment. Sophie adamantly opposed her brother, accusing him of reversing the laws of charity and nature. "I tried to prove to him . . . that the law of charity would not let a child be separated from her mother. I was pleading a weak case which I lost."

Reluctantly Sophie acquiesced, and in the spring of 1796 the timid but determined sixteen-year-old journeyed to Paris, a place she feared, trusting the Holy Spirit to see her through. Her first years in the ravaged city were spent in a small house owned by a family friend, Mademoiselle Duval, on the rue de Touraine. Here she taught catechism to neighborhood children and, at her brother's insistence, spent many hours each day reading Scripture and studying theology. It was a difficult, lonely time, a time of prayer and preparation for what lay ahead, but Sophie persevered, submitting always to her brother's strong, harsh, and sometimes unjust criticisms.

"I suffered at first," she said, "and thought that my brother was very hard on me. But I got used to it, and what had at first made me suffer ended up by making me laugh."

Her days brightened somewhat in the friendships she made with several young women, Octavie Bailly, Marie Françoise Loquet, and Marguerite Maillard, who sought Louis as their spiritual adviser. Together the young women read and studied the great mystics of the

Church while submitting themselves to the rigors of Louis's high standards of self-examination and denial. Rarely pleased with the way they responded to his challenges, he encouraged them in further acts of suppression of will and physical penance. More than once he taunted Sophie, saying she would never be a saint. Her reply was that she would get even by being very humble.

With the dawn of the new century, convents began to reopen in France. A new pope, Pius VII, was elected, Napoleon was attempting to restructure the government, and Madeleine Sophie continued to dream of one day becoming a nun. After she read the life of Francis Xavier, the Jesuit missionary, her thoughts began to turn more to the apostolic rather than the contemplative aspects of religious life. She was now certain that she would find a way to do what God was calling her to do.

That way came in the person of Joseph Varin, a young priest who arrived in Paris in June 1800, having walked for three months with a small band of priests from Austria. For Joseph Varin, the road to Paris had been paved with hardship, adventure, disappointment, and hope. In 1794 he had joined a group of other young priests in attempting to revive the spirit and rule of the Society of Jesus, which had been suppressed in France for thirty years. The small group founded an order called the Fathers of the Sacred Heart and dedicated themselves to the motto "One heart and one mind in the Heart of Jesus." After five years, they merged with another order, the Fathers of the Faith, taking on the latter's name and hierarchy.

Just as Sophie never relinquished her vision of a religious life, never far from Varin's sight was his dream of founding a sister order for the Fathers of the Faith. When he met Madeleine Sophie in Paris in the summer of 1800, Varin realized that here was the woman capable, as no other woman had so far proved to be, of leading such a challenging undertaking.

Varin recorded his initial impressions on being introduced to Sophie by Louis Barat: "I found a frail-looking person, extremely modest and timid. The inner conviction that I had felt when her brother spoke to me of her for the first time became more intense and the light shone more vividly. Then I understood everything! 'What a foundation stone!' I said to myself. In fact, it was upon her that God willed to build the Society of the Sacred Heart."

Shortly after that first encounter, Joseph Varin listened with interest as Sophie deliberated with him about her future. He suggested that instead of entering one of the contemplative religious orders to which she remained attracted, she might join him in founding a women's order, consecrated to the Sacred Heart of Jesus and dedicated to the education of youth. He argued that a spirited and inquisitive intellect like hers would be wasted locked behind the grilles of Carmel but would be challenged to greater heights in a more open environment, one that combined religious life with the work of education. It was a persuasive argument, and the peasant girl from Joigny eventually agreed. Thus began a friendship that would grow and deepen over fifty years, linked to an adventure that would consume them both.

The Society of the Sacred Heart began officially on November 21, 1800, when Madeleine Sophie Barat, Octavie Bailly, Marguerite Maillard, and Marie Françoise Loquet made vows of consecration in a tiny attic chapel in Paris. Father Varin said the Mass and each candidate, dressed in white, received a medal of the Sacred Heart with the words "I have come to cast fire upon the earth" engraved on one side and "My heart is joined to yours" on the other. Remembering that time, Madeleine Sophie wrote, "I knew nothing, I foresaw nothing, I accepted everything."

During its first years of precarious existence, the Society of the Sacred Heart had little beyond the spirit, optimism, and dedication of four enthusiastic novices and the unwavering support of its mentor, Joseph Varin. In the beginning the small community remained in the house on the rue de Touraine and applied themselves to the daily tasks of the novitiate hastily devised by Father Varin.

The Society moved from Paris to Amiens, France, in 1801, acquiring along the way two more pioneers: Henriette Grosier and Geneviève Deshayes, a thirty-four-year-old aristocrat who helped support the struggling congregation by selling off her fashionable wardrobe. The first Sacred Heart school for young girls was opened on the rue Martin Bleu Dieu and in the spring of 1802 a free school for those unable to pay tuition was started in a rented building nearby. When the enrollment of the free school began to increase and the building to overflow, larger quarters were sought and found on the rue Neuve. It was in Amiens that Madeleine Sophie made her final vows as a religious of the Sacred Heart, and in December 1802, at age twenty-three, she was named the first superior of the Society.

Father Varin recounted, "I spoke to them [the young novices] about Our Lord, and then told them I wished to assure myself that they were sufficiently well instructed to teach Christian Doctrine to their pupils. So I put to them some questions in catechism. . . . When it was Sister Sophie's turn I said: 'You are the youngest and I must give you the easiest question. Why did God make you?' 'To know Him, to love Him and to serve Him,' she answered. 'What do you mean by *serving* God,' I continued. 'Doing his will,' she replied. She would have said more but this was enough for me. I interrupted her: 'To serve God is to do His will, you say. You wish, no doubt, to serve Him?' 'Yes, Father.' 'Well HIS WILL is that you should be Superior.' "

On hearing the words Sophie fell to her knees and tears rolled down her cheeks. In keeping with the threat she had made to her brother to be "very humble," she felt unprepared and unworthy of the honor. Father Varin said later, "I never found any obstacle in her but her humility."

"When I was first launched I couldn't put two words together," she recalled, "but I had to do everything and get on somehow."

The Sacred Heart community was enlarged again in 1803 with the admission of three more women of courage to its ranks: Catherine de Charbonnel, Felicité Desmarquest, and Anne Baudemont. By the fall of 1804 the Society had acquired its first permanent house, Le Berceau in Amiens. There the first roots of the Society were planted in the form of a boarding school with high academic standards and a strong emphasis on the written word. Here too the first Plan of Studies was conceived combining traditional subjects with moral and religious training, and the foundation was laid for the distinctive Sacred Heart traditions that would encircle the globe.

Le Berceau was more commodious than the house on the rue Neuve, but the rooms for the community, which now numbered sixteen, were spare and austere. A mural on a wall in the cloister depicted a group of nuns floating in ecstasy around the Sacred Heart. "It was done by one of ours without artistic talent," Sophie observed, "but it edified us." She later called these early days "the golden age, when poverty was real and each day brought new challenges."

As the Society grew and expanded, unity of style and purpose was the key to its survival. The mission Madeleine Sophie envisioned for her "little society" was in keeping with the motto Father Varin had passed on: "One heart and one mind in the Heart of Jesus." Her vision was broad, her expectations high, and her courage unwavering as she set out to "cover the world with Convents of the Sacred Heart."

It was Sophie's idea that Sacred Heart convents be structured like family units. The schools were called houses; the students were referred to as children and the nuns as Mothers. (The term "Madame" had been used as a precautionary measure after the Revolution when all French religious orders were forced to keep a low profile. Eventually the term Mother was adopted, but "the Madames of the Sacred Heart" was a phrase that plagued the Society ever after and became a characterization the nuns strongly disliked.) In addition to the "choir religious" (the Mothers) were the coadjutrix, or domestic, religious, who were referred to as Sisters. The distinction between the coadjutrix and choir religious was mainly one of class and education. Establishing two classes of religious within one order, a tradition begun in the Middle Ages and continued into the twentieth century, permitted women of the lower classes to enter religious orders they would otherwise have been unqualified for. In the Society of the Sacred Heart, the coadjutrices served in domestic positions that were essential, even crucial, to the running of the convents and schools. Although they wore a different habit and were not permitted to say the daily Office or participate in administrative or academic activities, their presence brought a special spirit of dedication and devotion to the grand houses of the Sacred Heart. In the performance of their daily chores, which often went unnoticed and unappreciated, they lived and represented a real lesson in humility.

The habit that the Society adopted for the choir religious changed only slightly during the hundred and sixty years it was worn throughout the world. The simple black two-piece widow's dress, with fluted white bonnet and thin black veil, was in keeping with the dress of the time. It was unique among habits for the simplicity of its design and the gracefulness of its lines.

The school in Amiens, Le Berceau, was the first of the 111 permanent houses of the Sacred Heart established by the Society during

Mother Barat's lifetime. Father Varin found the second in 1804, six hundred miles away in Grenoble. At his urging the young foundress traveled from the small, thriving community in Amiens to begin her work anew with the remnants of a Visitation community whose numbers had been nearly depleted by the Revolution. As the two friends climbed the stone steps of the old Visitation monastery, Sainte-Marie-d'en-Haut, they were greeted by the unbridled enthusiasm of one of the novices, who threw herself prostrate at Madeleine Sophie's feet. "I was speechless at the sight of such humility," Sophie later wrote, "and curious to know more about her."

The novice, who was to play a prominent role in shaping the Sacred Heart destiny, was Rose Philippine Duchesne. Daughter of a prosperous, aristocratic lawyer, she was born on August 29, 1769, on place de Saint-André in Grenoble. Privately educated with her male cousins, she had received early exposure to a broad range of classical academic subjects, as had her new superior, Madeleine Sophie. Philippine was tall and craggy-faced. A woman of great physical strength and indomitable will, she was ten years older than the petite foundress of the Society of the Sacred Heart. She too had been convinced early of her religious vocation and was strongly attracted to missionary work. She had taken the habit of the Visitation order at age nineteen, on September 10, 1788. After she had been in the novitiate for four years, the Revolution had forced her convent to close and Philippine to assume her former secular life and dress. Anxiously she awaited her return to the active religious life she had chosen, but that time was eleven years away. At the end of the Revolution, in 1801, with the help of her family, Philippine had reclaimed the old monastery, but the dream of a revitalization of the community was not to be. Only a few of the fragmented group returned, and after a short time all but Philippine and two companions left. A young schoolgirl, Emilie Giraud, also remained to teach a handful of village children who came up the hill for their lessons every day.

When Father Varin made a visit to the almost deserted monastery in 1804, he knew he had encountered another highly talented woman, one who could be, as Madeleine Sophie had been, a foundation stone. "If she were the only one," he said, "it would be worth going to the ends of the earth to find her." Convinced that the Society of the Sacred Heart was ready to branch out and that the monastery at

Sainte-Marie was a perfect location, he had urged Madeleine Sophie not only to see the monastery but to meet Philippine Duchesne. As had been true in the past, his instincts proved right. The young superior and her new recruit made a dynamic pair. Strong-willed and intellectually independent, each had a missionary vision and sought a destiny that would bring that vision into focus.

Almost immediately Mother Barat, with the two religious who had accompanied her from Amiens, began to remodel the old monastery and restructure the tiny community, creating a physical environment compatible with the spirit and mission of its new affiliation. As she instructed the new Sacred Heart novices on the routine they would follow, Visitation ways were replaced by less rigid and more experimental ones.

The grilles that had separated the nuns from outside visitors came down. At times Philippine exclaimed in wonder at the young superior's revolutionary spirit. "O my dear grilles!" she cried. But Mother Barat responded pragmatically, "Don't talk to me of grilles! Our intentions, our actions, cannot be shut up in grilles."

Rather than follow the oldest religious rule, written by St. Augustine, Father Varin and Mother Barat chose to base the rule for the Society of the Sacred Heart on one written in the mid-sixteenth century by St. Ignatius of Loyola, founder of the Society of Jesus, which combined monastic life and apostolic work. Mother Barat and Father Varin knew there would be problems in modifying a constitution written for men to govern a community of women, but they believed the Ignatian rule offered the new Society the monastic structure and spiritual life it sought. Like the Jesuits, the Society of the Sacred Heart required its members to take a vow of education along with vows of poverty, chastity, and obedience. Each had a central government elected for life, but, unlike the Jesuits, the nuns were required to observe cloister, which meant that their lives were confined to the convent schools where they lived and taught. They were also required to recite the Little Office of Our Lady in chapel three times a day, a substitution added by Madeleine Sophie to replace the perpetual adoration of the Blessed Sacrament she had first envisioned. Other changes were made to conform to the uncertainty of religious life at the time. During the early years life in the cloister was far more flexible and ambiguous than it would be later. Napoleon's disapproval made it unsafe for French religious orders to be overtly religious. Even cloistered nuns moved around the cities in mufti for safety.

The first General Council of the Society of the Sacred Heart met in January 1806 at the motherhouse in Amiens. Madeleine Sophie Barat was elected superior for life by one vote over Mother Anne Baudemont, who had remained in Amiens as superior when Mother Barat traveled to Grenoble. The council spent most of its time working on a draft of the Society's constitutions and approved the official seal, which depicts the Sacred Hearts of Jesus and Mary entwined between two branches of lilies. On March 10, 1807, the Statutes and Rules of the Religious of Christian Teaching (a bogus name that the Society assumed for a time to shield its identity from the government) was approved by Napoleon.

Three new convents and schools of the Sacred Heart were established in 1808, one at Ghent in Belgium, one in Cuignières, and one at Niort near Poitiers. Mother Barat traveled extensively now, overseeing every detail in the new schools and keeping in close touch with Father Varin by mail as they continued to hammer out and revise the constitutions.

In April 1814 the Napoleonic Empire fell, and Louis XVIII took the throne. In that same year the Society of Jesus, long suppressed, was reconstituted by the papal bull *Solicitudo Omnium Ecclesiarum.* Joseph Varin and Louis Barat were finally able to fulfill their dream of becoming Jesuit novices, but each continued to advise Mother Barat on the complex and delicate task of getting the Society's constitutions approved by Rome.

On November 16, 1815, the second General Council met in Paris, and the Society's new constitutions were approved by the Sacred Heart membership, represented by the superiors of the eight Sacred Heart houses then in existence.

In the spring of 1816 Mother Barat wrote, "We are very satisfied now. The Society has now but one heart and one mind; everywhere we are 'the religious of the Sacred Heart'; everywhere we have the same Rule and Constitutions." The time had come to take this unified Society to the ends of the earth.

A house of the Sacred Heart had been established in 1816 at 40 rue des Postes in Paris, with Philippine Duchesne as superior. For eleven years Philippine had shared with Mother Barat her ambition to be a missionary, to spread the spirit of the Sacred Heart to foreign lands, and each time the subject was raised Madeleine Sophie's response was always the same: "Wait and pray. Later perhaps, we may think of it. It is out of the question now." But Philippine never lost hope.

Then on January 17, 1817, Bishop William Dubourg of Louisiana arrived to call on the Paris convent. Louis Barat had previously met the missionary bishop, who was seeking a group of religious women willing to cross the ocean to open a school in his diocese. Louis had suggested his sister's order as a possibility. The day of the bishop's visit, Mother Duchesne, who had heard the rumor of a possible mission to America, posted herself as portress near the doorway. She was determined that the bishop not leave without Mother Barat's consent to his request. While the bishop sat with Mother Barat urging her approval, Sophie thought to herself, "Things are certainly looking up for Mother Duchesne." Then she sent for Philippine, who fell to her knees and asked the bishop's blessing.

"I am ready to leave at once," Philippine informed them, "even if I have to go to the end of the world on foot." Mother Barat replied to her most impatient daughter, "I am well aware that you have good legs, but can your heart stand the sea voyage?"

On March 21, 1818, Philippine Duchesne with two coadjutrices, Sisters Catherine Lamarre and Marguerite Manteau, and two choir religious, Mother Eugénie Audé and Mother Octavie Berthold (daughter of Voltaire's secretary), boarded a ship called the *Rebecca* and spent eleven stormy weeks crossing the Atlantic. At the end of May they sailed into the Mississippi River past cotton fields and plantations. On May 29, the feast of the Sacred Heart, the *Rebecca* anchored twenty miles south of New Orleans. The nuns were lowered by armchair into a dinghy that carried them to shore.

The French missionaries spent their first weeks in New Orleans as guests in an Ursuline convent awaiting word from Bishop Dubourg concerning the school they had come to open in St. Louis. Mother Duchesne wrote long letters to her sisters in France, reporting on the profusion of mosquitoes and other "creatures that appear by the millions, swarm on people's heads, and even get in their mouths." She described the strangely constructed buildings made entirely of wood, with no brick.

By July, after receiving no word from Bishop Dubourg (his letter of welcome did not reach them for nine months), the impatient Philippine booked passage to St. Louis. On their arrival, the five nuns were escorted to the bishop's house. He settled the weary travelers temporarily, but on August 22 Mother Duchesne wrote to Mother Barat that the bishop's wish was that they establish themselves not among the French and Irish in St. Louis but in the more primitive town of St. Charles, twenty miles away.

The house that Bishop Dubourg had found for them, in which they would create the first convent of the Sacred Heart in America, was a modest wood structure. It consisted of a large central room with six smaller ones, three extending off each side. Two fireplaces provided the only heat for the compact residence, which would prove to be hot in summer and frigid in winter.

In keeping with the Sacred Heart constitutions, a free school for girls was opened on the property at St. Charles in September, the first school of its kind west of the Mississippi. The first boarding students arrived in October. They slept on mattresses on the floor of the house, as did Mother Duchesne and the other nuns. In her book *Education with a Tradition,* Mary O'Leary wrote of the first women who shared and lived Mother Barat's dream: "The first thing one notes about them is that they are all interesting and marked personalities; of many of them it may be said that they would have stood out in any circumstances." It was through their example, their daily courage and commitment through the early years of trial and error, that Children of the Sacred Heart came to know the meaning of Madeleine Sophie's phrase "For the soul of a single child I would have founded the Society." Each student became that single child and in her own way was formed by that sentiment.

Language was one of the many problems the group encountered at St. Charles. Some of the children spoke French while others spoke only English, but only a few spoke both. One of Mother Duchesne's most frustrating and challenging assignments was to learn the English language, a task she never completely mastered. Through the winter of 1819 the nuns faced numerous other challenges in their new school. The children were of different levels academically as well as spiritually. Some were unable to read and most had never heard of Jesus. Progress was slow and at times discouraging. Supplies were limited, food and water scarce. For most of the winter the Missouri River was blocked by ice, preventing supply boats from reaching the settlement. It was so cold that the water froze beside the fire, as did the laundry hung there to dry. Philippine wrote to her sister in France: "Neither doors nor windows close tight and there is no one here who knows how to make a foot-warmer. Our logs are too large for the fireplace, and there is no one to chop them for us and no saw with which we might cut them ourselves. . . . We have maize, pork and potatoes, but no eggs, butter, oil, fruit or vegetables. . . . We should . . . value a case of altar wine and some olive oil — the only edible oil to be had here is bear-grease, which is disgusting."

The care of the habit and its intricate undergarments was also a hardship for the nuns on the frontier. Each piece had to be washed separately, and the headdress had to be starched and fluted by hand in a complicated, time-consuming method. Letters to and from France took months to reach their destination, which sometimes forced Mother Duchesne to make decisions without Mother Barat's approval. She did her best to hold firm to the constitutions in governing the small community and to keep the spirit and form of the school rule in St. Charles as closely aligned with those of the French schools as possible. Bishop Dubourg tried in vain to persuade the nuns to Americanize their routine to make it more conducive to life on the frontier, but Philippine would have none of it. She was adamant that no change would be made without the permission of her superior.

"He said we were five heads in one bonnet," Mother Duchesne proudly wrote to Mother Barat.

Gradually, the pupils at St. Charles began to catch on to the traditions of the Sacred Heart, although it was obvious from the start that they would never match their European counterparts in manners and deportment. They were introduced to feast days, First Fridays, and the crowning of the Blessed Mother in May. But while enrollment in the free school increased, the boarding school progressed less well. Parents in St. Louis were reluctant to send their daughters across the often unnavigable Missouri, and this presented Mother Duchesne with a real dilemma. She saw the enthusiastic response of the children in the free school to the training they were receiving and knew that a great need was being filled there, but it was becoming increasingly evident that the boarding school, the only source of revenue, was a failure.

Then Mother Duchesne was asked by Bishop Dubourg to establish a new boarding school at Florissant, a small village nearer St. Louis. Mother Duchesne conceived of dividing her community in two, leaving two nuns to oversee the free school at St. Charles and moving the rest to Florissant. But Bishop Dubourg, who controlled the funds Mother Barat provided for the American foundation, adamantly opposed Mother Duchesne's plan, pointing out that the number of nuns was too small to divide.

Madeleine Sophie concurred with the bishop's advice and advised Philippine to keep the mission together: "Do not succumb to that temptation, my daughter," she wrote, "it would be your ruin. Once your little band were divided you would become mere school teachers, unable to observe any rule. Before thinking of other missions, you should begin by forming one house as well established and regular as circumstances permit, in order to attract vocations."

Students began arriving at the new school in Florissant almost the moment the new building was finished, and by May 1820 twenty-two students were enrolled. This time the nuns were well acquainted with the hardships of rural life, but they continued to be amazed that American parents were so willing to expose their children to such primitive conditions. One nun wrote, "People are so accustomed to poor lodgings in this country that they do not hesitate to send their children as boarders, even daughters of the wealthiest families." The nuns were delighted by their newfound success, particularly that their new brick building was filled to capacity. Philippine was now fifty-one years old, but her willingness to do whatever was required of her was never compromised by personal inconvenience or physical discomfort. The characteristics Father Varin recognized and admired in the determined young woman he met in Grenoble proved worthy of the course the Society of the Sacred Heart set for her. By 1824, within five years of the foundation of the school at Florissant, twenty-two postulants had entered the order under Mother Duchesne's strict supervision. The Society of the Sacred Heart had taken root in America.

While Mother Duchesne was successfully establishing the Society in America, Mother Barat was struggling to gain the civil and ecclesiastical approval that she felt would ensure the permanence and stability of her international Society. To receive canonical status and the approval of Rome, a religious congregation required papal approbation. Mother Barat's first request for approbation was submitted to Pope Pius VII in 1823, but his death a few months later prevented the Society's petition from being approved. Under his successor, Leo XII, approval was complicated by the papal requirement of solemn vows, which only the pope could dissolve and which included papal enclosure, the erection of grilles in the convents. Mother Barat regarded grilles as incompatible with the Society's apostolic work but strongly advocated cloister — which simply required that the community remain shut away from the world except while teaching children in its schools — for she felt that cloister provided necessary and sufficient protection for the Society's contemplative life. "We insist we have no grilles," she wrote Mother Duchesne. "Now I ask you, where would you be in Louisiana if you had that to contend with?" To keep the Society united and to preserve the essence of its double identity, contemplative and apostolic, Mother Barat agreed to incorporate a vow of stability along with the vows of poverty, chastity, obedience, and education.

In a letter to Pope Leo XII, Mother Barat described the urgent need for the Church's approval: "The Society desires to spread devotion to the Sacred Heart over the whole earth and set everyone on fire with divine love.... But since our Institute embraces various countries where our Society can do good, it is indispensable that we have a uniform rule in the places to which we shall be called, and this uniformity can only result from the will and approbation of your Holiness."

On July 31, 1826, papal approbation was granted. King Charles X signed the document giving the Society civil approbation on April 22, 1827. This protected the Society's legal rights, but only marginally, for the state still controlled the teaching orders it approved.

The struggle to attain the stamp of approval from the Vatican had only increased Mother Barat's belief that for the Society of the Sacred Heart, as it grew and expanded throughout the world, unity and obedience would be the keys to a common life and a common end.

For the Sake of a Single Child

4

TWO YEARS after the successful move from St. Charles to Florissant, Missouri, Philippine Duchesne with consent from the motherhouse in France agreed to a request from Mrs. Charles Smith, widow of a wealthy Louisiana landowner, to establish a school in Grand Coteau, west of the Mississippi River. Mother Duchesne knew that more nuns were on their way from France and that the Society's American branch was being swelled by American girls who felt called to religious life. The time was right to divide the community and embark on a new adventure. For this important mission she chose her friend and trusted aide Mother Eugénie Audé. For three years Mother Audé had labored with Mother Duchesne in rooting the Society in Missouri; now she would go it alone in Louisiana.

The rustic colonial plantation house donated by Mrs. Smith had had several additions since it was built in 1729 but retained its original Jeffersonian architecture: brick exterior, white trim, and green shutters. The brick for the first addition, commissioned in 1830, was manufactured on the property. The windowpanes were hand-blown in Paris and the wood used for the interior was Louisiana cypress. Huge, graceful limbs of oak trees overlapped to form a sheltered pathway connecting the school with a Jesuit college nearby. The formal garden was laid out according to plans belonging to a French bishop.

When the Academy of the Sacred Heart at Grand Coteau opened in 1821 as the Institute for the Education of Young Ladies, public school education in Louisiana was nonexistent. Thus, the Society of the Sacred Heart played a major role in forming the educational history of the state. Today the school holds the double distinction of being Louisiana's second oldest institution of learning and the oldest continuing Sacred Heart school in the world. Through flood, fire, cholera, and the Civil War, its doors have never closed.

During the Civil War, the religious and students watched from the second floor porch as the Battle of Grand Coteau was fought only yards away. Union soldiers under General Nathaniel Banks outnumbered the Confederates ten to one. Both armies had bivouacked in the area for weeks and were in desperate need of food. They stripped the land and raided plantations to obtain supplies. The school was cut off from its food supply and probably would have closed had it not been for a strange coincidence. It happened that General Banks's daughter was attending Manhattanville, the Sacred Heart school in New York City. This fact was brought to the attention of Manhattanville's superior, Mother Aloysia Hardey, herself a Grand Coteau graduate, and she immediately asked the general's wife to intercede with her husband on behalf of the nuns and children at Grand Coteau. Almost at once Mother Hardey received word from the battlefield that no harm would come to the convent, that General Banks had ordered his commissary chief to provide the convent with food and had issued a statement saying any unauthorized persons found on the convent grounds would be shot on sight. The convent doors stayed open.

Today the school boasts a student body of approximately three hundred, eighty of whom board, coming from forty parishes in Louisiana, seven states, and seven foreign countries. The original grounds have been expanded from fifty acres to two hundred fifty, which now include riding stables, a swimming pool, a gymnasium, a chapel, and a cemetery where white crosses bear the names of nuns instrumental in the school's history.

In June 1826 Mother Barat wrote to Mother Duchesne of meeting a priest named Father Neil, who was a pastor in St. Louis. "He is thinking seriously of having you establish a house in St. Louis, and after all the details he has given me of conditions there, I have not the slightest doubt that such a foundation is necessary." In the meantime, Mother Duchesne had written to Mother Barat telling her of an offer she had received to return to St. Charles.

Mother Barat responded negatively: "You must have a center, a Mother House in that part of the world which will be able to support the other houses. St. Louis is the place to choose. . . . Do not think of St. Charles until this is done. All our thought should be concentrated on St. Louis now. Our foundations must be solid, our work a basis for the future. A Mother House for America is absolutely necessary. What city would be more suitable than St. Louis?"

Acting on her superior's word, the enterprising Philippine began spreading her nets seeking support for the St. Louis project Mother Barat had recommended — and she found it. It seemed that whenever the Society was in need of assistance, especially in the early days of its American foundations, support from clergy and generosity from the laity were always at hand.

John Mullanphy, a successful St. Louis real estate and cotton merchant, offered the Society a brick house that Philippine wrote was "less smiling than that of Sainte-Marie-d'en-Haut, but resembles it slightly, being elevated, solitary, in a healthful locality overlooking the Mississippi and the city." What Mr. Mullanphy offered, in addition to the house, was a twenty-acre tract of farmland that he agreed to lease to the nuns for one dollar a year for nine hundred and ninety-nine years. This was contingent on the stipulation that the religious "board, lodge, clothe, provide for and educate all such indigent female children who are orphans [for each he would pay the sum of five dollars per year], not exceeding the number of twenty at any one time, as shall be designated by said Mullanphy during his life time." The lease further stipulated that in order to keep the children in the orphanage from rising above their station in life, they would be "required to go barefoot in the summer, eat corn-bread and drink neither coffee nor tea."

Mother Duchesne's plans included establishing a convent school in the Mullanphy house and a free school in a log cabin on the property as well as building an orphanage on the grounds. The entire complex would come to be known as City House. The idea of an orphanage connected with the school was in keeping with Mother Barat's original conception of including in the Society's constitutions the education of the poor as well as the rich. But she perceived the strange terms of the Mullanphy contract as less than equitable, especially the payment of five dollars a year for the care of each orphan. "This is a heavy burden," she wrote to Mother Duchesne, "but God will aid you, I am sure."

The nuns gave a broad interpretation to the Mullanphy lease and never required the orphans to go barefoot or restrict their diet. Nor was the number of orphans always kept to twenty. Throughout the Civil War and the years following the cholera epidemics in St. Louis, the orphanage often housed forty children at a time. By the end of the century more than six hundred girls had been cared for and educated. Many went on to profitable jobs while others joined various religious communities, including the Society of the Sacred Heart.

When Mother Duchesne moved from Florissant to St. Louis on May 2, 1827, she brought with her Mother Mary Ann O'Connor, four orphans, and her undaunted, optimistic spirit. "It is here that we were meant to be from the beginning," she said, remembering that it had been nine years since she arrived in St. Louis hoping to establish a school. The house Philippine had been given by Mr. Mullanphy was a far cry from some of the lavish mansions the Society owned in France. It was unfurnished, in need of repair, and rumored to be haunted, but Mother Duchesne was not intimidated by poverty or ghosts. She fully ascribed to her superior's belief that God would come to her aid, and soon the orphanage was gifted with a cow, an ample supply of vegetables, and a cartload of school equipment, a gift from the defunct St. Louis College. A chapel was set up in the old kitchen of the house and the first Mass was offered on May 6. Mother Duchesne postponed accepting pupils into the convent school for several months, busying herself with construction of the orphanage and remodeling of the other two buildings while awaiting the arrival of the nuns from France. The recruits from France finally appeared on September 9, and shortly thereafter City House opened. By the year's end the convent school had twenty pupils, the free school twenty-six, and the orphanage nine. For several years the Society of the Sacred Heart was the only order offering education to the poor in the Midwest. As in the other places where the Society established the first schools, the schools it started in St. Louis became models for educational institutions in the city.

A notice from the *Catholic Almanac* for 1843 permits a glimpse into life at the Young Ladies' Academy of the Convent of the Sacred Heart (City House).

Instruction — The following branches of useful and ornamental education are taught in the Academy.

English and French — Reading, Writing, Grammar, Arithmetic, Sacred and Profane History, Geography, Use of Globes, Projection of Maps, Mythology, Poetry, Rhetoric, Natural Philosophy and Domestic Economy, Sewing, Marking, Lace, Muslin, Tapestry and Bead Work; Painting on Velvet and Satin, Drawing, Painting in Water Colors and Crayons, Shell and Chenille Work, Artificial Flower Making, Filigree, Hair Work and Crystallized Parlour Ornaments, Music, Vocal and Instrumental.

Terms: Boarding $120 per annum, payable in advance.

Dress and Furniture — Each pupil must bring, at her entrance, her bedding, consisting of a mattress 5½ by 2½ feet, a pillow, two pairs of sheets, two blankets and a coverlet. Six changes of linen, stockings, neck and pocket handkerchiefs, one green sun bonnet, a sufficiency of underdress, a white muslin veil, a silver spoon, a knife and a fork, a cup, a bag for her linen, a trunk, a work basket, six capes of cambric and one of black velvet, one cloak, six towels, one pair of gloves.

General Regulations — The academic year commences on the 1st of October and ends on the 8th or 10th of September.

The religious exercises of the Academy are Catholic. Young ladies of all denominations are admitted, provided they be willing for the sake of order to assist at public duties of religious worship performed in the house.

The young ladies are permitted to spend the time of vacation at the Academy, nay, the mistresses prefer that they do because even that time, though granted for relaxation, may be very usefully improved.

The parents are requested not to pay visits to their children except on Thursdays.

All letters are to be addressed to the Superior of the Academy, and they are opened, those of the parents only excepted.

Frontiersman Kit Carson's daughter was once a pupil at City House, as was author Kate Chopin. In her biography of Phyllis Schlafly, Carol Felsenthal writes, "Devotion, stability, continuity, direction were at City House's core. It was the sort of place where generation after generation of a family's daughters got educated. The nuns would stretch the rules and shrink the tuition to keep a Sacred Heart education in the family. . . . The nuns knew every student personally. City House standards were as rigid as they were exalted. The student who failed to meet them or flouted them was likely to bring down upon herself, if not the wrath of God, then, at the very least, the wrath of Reverend Mother. A girl curtsied when she passed Reverend Mother or the Mistress General in the hall. If a girl slipped up, she came in on Saturday and polished the giant brass doorknobs on the massive oak doors. There were History medals and English medals and Latin medals for outstanding academic achievement, but there was also an equally coveted politeness medal. The City House curriculum was rigorous and rigid. There was no such thing as an elective. Students took French and Latin and they took them simultaneously, and they took them in addition to all their other academic courses. The Sacred Heart schools in St. Louis were symbolic of the Society's American history, its growth, its continuity, and its commitment to education."

In the summer of 1834 an outbreak of fever struck the Sacred Heart community in St. Louis. Students and nuns were felled by the dozens. The convent was temporarily turned into a hospital and the schools were closed, but because the orphans were separately housed, they escaped illness. When the sick nuns were sent to Florissant to recuperate, only Mother Duchesne stayed behind. In the fall when the school reopened, word came from France that Philippine had been relieved of her position as superior in St. Louis. Mother Barat felt that the burdens her friend had carried for six years had been sufficiently wearing: "You have need of rest, dear Philippine, and also of an easier administrative position." Mother Duchesne was asked to exchange places with Mother Catherine Thiefry at Florissant, which she regretfully did. Her duties at Florissant consisted of much the same work she had done in St. Charles. Later she would write to a friend, "I wake the religious in the morning, make the last rounds at night, clean the outhouses, scrub, sweep — these are my ordinary occupations."

Because of the continuing political unrest and the threat of another revolution in France, Mother Barat summoned the Society's sixth General Council to meet on June 10, 1839, in Rome at Trinità-dei-Monti, the Society's beautiful school for the daughters of Roman nobility built at the top of the Spanish Steps. Since 1816, when the constitutions had been framed, the number of Sacred Heart schools had expanded from six to forty. This rapid growth was both frightening and challenging to Mother Barat, who was forced to use every ounce of her ingenuity and creativity to keep the Society's books balanced, its schools filled, and its religious community on track. Regularly she dispatched trusted aides to iron out problems in distant places when she was too busy to go herself. One of her most valued assistants, Mother de Charbonnel, was made treasurer of the Society in 1815 and founded schools in Le Mans (1821), Autun (1822), Besançon (1823), and Metz (1824). By the end of her life she calculated that she had traveled enough miles to take her around the world three times. She was a crack mathematician, so no one dared question her equations.

It soon became obvious to Mother Barat and the members of the General Council that she could no longer personally supervise each school, and a decision was made to divide the Society into provinces governed by Mothers Provincial, whose duties would include directing and visiting those convents placed under their control. It was in the spirit of that decision, in the spring of 1840, that Mother Barat dispatched her secretary, Mother Elizabeth Galitzin, as temporary provincial of the Society's American houses to visit the Sacred Heart convents and schools in the United States.

After forty-five days at sea, this daughter of Russian royalty, who had been converted to Catholicism by the Jesuits, arrived in New York. With her were seven French religious who had been given the coveted assignment. From New York, Mother Galitzin and her companions traveled across Pennsylvania to the Ohio River and on to the convents at St. Louis, Florissant, and St. Charles, which had been reopened in 1828. They made rapid inspections of the schools and convents, noting the needs of each.

Mother Aloysia Hardey, who was among the Society's first American members, then superior at St. Michael's, Louisiana, had received a letter from Mother Barat urging her to "enter fully into Mother Galitzin's views for the greater glory of the Sacred Heart of Jesus and the good of souls." Mother Barat knew well that her Mother Visitatrix, the title Mother Galitzin assumed with her duties, was uncompromising in upholding the Society's rule. The wise Mother General cautioned her American daughter that it would "not be contrary to the perfection of obedience to make known to [Mother Galitzin] the customs of your country and the inconveniences that might arise from the adoption of certain measures or regulations proposed by her." It was clear to Mother Barat from the beginning that although "Unity in all things" was the most desirable approach, there would have to be flexibility in many areas as the Society moved into countries where the cultures and customs were different from those in France.

Mother Galitzin's visit to St. Michael's went smoothly. She and Mother Hardey hit it off immediately and Mother Galitzin informed Mother Barat in one of her reports that Mother Hardey "is endowed with rare capacity for government" and suggested that she be named provincial of the American houses at the next General Council. Mary Anne Hardey, who had changed her name to Aloysia when she entered the Society in Grand Coteau, would in fact become not only provincial of the American houses on the East Coast but also one of the Society's most prominent American nuns. As provincial, she would found twenty-five houses of the Sacred Heart along the eastern seaboard, from Nova Scotia to Cuba. A woman of intelligence, imagination, and boundless energy, she has been characterized by the Society's historian, Sister Margaret Williams, as the one who kept the Society balanced between tradition and innovation in its early days in the United States.

While Mother Galitzin was in St. Michael's, she received a plea from Philippine Duchesne that the Society consider expanding its mission into Indian territory west of St. Louis. It had always been a dream nestled in the noble heart of Philippine that one day the religious of the Sacred Heart would find a place with the American Indian. Finally, when in 1841 the Society was asked to open a school for the Potawatomi tribe in Sugar Creek, Kansas, Mother Duchesne sought Mother Galitzin's permission for this extraordinary venture. Her letter to Mother Galitzin at St. Michael's was only a small reflection of the passion she felt. "Beyond the western boundary of Missouri," she said, ". . . there is a very good tribe that comes from Canada, already partly converted to Christianity. They are called the Potawatomi. . . . The missionary whom I saw yesterday considers it a duty for us to seize this opportunity before others of non-Catholic faith do so." At the end of the letter she listed the names of those she considered suitably fit for the special mission and at the bottom added her own. "I shall just be an extra member of the group, helping with the housework and other labors." She was over seventy years old, ill and unfit, and still she believed that God would make her strong enough to go to Sugar Creek. She was also convinced she could count on Mother Barat to support her in this effort. The support came in a letter from Mother Barat to Mother Galitzin: "This matter should not be neglected. Remember, dear Mother, that good Mother Duchesne in leaving us for America had only this work in view. It was for the sake of the Indians that she felt inspired to establish the order in America."

With those words permission was granted, and within a few weeks Mother Lucille Mathevon was selected as superior and Mother Mary Ann O'Connor, Mother Duchesne, and Sister Louise Amyot as her assistants. On June 29, 1841, the four nuns, accompanied by two Peters, Father Verhaegen, superior of the Jesuits in Missouri, and Father De Smet, left St. Louis by steamboat and traveled up the Missouri River for four days. A French settler's house, located eighteen miles below Sugar Creek, provided lodgings for the night. The following morning as they walked toward the reservation, they encountered Indians mounted on horses posted every two miles along the trail to ensure their safety.

"We were given a reception that far exceeded anything we had expected," Mother Mathevon wrote; "a half breed named Joseph Napoleon Bourassa made a fine speech in the name of the tribe and the 700 who were assembled to greet us. . . . I do not remember what Father Verhaegen said in reply, but he presented Mother Duchesne to the Indians, saying, 'Here is a religious who has been asking the dear Lord for thirty years to let her come and teach you, and how happy she is that at last He has heard her prayer.' "

Soon the nuns were set up in a small cabin that was primitive but clean. A wood stove provided the only heat, and when winter came the nuns and their pupils huddled around the fire. Mother Duchesne struggled against the harsh conditions and her own infirmities, which were growing worse with age, while the new convent was slowly being constructed nearby. Although Mother Duchesne spent most of her time in prayer at Sugar Creek, the Indian children loved her. While the other nuns gave their best efforts to engage the children in lessons, finding them not unwilling but easily distracted, Mother Duchesne only tried to love them. Mother Mathevon taught them singing and gave them tips in sewing and cooking. Mother O'Connor taught catechism, prayers, reading, and elementary exercises in writing and mathematics. And Mother Duchesne let the children hold the strange gold piece she wore that ticked and had moving hands or let them play with the oversized rosary beads at her side. They had never seen a watch, or a rosary, or a nun.

When the two-story log cabin convent was completed, the nuns did their best to follow the Society's rule and keep cloister. But it was not always easy. The weather was severe and space in the log cabin was limited: Provisions were kept under the kitchen floor while prayers were said on top of it. Mother Duchesne had known hardship and adversity in St. Charles, but what she experienced at Sugar Creek was far more taxing. She prayed for perseverance and understanding, trusting that God would provide the other ingredients necessary for making the Indian mission successful.

Mother Galitzin visited the Sugar Creek mission on Palm Sunday 1842 and received an enthusiastic welcome from both the nuns and the "good savages," as Philippine called the Indians, who stood in line to shake her hand. Mother Galitzin observed the numerous physical sacrifices the religious were required to make as they struggled to survive. She saw them gather wood, wash and mend clothes, cook meals, and carry water before their day began. Dirt, disease, and cold were constants in their lives, and since there was no private chapel they were forced to walk to the Jesuit church several miles away. Although she tried valiantly to hide it, Mother Duchesne's deteriorating condition did not escape Mother Galitzin's attention. Soon Mother Duchesne was ordered back to civilization, a decision that broke her heart. "I can only adore the designs of God, who has taken from me the thing I had so long desired," she said, but once she received the word, she accepted it with humility.

Despite the severe impediments that plagued their every move at Sugar Creek, the missionary Mothers succeeded. By 1843 there were twelve hundred Catholic Potawatomi on the reservation, and as the religious community enlarged, the classes grew, boarders were accepted, and progress accelerated. When in 1848 the Potawatomi were deeded new land by the government on the other side of the Kansas River, the nuns moved with them, eventually opening an Academy of the Sacred Heart at St. Mary's, the mission they shared with the Jesuits. They remained there for twenty-five years.

At the same time as the nuns from St. Louis had set off to establish their mission among the Potawatomi, a small group of religious, under the supervision of the peripatetic Mother Galitzin, headed for New York City. For fifteen years Mother Barat had hoped to establish a Sacred Heart school in New York, which had become not only the first city of culture and industry but a Catholic city as well. Bishop John Dubois had offered an invitation to the religious of the Sacred Heart in 1827, but for various reasons including lack of money and personnel Mother Barat had turned him down. In 1841 John Hughes, the new bishop of New York, visited the Mother General at the motherhouse in Paris and petitioned her to bring her nuns to New York. This time she agreed.

Much like the first Sacred Heart missionaries in St. Louis, the nuns had been promised a residence, but when they arrived on May 6 no house had been provided and they were forced to ask the Sisters of Charity for temporary quarters. Soon the search was on for a building that would house the school they had come to open, and when they came upon a run-down boarding house near the bishop's residence at the corner of Houston and Mulberry streets, they rented it. The New York community, which originally consisted of Mother Catherine Thiefry and Mother Johanna Shannon, was joined by Mothers Aloysia Hardey and Ellen Hogan from St. Michael's, Mother Adeline Boilvin from St. Louis, and Mothers Bathilde Sallion and Elizabeth Tucker and Sisters Battandier and Louf, along with several others, from France. Mother Sallion was appointed superior of the school.

Throughout the history of the Society of the Sacred Heart nuns were frequently shifted from one school to another, and often from one country to another. Mother Barat's vision of a worldwide network of schools made mobility an essential part of the Society's missionary spirit and required the nuns to travel large distances and experience great adversity, especially in the early days. It was a rare religious of the Sacred Heart who stayed in one place for more than five years. The shifting of personnel was, in Mother Barat's opinion, a safeguard against the staleness that often comes with routine and at the same time provided the growing Society with a continuity of character. Because the Society now had a universal Plan of Studies, a set of unique traditions, and a common method of formation of novices, the movement of nuns from one school of the Sacred Heart to another was, in most instances, accomplished smoothly and efficiently.

When Mother Galitzin's long mission was finally completed in 1842, she sailed for France with Mother Aloysia Hardey as her companion. For the first time the young nun from Louisiana would have an opportunity to meet her Mother General face to face. But finding the elusive superior, who was traveling herself, proved difficult. She was not at the motherhouse in Paris, and so Mothers Galitzin and Hardey set out for the Trinità-dei-Monti in Rome. (It was here that the famous fresco *Mater Admirabilis* would be painted two years later on a corridor wall, a picture of the young Virgin in the pink dress that would come to be a significant spiritual symbol for all Sacred Heart students.)

Again the travelers were disappointed, but they were given a letter from Mother Barat directing them to Lyons, where there were now three Sacred Heart schools: one on the rue Boissac, where the Children of Mary sodality was started, a country house called Les Anglais, and another called La Ferrandière. At the latter the much anticipated introduction between Madeleine Sophie Barat and her American daughter Mary Aloysia Hardey took place.

When the words *"Notre Mère Générale"* were whispered in her ear, Mother Hardey moved forward to kneel and kiss the foundress's hand. The hand that had governed the Society of the Sacred Heart for almost forty years was strong and firm, for although she had accomplished much, Mother Barat was not an old woman. She still moved with vigorous strides, spoke with spirited enthusiasm, and offered her time and attention generously to her American visitor as they walked together in the gardens of La Ferrandière. Mother Hardey recognized in Mother Barat many of the characteristics she had come to know in Mother Duchesne — the strength, the resolve, and the wisdom. The days spent at La Ferrandière provided Mother Hardey an opportunity to speak to her Mother General in detail about the school in New York and to ask her if she might someday make the trip across the ocean to see in person what had been accomplished in her name.

For an instant Madeleine Sophie's eyes clouded as she shook her head. She could not come — long ago she had put aside the dream of it — but now she would count on Mother Hardey to be her eyes and ears in the way Mother Duchesne had once been. With that in mind Mother Barat named Mother Hardey superior of the New

York house. On her return to Houston Street Mother Hardey replaced Mother Sallion, who was on her way to found a school in Canada.

In July 1843 Mother Galitzin returned briefly to New York and then once again set off for St. Louis and St. Michael's, where she contracted yellow fever and died. Mother Hardey was deeply saddened by the news, for the two nuns had grown to know one another and had become friends. The next shock Mother Hardey received came in a letter from France informing her that she had been chosen provincial of the American houses along the eastern seaboard, which now included a novitiate in McSherrystown, Pennsylvania, founded in 1842, and a school in Canada, St. Jacques de l'Achigan. Acquisition of larger quarters for the New York school was among her many concerns. The house on Houston Street was already filled with sixty pupils, half of them boarders. With more applying each day, Mother Hardey knew that expandable space was needed. Bishop Hughes had suggested that the nuns move their boarding school to the country and keep the Houston Street property as a city school for day pupils.

After receiving permission from the motherhouse to purchase a country estate, Mother Hardey found one in Astoria, formerly owned by the Delafield family, called Ravenswood. In addition, a free school was started in a house on Bleecker Street, and a second school for girls was founded there in February 1848. The annual tuition was $50 a year and life there was very bleak indeed.

"We were very poor," one nun wrote. "We had no regular beds and could not afford fuel for fires except in the classrooms and there we stretched out our mattresses for the night."

Poverty, in the real sense of the word, was rarely connected with the religious of the Sacred Heart by those who saw their glorious mansions and knew their haughty, intellectual reputation that first took hold in Europe and spread to the United States. But during the early years of establishing schools in the plains and cities of nineteenth-century America, poverty was not only practiced; it was lived.

In 1847 the boarding school in Astoria was closed at the urging of Bishop Hughes, who had visited Mother Barat in France and received her permission to move the school to a new location. That location was the Jacob Lorillard estate, which stood on a hill between the villages of Harlem and Manhattanville in New York City. The brownstone mansion had been built in 1833 and was put up for sale in 1846 by Jacob Lorillard's widow and children. When Bishop Hughes set out to acquire it for the Society of the Sacred Heart, negotiations proved difficult at first. The price of seventy thousand dollars was too high for the Society, and the Lorillard children refused to sell without the consent of their mother, who was opposed to a lower figure. Mother Hardey, her community, and students immediately began a novena, which proved to be more successful than intended. Mrs. Lorillard died suddenly and the property was offered for fifty thousand dollars with an additional twenty acres. Bishop Hughes commented, "Be careful not to oppose Mother Hardey's wishes, for if necessary she will kill you with her novenas." On November 6, 1847, the sixty-three-acre estate, once the camping ground for George Washington's army during the Revolution, became Manhattanville Convent of the Sacred Heart. In a matter of months, Manhattanville, like other Sacred Heart institutions before it, was quick to establish a reputation for high scholastic standards and a strict code of discipline. Wings were added to the main house to accommodate the boarding population, which began to increase steadily from all parts of the country. By 1870 there were three hundred students. Mother Hardey's natural wisdom and prophetic vision were a crucial factor in the speedy development of the school, which would eventually become a women's liberal arts college known as Manhattanville College of the Sacred Heart.

Meanwhile, after a ten-year stay, the Bleecker Street academy moved to Fourteenth Street in 1852 and then to a new house on Seventeenth Street, where for fifty years the Society operated a parochial school for immigrant children as well as a center for religious instruction and adult education.

The Society opened a school on Madison Avenue in 1881 to offer a Sacred Heart education to those who lived in the new residential sections of the city. For although the school on Seventeenth Street continued to attract a large student population (until it became Maplehurst and moved to the Bronx in 1905), that section of the city was no longer the center of metropolitan activity. Manhattanville relinquished its day school to the school on Madison Avenue, which consisted of three town houses with connecting passageways.

An early catalog reflects the plan of the day and studies.

Academy of the Sacred Heart
533 & 535 Madison Avenue
New York

The aim of the Religious of the Sacred Heart is to give their pupils an education which will prepare them to fill worthily the place for which Divine Providence destines them. The training of character and the cultivation of manners are therefore considered matters of primary importance.

Hours of attendance are from 9 A.M. to 3:30 P.M. Classes in the junior department end at three o'clock.

It will not be necessary for the pupils to study lessons or write compositions at home, as time will be allotted for this purpose during school hours.

The pupils will dine at one o'clock and will be required to converse in French while at the table.

The course of studies comprises, besides the thorough grounding in the ordinary branches of education:

A complete course of Christian Doctrine.
Elements of Philosophy.
Ancient and Modern History, special attention being given to Sacred and Church History.
Literature, Ancient and Modern.
The English Language in all its branches.
Latin.
Mathematics and
The Natural Sciences.

TERMS

Senior Department — $200 per Annum
Junior Department — $150 per Annum
Bills Payable Semi-annually, in Advance.

References required. No deduction on account of absence or withdrawal before the expiration of the session, except in cases of protracted illness.

The Madison Avenue school was distinctive for its serious curriculum, its French influence, its strictness, and its acceptance of Protestant students.

Discipline was a primary factor incorporated into every phase of student life. There were as many "exercises in behavior" as there were exercises in academics. In response to parental criticism for imposing such an inflexible, military-like code of conduct on their female students, Mother Janet Stuart, the Society's sixth superior, wrote during her short generalate (1911–1914): "The discipline in schools of the Sacred Heart has met with a great deal of criticism. Why these moments of strict silence? Why this supervision? Why this insistence on play? This opposition to cliques and private friendships. Why such exacting persistence as to manners? All, in the main, for the same reason, because they conduce to the training of character, they exact self-control, and attention, and consideration for others, and remembrance, not in one way but in a hundred ways."

At the Sacred Heart school on Madison Avenue and elsewhere, the students were credited, at an early age, with having sufficient internal resources to endure the pain of restraint and the high level of control in their lives and to respond appropriately.

"I wouldn't repeat the experience for a million dollars," one graduate said, "but I wouldn't take ten million for what it taught me."

Even in the early days the nuns mixed a heady concoction for their students' consumption, peppering their classes with antiquity as well as the avant-garde. In 1900 the girls at Madison Avenue were given talks on physics, and in 1905 courses in Milton and Dante were added to the English department. There were lectures on Shakespeare's plays as well as on Lincoln, Hiawatha, and the poet Gerard Manley Hopkins, and lectures were frequently given on a variety of other subjects by visiting professors and Jesuits.

Founded in an era of revolution, suppression, and anticlericalism, the Society of the Sacred Heart celebrated its golden jubilee in 1850, with sixty-five schools under its international umbrella. But even as it celebrated, war once again threatened its stability. In February 1848 civil war had broken out in France between worker and Royalist. As King Louis Philippe scurried in his coach toward England, an obscure professor of economics, Karl Marx, was encouraging workers of the world to unite. In the name of social reform, houses of the Sacred Heart had already been confiscated in Switzerland and now the same fate threatened those in Paris.

"Fribourg is invaded by the radicals," wrote Mother Barat, who was no stranger to the smell of gunpowder or the sound of cannons. When the uprising began, she resolutely told her surveillant at the Hôtel Biron, one of the Sacred Heart houses in Paris, to engage the children who remained there in a noisy game of *cache-cache* (French hide-and-seek) to distract them from the shooting nearby. She would not hear of closing the school. "That's running away," she said. "We shall stay and be reasonable." She walked through the bloody streets in mufti, and what she witnessed made her weep. She took in a wounded man who stumbled into her courtyard and personally nursed him back to health. She provided food for hungry workers, establishing a soup line at the well-appointed convent kitchen until the police put an end to it. In the spring she offered a tree from the convent garden to be planted in honor of liberty, but in June the revolution heated up again, resulting in more bloodshed, destruction, and death.

In November Mother Barat again donned secular dress and set out to check on the welfare of her other houses in France. As she moved from Beauvais to Tours, Nancy to Amiens, Niort to Poitiers, she found each one safe and secure but in need of moral support, which she provided by her mere presence. Her personal interest and personal affection for every student and every religious were an essential factor in keeping the Society unified when the world around it was in turmoil.

The revolution ended in December when Louis Napoleon was elected president of the Second Republic. And then it was Rome that was under siege. The pope's minister was assassinated on the steps of the Vatican and Pope Pius IX himself fled the Holy City for Naples. In the spring Garibaldi knocked at the Society's Villa Lante, wedged into the slope of the Janiculum Hill. He was seeking Cardinal Lambruschini, the Society's cardinal protector. When the nun in charge refused to allow the school to be searched, Garibaldi returned with seventy men who vandalized the convent as they hunted the missing priest. The cardinal was nowhere to be found.

That night the resident nuns were forced to evacuate. Transported through the streets in open carts, one of them overheard an officer comment to his comrade, "What women they are! They are dragon-hearted." The exhausted group reached Trinità-dei-Monti at midnight and took refuge there.

In March 1850 the National Assembly passed the Falloux Law,

which granted all French religious congregations freedom to run educational institutions. During that year, 251 Catholic schools opened in France. Both the Society of Jesus and the Society of the Sacred Heart were inundated with requests to make foundations, and each turned down more offers than it accepted. Between 1850 and 1860, Sacred Heart schools were opened in Orléans, Layrac, Moulins, Brittany, Calais, and Montigny-lès-Metz. Second houses were opened in Marseilles and Besançon, the latter called Saint-Ferréol, an orphanage. At Moulins in 1857, the Dames de Saint-Paul merged with the Society. During this productive decade Roehampton opened in England and a school was started in Ireland as well. Meanwhile Sacred Heart schools sprang up in Germany, in Milan, in the Tyrol, and in Poland. An estate given by the duke of Pastrana became a Sacred Heart school near Madrid.

Emperor Napoleon III was perceived as sympathetic to Catholic causes and proved it by crowning a statue of Our Lady of Victories in Notre Dame. In the summer of 1854 Mother Barat felt the Society was secure enough and the political climate calm enough to purchase another magnificent piece of property for the Society, Les Feuillantines, near the rue de Varenne in Paris. Here she hoped to establish a new and permanent motherhouse. Like so many of the other houses acquired at that time, the new property included an ancient monastery, this one built by Anne of Austria in the seventeenth century. "Here," Mother Barat commented, "is the little nest where I shall die," but her hope for a long stay vanished two years later. With the restoration almost complete, France was plunged into the Crimean War, which proved a disaster for both the French army and the Society of the Sacred Heart. Mother Barat's newly acquired land in Paris was confiscated and divided into four parts to facilitate the building of roads. She appealed to the courts but won only a year's reprieve of the evacuation date and a small indemnity. The demolition began in March 1857.

Among the many strong personality traits that characterized the Society's first Mother General, her tenacity and determination were legendary. She rarely allowed circumstances beyond her control to dictate a conclusion she deemed unacceptable. A woman of great pragmatism and even greater imagination, she refused to be vanquished. If the government would take Les Feuillantines, then she would simply find another spot on which to build her motherhouse.

She found the spot, on the western side of the Hôtel Biron, the house that the Society had transformed into one of the most opulent and well-known schools in France. Built in 1729 on rue de Varenne on the Left Bank of the Seine, the house was described as having been built in "the insolent splendor of the baroque." Until it was confiscated by the French government at the end of the century, the Hôtel Biron served three functions for the Society: school, motherhouse, and novitiate.

When work on the motherhouse was completed in 1858, Mother Barat planted a cedar tree, as a symbol of life, its mystery, and its seasons. She often prayed under it, used it as shelter from the steamy Paris summers, and made it a special place to visit with those who sought her counsel. The children in the school at the Hôtel Biron loved her and when they saw her walking in the garden they often ran to greet her. She kept in touch, through letters and personal visits, with countless former students, with her own family, and always with her "dear daughters," the religious who represented her in the distant places the Society inhabited. Now she was not only the head of a major religious order, but a chief executive officer as well. She woke before five each morning and continued her work by candlelight late into the night. Her love of people, her belief in the profound need to educate women, and her devotion to God were stimuli for the positive energy that urged her on.

The Society and the foundress suffered a profound loss when its founding father, Joseph Varin, S.J., died on April 19, 1850, followed two years later, on November 18, 1852, by its first missionary, Mother Rose Philippine Duchesne, in St. Charles, Missouri. Only weeks before her death Philippine had written her friend and superior, "At present I do not know when the end will be, but I come once more to kneel at your feet, beg your pardon, and assure you of my loving veneration." Although Mother Barat was deeply saddened by both losses, she took courage from the knowledge that Father Varin had given the Society its most precious gift, the gift of life, and that by her lifework Philippine Duchesne would be an enduring role model and inspiration to hundreds, even thousands, of nuns who would follow in her dogged footsteps, spreading the "little Society" to remote parts of the world.

Despite the political turbulence that swirled around them and the numerous unforeseen obstacles inherent in founding and rooting schools at home and abroad, Mother Barat's nuns persevered in her commitment to "cover the world with Convents of the Sacred Heart." Between 1818 and 1850, fifty-five French nuns traveled from France to North America to support and carry on the mission Philippine Duchesne had begun. Sacred Heart convents and schools opened in Baton Rouge, Louisiana, and St. Joseph, Missouri, in 1851, and in Chicago and Cuba in 1858. Two foundations were made in Chile, one in Santiago (1854) and one in Talca (1859). Mother Aloysia Hardey went to Detroit, where the Society was welcomed, and after opening the school on Seventeenth Street in New York City, she moved the Society north to Canada. "The charity of Christ drives me on," Mother Barat said as she communicated through thousands of letters with her peripatetic, international community.

As they struggled to establish Sacred Heart schools in newfound lands, the nuns were often subjected to harsh weather, impossible living conditions, long months of travel, and bouts with disease. They were constantly required to adapt to new languages, new customs, and new territories. Monetary problems and the difficulty of communicating with the motherhouse on another continent were severe stumbling blocks in the planning and building of each new foundation. This was on-the-job training under the most trying circumstances, requiring courage and strength as well as an excess of determination in the Duchesne mold. To be a missionary was in itself a dangerous occupation; to be a woman missionary was an act of heroism.

Following the Society's golden jubilee Mother Barat continued to travel and scout new locations for schools and convents in Europe, although to a lesser degree than before. Her authority now flowed more through the provincials she had appointed than through personal contact. Still she retained an abiding interest in each new school and always in the children. "Our Lord and the children are all that I care about now."

She spent countless hours at her desk at the motherhouse, attending to her mounting correspondence, which included ninety-eight letters to the worldwide community and more than fourteen thousand personal letters written during her lifetime. The years had begun to take their toll on her physically, but she refused to give in to infirmity or old age, slowing her pace only when she thought some- one who was especially concerned with her welfare was watching. One who observed her during this time drew this verbal sketch: "She was small and thin, with olive-tinted complexion, quick walk, rapid and expressive gestures, a gay laugh, and a way of holding her cross in her hands."

She summoned the eighth General Council in June 1864 and, in what would be her last official communication to the councilors, she wrote of her wish "to gather together once more in this land of exile my old mothers and daughters who have helped me for so long and shared with their First Mother the constant work of our diffi- cult mission, who have so often lightened my burden and consoled me by taking the hardest and most tiresome part of it. Yes, I want to see them again, to tell them of my feelings and of my gratitude, and to urge most earnestly those who will live after me to redouble their devotedness, if possible, and to strengthen our Society on the foun- dation of the solid virtues, especially those most proper to our voca- tion: humility, an ardent zeal for the salvation of souls, and an unlimited generosity that no obstacle can check when there is ques- tion of the glory of the Heart of Jesus."

During her life she had seen one school become 89 in fifteen countries (she founded 111 but 22 had been forced to close) and 4 nuns become 3,539. For the little girl from Joigny whose father made wine barrels, it had been a most extraordinary journey. "For the sake of a single child" she had founded the Society of the Sacred Heart, and for those religious who shared in that foundation, in Europe and North and South America, and for those who would carry it in her name to Africa, Asia, and Australia, her legacy was inspirational. "We shall have no limits but the horizon," she prophesied.

Madeleine Sophie Barat died on Ascension Day, May 25, 1865, and in a letter left behind asked her "dear daughters" to remember her in their prayers but, more important, to "maintain, at the price of every sacrifice and with a persevering zeal, fidelity to our holy rules, to spread as far as we can the knowledge and love of the Sacred Heart of Jesus and to become, in every place where we shall be, the good odor of Him whose name we bear in spite of our unworthiness." Her own personal holiness and earthly accomplishments would be attested to in St. Peter's Basilica when Pope Pius XI declared Madeleine Sophie Barat a saint, confirming what those who knew her had always been sure of.

The three Mothers General who succeeded Mother Barat as superior of the Society of the Sacred Heart had terms of varying length. Josephine Goetz (1865–1874), Adele Lehon (1874–1894), and Augusta de Sartorius (1894–1895) were all known by the foundress during her lifetime. Each had come up through the ranks of the Society and each governed with strict adherence to her own interpretation of Mother Barat's original blueprint. During the thirty years after her death, the Society doubled in membership from 3,539 to 6,649 while the number of schools increased from 89 to 137. Vocations were on the upswing, reaching a peak in 1894, when 680 novices were studying to become Sacred Heart nuns. At no time in its history was the Society rolling along with more confidence. Letters from the motherhouse to the worldwide community emphasized preservation of established traditions and routines.

When Mother de Sartorius died after a generalate of less than a year, she was succeeded by Mabel Digby, a convert to Catholicism who had entered the Society on February 19, 1857. She had been superior at the school in Marmoutier and later vicar of the Sacred Heart's English-Irish vicariate (provinces had been changed to vicariates in 1851). At the school known as Roehampton in England Mother Digby established herself as one of the Society's most impassioned and gifted Mistresses of Novices. After her election as Mother General in 1895, she sailed to America with her friend and assistant Mother Janet Stuart. During the nine months she spent abroad, she inspected houses in the United States, Canada, and Mexico. One major decision made during that trip was to consolidate the twelve Sacred Heart novitiates in North America under one roof at Kenwood near Albany, New York. Here all American aspirants to the Society of the Sacred Heart would be exposed to the same spiritual exercises, teaching method, and personal formation.

On November 21, 1900, the Society of the Sacred Heart marked its centennial and again was faced with a political crisis that threatened the extinction of its forty-seven French houses. By the end of the nineteenth century, government control and repression of religious orders, which had abated somewhat in mid-century, were again in a resurgence.

Mother de Sartorius, who had been in Germany in 1872 when Bismarck forced the Jesuits into exile there, knew the signals of repression well. She knew that although many anticlerical laws in France were unenforced, they remained effective tools that could be used against religious congregations at any time. She hoped that despite the mounting tensions, the Society of the Sacred Heart could maintain a low profile and continue its educational work, which it did until 1901. Because taxation was used as a form of anticlericalism, the Society was forced to pay taxes of nine hundred thousand francs a year on the motherhouse, for which it dug deep into its treasury pockets. Then on July 9, 1901, new legislation leveled against all French teaching orders went into effect. Pierre Waldeck-Rousseau was responsible for the law that forced all religious teaching congregations to be authorized by the state according to certain conditions set by the government. Any order refusing to comply risked expulsion.

Mabel Digby, then Mother General, was as intractable in her view of secularization as Madeleine Sophie would have been. Before her petition for authorization had been refused, her mind was already made up. The Society of the Sacred Heart would, under no conditions, submit to the government's demands. "We must not hold to our houses more than our Lord holds to them," she said. "What would be the loss of them all in comparison to one deliberate infidelity on the part of one of us?"

The closing of the French Sacred Heart schools began in 1902 and continued for seven years, the time allotted by the state for all orders to leave the country. Mother Digby decided that the Society would use every day of that time to continue running its schools, and when the time for departure was at hand she gave careful thought to the destination of each religious who was to be separated from her convent and her country. Many of the elderly were sent to French-speaking communities, the younger ones to more distant missions such as the United States, and others to boarding schools in Spain, Belgium, and England, where many students from the French schools joined their teachers. On meeting one prospective but optimistic exile, Mother Digby asked where she would make her new home. "I don't know, Reverend Mother," came the reply, "but it's written on my trunk."

The furnishings of many of the French schools were saved from the hands of the "liquidators" by the nuns' care and cunning. The contents of each house were inventoried, and lists were sent to schools abroad so that special needs could be filled. Clocks, altars, school furniture, stained-glass windows, even entire libraries were packed and sent away. Many of the houses were sold on the open market, with the remainder given to friends to hold in safekeeping until the day the Society would again have access to its homeland.

One curious adjunct of the anticlerical legislation that proved advantageous to the religious of the Sacred Heart was the law regarding personal property. Since only the Society and not the state recognized the vow of poverty, all property that belonged to individual nuns at the time of their vows or any inherited by them afterward, although given to the Society, was considered individually owned. The law stated that compensation for the confiscated land could be obtained from the courts and, additionally, that a life pension would be dispensed to every property-owning religious regardless of her personal resources.

Mother Digby hired a lawyer who presented more than two hundred cases to courts, nearly all of which were handsomely settled. The Society, it was said, realized a larger profit from this process than any of the other orders that applied. After paying off its legal fees, nine million francs remained in the till. This sum was set aside and used in reestablishing the Society in France after World War I.

When the time finally came for the closing of the motherhouse, Mother Digby sat in the chapel as the altar was removed and the tree planted by Mother Barat, which had grown no taller since her death, was chopped down.

Spirit Seeking Light and Beauty

5

◖DURING THE THREE-DAY retreat given annually at each Sacred Heart school, the students were exempt from class but were required to participate in a variety of spiritual exercises given in the chapel by a priest from the "outside world." There was no speaking during the seventy-two hours, which were meant to be a time of personal reflection and spiritual contemplation. In the students' refectory the dining tables were covered with white tablecloths to reduce the noise level, and during the meal a nun read from an inspirational book especially selected for the occasion. At Eden Hall a low, mellifluous voice began the life of Mother Janet Stuart, perhaps the most brilliant, gifted, and scholarly woman to enter the second generation of the Society of the Sacred Heart.

Born in Cottesmore, England, on November 11, 1857, she was the daughter of a twice-widowed Anglican minister. Her father's two marriages produced thirteen children. Janet was the youngest of the second family. She was only two years old when her mother died, and she later wrote that the sorrow and trauma of that event precipitated her tumultuous relationship with God.

"It was on the subject of death that my faith, such as it was, received its first shock, when I was six years old. Having heard of the resurrection of Lazarus, and that miracles equal to that could be worked by faith and prayer, I resolved to raise my mother from the dead and escaped from my nurse into the church yard to perform the miracle. Having prayed with all my might, I shouted as loud as I could: 'Mama come forth,' without the slightest doubt I should see the grave open at once. The disappointment was very great and left a seed of doubt in my mind that bore fruit later."

A tomboy in what she described as an old-fashioned and tradition-bound home, she questioned whether "homes [are] more cere-monious when there is no mother." She was tutored in the parson-age with her siblings by German and French governesses and loved to read and to ride horses. Since her father had a fine library and farmed land near the parsonage, she had ample opportunity to do both. She loved livestock and animals of all sorts and became an expert in animal husbandry. After she entered the convent, a farmer from her village exclaimed, "What a shame, she is a great loss to the agricultural world." What he could not know was that the agricul-tural world's loss would be the Society's extraordinary gain.

After a long, difficult struggle, she resolved her doubts about the existence of God with the help of a Jesuit priest and made the deci-sion to convert to Catholicism. This unexpected conversion caused her father great pain and created a breach between them that was never repaired. Reverend Stuart was bewildered and disappointed at his daughter's determination to seek her answers outside the Anglican Church. He did his best to dissuade her from joining an-other religion, going so far as to set up an appointment for her with his friend William Gladstone, for whom Janet had "great venera-tion." "Mr. Gladstone," she wrote, "took the line of loyalty to the church of one's baptism." He told her that the Anglican Church was a branch that had not cut itself off from Rome but was undergoing persecution from the Roman branch and that "it was a dangerous cause, but one that should be held on to until unity comes back." He suggested that her mistake was in seeking a philosophy as well as a religion. After the visit she pondered his words and admitted they had given her "a certain shiver," but her intention to convert to Catholicism remained firm. For her it was not a choice between Catholicism and Protestantism, but between Catholicism and agnosticism.

On March 6, 1879, with the advice and counsel of her friend and spiritual director Father Gallwey, Janet Stuart entered the Catholic Church. The following day she made her first communion and never again lived in her father's house. As rector of an Anglican parish he felt it would be inappropriate for a Roman Catholic to be part of his household. It was a painful separation for father and daughter.

Three years later, while making a retreat at the Sacred Heart school at Roehampton, England, Janet Stuart received the call to religious life. She asked and received permission from Mother Mabel Digby, the Mistress of Novices at Roehampton, to enter the Society of the Sacred Heart.

"The day of entering is a very wonderful one," she wrote. "I remember the feeling of every hour of it. . . . I think it is more like death than anything I can imagine, and in fact that is just what it is, the death of one's first life and rather sharp agony; but one knows that as far as soul and will and resolve go, it is the intensest day of life, when they are put out to the full, and one simply gives all and goes in for death or for life whatever God chooses, and that is better than any high spirits or excitement."

She took the habit on November 13, 1882, and thus began one of the most remarkable careers in the history of the Society. Her life as a nun commenced with the novitiate, where she submitted to the exacting training period directed at reshaping body and will, mind and matter. She took the imposed discipline, acts of humility, and self-sacrifice in stride. A fellow religious who observed the novice during the early days of her religious life said, "She was always the same, first rate. She helped gladly whenever she was asked, but she never put herself forward, and it was by degrees that we realized that she really could do anything and everything. Her talents were multiple, she was a fine musician and poet, she was a deep thinker, a perfectionist who offered and expected the best." As a novice her goals were mortification, to obtain interior freedom; obedience, to be dependent on God; and simplicity, to lead the "common life." She believed the way to freedom was through renunciation and mortification. Before she entered the convent she had prepared herself well for religious life, submitting each day to self-imposed, time-consuming spiritual exercises in pursuit of the lofty goals she aspired to achieve. Thus she found life in the novitiate far less demanding than she had anticipated. Yet there were times, as there are for even the most gifted and committed, when she battled within herself against those elements of her nature that sought to destroy her resolve. She was innately shy and painfully self-conscious, but through Mother Digby's influence she learned that shyness was not a virtue.

She shared the fate of Mother Barat, who because of her many talents was denied the role of teacher in the conventional sense. Janet Stuart felt that she was most suited for teaching in a classroom. "I would not have minded what I taught," she said, "as long as I could have caught anyone and taught them anything." But four years in the classroom was all she was given before the Society called on her other considerable talents. She accepted the disappointment with cheerful resolve: "I live in confidence because I have nothing else to live for."

After her six-month probationary period in Paris before making her final vows, she returned to Roehampton as Mother Digby's assistant Mistress of Novices. Six years later, in 1894, when Mother Lehon, the Society's third Mother General, died, Mother Digby was called to Paris to work with the new Mother General, and Janet Stuart assumed her responsibilities, becoming Mistress of Novices and superior of Roehampton. The dual roles meant that her duties were multiple and exacting. By her example and leadership, hundreds of young women who had chosen or had been chosen to join her on the road to perfection were formed and trained in the well-established Sacred Heart tradition. She brought her own special brand of instruction to the novices, often employing her equestrian background in her lectures: "Sit your saddle more loosely, don't let the sportsman die within you." Her instructions on formation were frequently peppered with stories of fox hunting or sailing: "Certain great traditions," she said, "are in the Church of a consecrated life under the veil; these drew you to the cloister. . . . Bear in mind that you are on a sea-worthy ship, but that you are in port. You have to spread your sails, tend your helm, ply your oars — if ever you forget this and sit idle, swiftly comes the punishment of little-souledness. . . . Be watchful, temperate, humble, indomitable, serene, intrepid and strong."

The novices under Mother Stuart's supervision bore an unmistakable mark of excellence. She used texts from *Alice in Wonderland, Through the Looking-Glass*, and Kipling's *Jungle Book* to emphasize that things spiritual need not be dull or ponderous. As a natural sociologist she was continually amused by the comic frailties of her novices' human nature and the natural enthusiasms of their youth. She cautioned them to "be brave and laugh at the funny things; it will often save you from crying." Along with the formation of mind and body, she was keenly aware of the benefits that a good, healthy laugh and the counsel of good common sense could produce. She took a personal interest in all her novices, following their progress long after the formation period was over, and often referred to those with whom she had shared a special rapport as "my dear sons." She was determined to squeeze every ounce of character from their unformed and sometimes unfocused personalities by asking them to think of themselves as poppies in a wheat field, not violets in a wood. "You must grow like a tree, not like a mushroom. . . . Set your life to music." She wanted to give them the self-confidence Mother Digby had given her. "I have often thought that if I had fallen into other hands than yours," she wrote to her beloved superior, "I should have remained an un-opened oyster all my life or else gone wildly wrong."

Because she understood the complexities of life's stages and believed in the potential of women to achieve great things and perform great acts of courage and heroism, she was able to extract and refine the finest qualities of those she instructed. In the process she opened countless oysters. She believed that the strength of women lay in the formation of their character and that if their character was suitably molded it could alter and even change the process of education. "Their mission is civilization in its loftiest and widest sense," she said. For her, the greatest thing in creation was the inward life of the soul, "its acts of faith and hope and love and self-oblation, even the smallest." Those words reflected not only her appreciation for the unseen but her desire to touch it. This was another personal goal she sought to achieve and one she continued to address throughout her life, through letters, lectures, books, poetry, plays, and hymns.

An indefatigable student of words and language, she advised her charges never to give up trying to express themselves in more creative and imaginative ways. She stressed the importance of reading and attempted to extract from each encounter with the written page a new thought or idea. She challenged her intellectual self at every possible turn, viewed expression as the most fundamental instrument for everything that followed, and sought to instill in the young women in her care a disciplined mind and artistic eye that would be enhanced by moderation, patience, and self-control. This philosophy was incorporated into Sacred Heart education, where language, expression, and gracefulness were emphasized in every aspect of student life.

Nine months after her elevation to the office of Mother General, Mother de Sartorius died on May 8, 1895, and Janet Stuart's friend and mentor Mabel Digby succeeded her. Janet Stuart's responsibilities in the Society increased again when Mother Digby named her vicar of the Sacred Heart schools in England and Ireland. In August 1898 she accompanied Mother Digby on a trip to America. This would be the first of many such voyages for Mother Stuart. The two nuns spent ten days on board a ship called the *Dominion*, which docked at Montreal. They were driven to the banks of the St. Lawrence River, where they began their inspections of the North American Sacred Heart schools. Their first stop after Montreal was Rochester, then a hasty glimpse of Niagara Falls. Their next stops were in Chicago, Cincinnati, St. Louis, Omaha, San Francisco, and Mexico. Grand Coteau, New Orleans, and St. Michael's followed. Philadelphia, Atlantic City, New York, Boston, and Providence were the last cities on the exhausting schedule.

The final month of the thirty-six-week visit was spent at Manhattanville, the Sacred Heart college in New York City, which was the Society's "jewel in the crown" from its founding in 1847 until 1977, when it gave up its religious identity. It was here that all the North American vicars and mistresses of study gathered to hear Mother Stuart's famous lectures on education. She spoke to them of simplicity of aim and reiterated that their mission was "to educate children, to fit citizens for the kingdom of heaven, to train them that they so pass things temporal that in the end they might not lose the things eternal."

The dawning of the new century found Mother Stuart where she most loved to be, among the students, novices, and community at Roehampton, but her respite was to be short. In January 1901 she was nominated to be visitor to the Sacred Heart schools in South America and the West Indies. In a letter to a priest friend she wrote, "Our Lord is quite determined to teach me the lesson of confidence and make me overcome my shyness before I die. . . . It will be a long journey, about six months."

Letters postmarked Puerto Rico, Cuba, Panama, Chile, and Buenos Aires came back to England filled with her unique insights and observations about the students she met and the schools she visited. Sister Mary Quinlan comments in her book *Mabel Digby — Janet Erskine Stuart* that some of the letters Mother Stuart sent to Mother Digby during her Latin American visit were sometimes critical and often brutally honest. Speaking of a nun she encountered at one Latin convent, she said, "Do you know what we have [here]? A

Professed Sister who was a *sage-femme* . . . she acts as a bone-setter and consulting surgeon to the neighboring houses. They say she sets limbs and reduces dislocations beautifully. . . . Did you ever hear of anything so repulsive?" At another school Mother Stuart discovered that the nuns drank beer and wine between meals and ate "cold meat," which did not meet with her approval, and she made the observation that in one vicariate she foresaw trouble because "they have admitted [to the religious community] such dreadful people." The harshness of her comments were, as Sister Quinlan points out, probably due to language difficulties and a lack of understanding about unfamiliar customs and attitudes rather than to an ungenerous heart. But her prejudices and judgments were acutely felt by the superiors whose domains she invaded. She was convinced that the way to keep the Society unified was to allow as little flexibility as possible in the interpretation of rules concerning community life. Her standards were of the highest order and her expectations for her fellow religious, no matter their geographic location, were equally lofty.

The years 1902–1911 were busy and active for Mother Stuart as the Society continued to open more schools in England for her to oversee. In 1903 a school was started in Leamington Spa and later transferred to Tunbridge Wells. Foundations were made on the Devonshire coast, and the school at Carlisle was transferred to Newcastle. In 1904 Roehampton received accreditation from the board of education as a secondary training college where members of the Society could qualify as teachers. New schools were established on the Isle of Wight and at St. Charles. These additions not only enlarged Mother Stuart's area of responsibility but required her to spend much of her time traveling to each locale. She spent several weeks each year at the motherhouse in Paris, where she conferred with the Mother General and reported on the welfare of the schools under her care. Nuns like Janet Stuart who held high office were required to be not only women of God but women of finance, diplomacy, and executive efficiency.

In 1903 schools opened in Malta and Cairo under the supervision of Helen Rumbold, formerly Lady Rumbold, who had entered the novitiate with Janet Stuart after the death of her husband and child. Between 1898 and 1911 three North American Sacred Heart schools were added to the growing network, in Menlo Park, California (1898), Forest Ridge near Seattle (1907), and Point Grey in British Columbia (1911).

Mother Stuart attended the sixteenth General Council of the Society in 1904, the last held in Paris. Five years later, when the Society abandoned the last of its French schools under government order, the motherhouse was closed and moved to Ixelles, Belgium. Expansion and exploration had now become a well-accepted Sacred Heart tradition.

In 1879 five Sacred Heart nuns had left St. Louis for Timaru, New Zealand. Two years later they moved to the neighboring continent of Australia. The seed for the Australian foundation had been planted thirty-eight years earlier when a student at the school in Conflans attended a public audience with Pope Leo XIII in Rome. "Holy Father," she called out, "send my nuns to Australia." "And who are your nuns, my child?" the pope inquired. "The nuns of the Sacred Heart," came the reply.

The Society's first house in Tokyo, Japan, opened in 1908, for it was Mother Digby's plan that when the Society was expelled from France it would go to the Orient. Sister Margaret Williams, historian of the Society, writes, "At first they [the students] came in rickshaws, clad in bright kimonos; soon they came in automobiles, clad in trim navy blue uniforms."

Mother Digby died on May 21, 1911, and was buried at Roehampton four days later. Janet Stuart wrote of her beloved mentor, "In her presence one breathed in the truth, strength and peace which she communicated during life; she will still communicate them." On August 27 when Mother Stuart was elected sixth superior of the Society of the Sacred Heart, the first telegram she received was from the community at Roehampton, who knew they had lost her to a greater cause. It simply read, "Alleluia." Although her heart would always be at the school in England where she had begun her religious training and had lived for thirty years, her permanent residence was now the motherhouse in Ixelles, which in reality would be only a stopping-off place between her many trips. By 1911 the Society's numbers had increased to sixty-five hundred religious, and it was Janet Stuart's intention to know every one of them. Of the last three years of her life, she spent 672 days visiting schools in Belgium, Holland, Alsace-Lorraine, Austria, Hungary, Poland, Italy, Sicily, Malta, Spain, Egypt, Australia, New Zealand, Japan, Canada, and the United States. Her first journey took her to Italy and Malta, then to the Austrian vicariate, which included the schools of Alsace-Lorraine, Hungary, and Poland. She stopped briefly at the convent called Blumenthal, established in 1848 on the border between Holland and Germany, and in October 1912 she left the motherhouse for Spain, ignoring a warning that Barcelona was in a state of revolution and that crossing the frontier would be difficult and dangerous. "Tell them we are coming on," she said.

The practice of the superior's visiting as many of the Society's houses as possible was initiated in the early years by Madeleine Sophie, who saw it as a practical way to retain the unity she felt was essential to the Society's character advancement. She advocated a central novitiate and a constant flow of communication between the motherhouse and all the schools the Society founded around the world. Janet Stuart not only followed the tradition of visitation but made it the foremost activity of her generalate. She recognized the importance of personally meeting superiors in foreign countries when she traveled with Mother Digby, and she was determined to extend her support and exchange ideas and observations with as many as possible. Following in the footsteps of the foundress, who traveled from house to house in the early days, she studied the needs of each school in each country and made detailed notes on how best to implement the suggestions she felt to be practical and prudent. Mother Stuart's extensive travels not only put her in touch with the growing international community but put faces to names she had known only on paper. This resulted in a closer and more personal bond between the Mother General and her troops. As long as the general rule and constitutions were universally obeyed, she was willing to cut the jib to fit the ship. "Our things need native soil for growth," she wrote. "When transplanted they die, and what is worse, they decompose after death."

In 1913 she commenced a journey around the world that took her from Egypt to Australia, Japan, and North America. She returned to many of the houses she had visited with Mother Digby and some new ones, always extending herself to the ultimate, meeting and greeting thousands of students, nuns, and alumnae, giving lectures, viewing countless pageants, and accepting countless presentations. She took pride in the spirit and precision she witnessed, and although not everyone or everything measured up to her standards, she took heart from the unity she observed and the obvious affection the students felt for their schools. The unmistakable qualities of Sacred Heart education were in evidence everywhere and even in their sometimes less than perfect state were living examples of a working philosophy.

When she arrived back at Roehampton on June 24, 1914, it was apparent that Mother Stuart had paid a high physical price for her long and taxing journey. On June 9 she returned to the motherhouse in Ixelles in failing health but struggled to keep her commitments and meet her obligations. By August war had been declared and the motherhouse was soon cut off from all the other Sacred Heart houses.

"Yesterday evening the door closed between us and the outer world," she wrote, "by the entrance of the Germans into Brussels." It was decided that the Mother General would be safer if she temporarily moved her headquarters to Roehampton. Here among the women and at the school she so loved, Janet Stuart completed the cycle of her life. After undergoing surgery, she died of blood poisoning on October 21, 1914. She was fifty-seven years old. Buried in the beautiful chapel at Roehampton between Mother Digby and Father Varin, she left a job that would be taken up by another but a void in the Society that would never be filled. Mother Stuart, like every Mother of the Sacred Heart, had dedicated her life to educate young women and contribute to the perfection of their character and the salvation of their souls. But because her talents were so special and uniquely varied and her inquisitive intellect was so searching, she was able through her positions of authority to set a strong example of what thoroughness, spirituality, excellence, and exactitude could achieve. Many members of the Society revered her as a saint, and for many decades after her death her book *The Education of Catholic Girls* was praised and quoted by religious and lay educators alike. It was to the individual always that she directed her energies and her insights. "I must never be bored, never be offended, never be busy. To be busy is to be engaged in an occupation which makes it inconvenient to be disturbed." For the soul of a single child, a single person, a single purpose, she gave her life, always reflecting the words of the hymn she wrote (sung by Children of the Sacred Heart all over the world), "Spirit Seeking Light and Beauty."

Planned and Unplanned Studies

6

●MOST STUDENTS who came to reside in the grand and sometimes palatial schools of the Sacred Heart, where the blackboards bore the impeccable italic script and the class mistress in fluted white bonnet and black habit stood on a raised platform above her anxious charges, readily understood that these were not just places of education but houses abounding in a tradition that reached far beyond academics.

It took me a while to realize that the Society of the Sacred Heart was a worldwide organization that extended well beyond the perimeters of Eden Hall with a well-respected system of education as unique as its foundress. Wherever a Sacred Heart school, college, or mission existed, so too existed a communal spirit combined with an all-encompassing educative process. It was said that Sacred Heart education was like an extension ladder, "every rung a step in development, every extension a reach to a higher plane." Most who experienced its intensity never forgot what it taught them, and some never forgave.

Mother Barat's vision of education combined the development of body, spirit, and mind "to marshall a child's mental resources, stimulate her imagination, and strengthen her will." Her goal was the education of the whole person and she insisted that her nuns be not only teachers but educators. To this end she submitted them to a rigorous five-year period of formation before they were sent into the classrooms where most would spend their lives. It was through the education of women that the Society first attained recognition, primarily at first for its well-formulated Plan of Studies, which Mother Barat characterized as a plan of "life and advance." The original blueprint, drawn up in Amiens in 1805, was revised six times, the last in 1952.

The Plan of Studies for Sacred Heart boarding and day schools, followed at Eden Hall in the late fifties and early sixties, was aimed at duplicating Mother Barat's original theory of education, which sought to prepare young women for future roles by exposing them to a broad academic curriculum emphasizing moral, spiritual, and intellectual training. Imagination and memory were stimulated by literary contests and oral examinations, and courses in logic and psychology cultivated an early facility in defining terms and analyzing ideas. The Plan of Studies served as a guide for class mistresses and expressed "a clear idea of [the Sacred Heart spirit], a spirit which will hold good for every work of education and teaching."

Sister Margaret Williams, biographer of St. Madeleine Sophie, historian of the Society, and daughter of the founder of *Commonweal* magazine, wrote that the Plan of Studies was the product of many gifted minds, "incorporating the traditional sources of pre-revolutionary Christian education which had formed the first teachers of the Society." Among those influences were the Ursuline school in Paris and the Jesuits' plan of studies, the *Ratio Studiorum*. The Society's plan was flexible and subject to revision; it combined a liberal arts education with Catholicism at its core. In the early days, schools of the Sacred Heart were academically tough and sociologically democratic; children of peasants sat next to daughters of aristocrats. But as time went on, this began to change. Mother Barat constantly railed against the reputation for exclusivity and elitism that the Society began to gain in France. "My father made barrels," she said, "and I want everyone to know it."

The Hôtel Biron, the Society's exclusive school on rue de Varenne on the Left Bank in Paris, did nothing to diffuse the belief that the Society of the Sacred Heart educated only the rich. It was said that whenever foreigners came to Paris and asked for school recommendations, the response most often heard was "Sacré Coeur, rue de Varenne." The variety and scope of subjects taught at the Hôtel Biron and in the other schools of the Sacred Heart bespoke a broadening vista for women's education. Although Mother Barat's role as foundress allowed her only one year of teaching in the classroom, she was a creative instructor. Her own classical education, combined with her aesthetic eye and pragmatic sense of reality, inspired her pupils. Often she challenged them by asking, "What have you got in your head? Shut your eyes and think this out. Think!" Those words were echoed through the years by her many followers in Sacred Heart classrooms throughout the world.

Taking a page from the Jesuits, Madeleine Sophie adopted the practice of repetition in her schools, a practice that was still holding sway in my days at Eden Hall. Every day the class mistress reviewed the material taught on the previous day. Mothers Quinlan, Miller, Wheeler, Russell, and many, many others accepted no excuses for unpreparedness or lack of precision in speech or written expression from their students. Rote memorization was expected of the New Testament (never the Old), but there were also opportunities for individual definition and sometimes creative thought. Every process that resulted in the acquisition of knowledge was fostered and encouraged, and although a process might end in mutual frustration for teacher and student, the exercise in itself was often a memorable lesson.

A Graham Greene short story my class read in fourth academic (twelfth grade) English class was characterized by the central thought "God writes straight with crooked lines." I remember shifting in my brown oxfords as Mother Carmody, our class mistress, attempted to correct my impression of that simple phrase.

"No, V V, it does not mean 'All's well that ends well.' Think about the characters and what the author is trying to tell us. Consider the other stories we have read this semester and try to find a common thread."

"But Mother, I am thinking."

"Well, dear, I am glad."

The Plan of Studies as formulated by Mother Barat included classes in logic for the younger students and in philosophy for the older ones. The philosophy in my time at Eden Hall was dispensed to every twelfth grade Sacred Heart student from the book *The Image of His Maker*. Written by Father Robert Brennan, who had been encouraged and assisted by a Sacred Heart nun, Mother Elizabeth Young, the book explained the complex theories of St. Thomas Aquinas on mind and matter. Classes in philosophy were unusual in high school at the time, but at Sacred Heart schools it was assumed that early exposure to conceptual thinking would produce original and independent Catholic minds. This might appear to be contradictory, for the premises of Catholicism are restrictive even in the most elementary concepts, but it was a stimulus to a thought pro-

RIGHT *Madeleine Sophie Barat, who founded the Society of the Sacred Heart in 1800 in the aftermath of the French Revolution.*

BELOW *Sainte-Marie-d'en-Haut, the Visitation convent in Grenoble, France, where Madeleine Sophie and Philippine Duchesne met.*

ABOVE *The motherhouse in Paris until 1857.*

RIGHT *Convent of the Sacred Heart, St. Charles, Missouri, where Philippine Duchesne established a school in 1818 at the request of Bishop Dubourg of Louisiana.*

BELOW *The convent school in Florissant, Missouri, opened by Philippine Duchesne in 1819, the first of thirty-five Sacred Heart schools in the United States.*

ABOVE *Convent of the Sacred Heart, Roehampton, England where Vivien Leigh and Maureen O'Sullivan were schoolmates.*

RIGHT *Janet Erskine Stuart, the Society's sixth Mother General and influential Mistress of Novices at the Convent of the Sacred Heart, Roehampton, England.*

ABOVE *Old Manhattanville College on Convent Avenue in New York City, which was sold for more than eight million dollars in 1950.*

INSET *Mother Grace Cowardin Dammann, the courageous president of Manhattanville College who admitted the first black student in 1938.*

ABOVE *Trinità-dei-Monti, at the top of the Spanish Steps in Rome, Italy, since 1920 the headquarters of the Society of the Sacret Heart,*

TOP LEFT *The school at Grand Coteau, Louisiana, where the nuns and students watched a Civil War battle.*

Mother Eleanor O'Byrne, left, president of Manhattanville College from 1945 to 1966; Mother Josephine Morgan, head of Manhattanville's Pius X School of Liturgical Music, and Francis Cardinal Spellman.

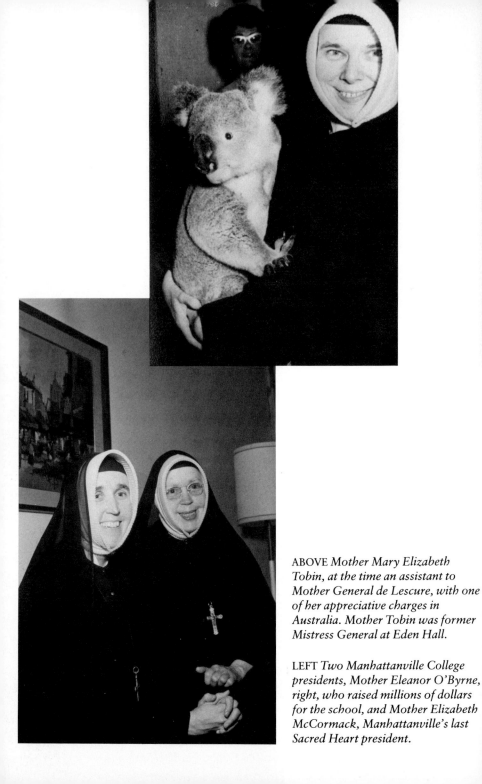

ABOVE *Mother Mary Elizabeth Tobin, at the time an assistant to Mother General de Lescure, with one of her appreciative charges in Australia. Mother Tobin was former Mistress General at Eden Hall.*

LEFT *Two Manhattanville College presidents, Mother Eleanor O'Byrne, right, who raised millions of dollars for the school, and Mother Elizabeth McCormack, Manhattanville's last Sacred Heart president.*

LEFT *Mother General Marie Thérèse de Lescure, left, and two assistants head back to Rome after visiting the Sacred Heart schools in the United States.*

BELOW *The Castle, the main building on the Manhattanville campus in Purchase, New York, once owned by Ben Halliday of Overland Express and later by Whitelaw Reid, owner of the New York Tribune.*

LEFT *Rose Philippine Duchesne, who brought the Society to the United States in 1818 and was canonized by the Catholic Church in 1988.*

ABOVE *The Rodin Museum in Paris, formerly the Hôtel Biron, the first of the Society's many elegant mansions in which the daughters of the privileged and the poor were educated.*

cess that some understood better than others — an early encounter
with abstraction that was another aspect of the educational process
advocated by the Plan of Studies. At the end of *The Image of His
Maker*, which still sits on a bookshelf in my room in South Carolina
(the only textbook I saved), is a paragraph about St. Francis de
Sales, who according to Father Brennan had "a most generous and
loving nature but a fiery and passionate disposition. Thus grace and
good will so worked together that his outstanding virtue — meek-
ness — was the flat contradiction of his strongest natural impulse —
to anger. As Saint Francis often said, 'One can catch more flies with
a spoonful of honey than with a barrel of vinegar.' " In the margin,
in a handwriting I no longer recognize, the words "So true, so true"
are penciled in.

Philosophy class was far from the only unique thing about Sacred
Heart education. The most memorable and certainly the most terri-
fying academic exercise was the oral examinations, common to every school and held twice a year on the subjects of doctrine, history,
and philosophy. Mother Janet Stuart, sixth Mother General of the
Society, wrote, "Self-control is so vital to the conduct of life that no
price is too great to pay for acquiring of the habit." Among the
many exercises geared to achieving that goal were the dreaded orals.
At Eden Hall all the students in the school assembled in the gymnasium with the entire religious community in attendance. The nuns
sat on rows of folding chairs facing the students. Some brought their
knitting, some their rosary beads, and others only intimidating, im-
perious expressions. The students wore white gloves, polished
shoes, and freshly starched blouses under their jumpers, which symbolized the seriousness of a ritual that was both chilling and challenging. From a silver tray passed around by the class mistress, each
student selected a strip of paper at random. On each a question had
been typed and numbered. When the tray was empty the student
with the first question rose from her seat, curtsied, and with the
words "Reverend Mother, I have question number one" began her
oratory. Never did I identify with my classmates more closely than
at the moment when thirty-two white-framed heads turned in the
direction of a shaky voice searching for an answer that was "brief,
cogent, and to the point." The results were usually mixed and it was
rumored that style counted more than substance, but on that rare
occasion when Reverend Mother's knitting needles fell from her lap

with a resounding clatter and the ominous words "You may sit down, dear" echoed in the silent gym, we all felt the inevitable moment of reckoning, a shared, unspoken knowledge that there but for the grace of God went each of us.

Once, in that memorable setting, I produced a moment of panic for myself when I compared an elastic clause in history to a piece of bubble gum, claiming that each had exceptional stretching powers. I remember being greatly relieved when one of the nuns told me later that she thought it a very creative metaphor.

Not every offshoot of Sacred Heart academic life was as contrived or as dramatic as the orals. In March 1960, with my own academic record hovering between poor and very poor, I turned my attention from academics to creative writing. This did nothing to endear me to Mother Carmody, who said more than once when we were gathered in her classroom, "March of 1960 is no time for one of us to be writing a novel." Her sentiments were shared by most of my other teachers who at various times had witnessed me smuggling assorted sheets of notebook paper into class, into study hall, and sometimes into chapel. After being reprimanded more than once for this unassigned, distracting activity I was ordered to see Mother Tobin, the Mistress General, which in my case was the equivalent of Brer Rabbit being thrown into the brier patch. Many of the nuns at Eden Hall shared the opinion that Mother Tobin offered me more time and understanding than I deserved, and they were probably right.

Mother Tobin listened patiently as I explained myself and in the process revealed the plot of my book, *When Spring Returns*, which revolved around the death of my hero's fiancée in a freak sailing accident. She knew I was perplexed about bad things happening to good people, and my hero, Christopher Mark Halloway, was as good and as sad as they came. Mother Tobin suggested that to prevent further complaints from my teachers I limit my creative writing to times of recreation and use the science lab for that purpose. I readily agreed, but I went there only once. In the midst of laboratory equipment, Bunsen burners, intriguing microscopes, and glass tubes I found I was quickly distracted from my book writing.

In writing fifty pages, which was where my novel stopped, I realized I did not know enough about "real life" to tell the story I wanted to tell. I was no Françoise Sagan. When I shared my frustration with Mother Tobin, she smiled and said, "Wait awhile. When the time is right you will know it." So the controversial pages were shut away in my trunk and eventually got lost somewhere between Torresdale, Pennsylvania, and Camden, South Carolina.

It was a scam of course, my novel writing, an excuse not to do the work assigned because I had invented something I viewed as more important, more personally rewarding, than Mother Carmody's assignments. It was another attempt to skirt the rules, assert my individuality, and test the tolerance of my teachers. It was a rebellion against the predictability of the endless routines that filled the indistinguishable days and nights. Yet like so much of my life at Eden Hall, it turned into a learning experience.

Madeleine Sophie's intention was not only to give the schools she founded a distinctive character and spirit but to incorporate into each an element of social awareness directed to moral development that went beyond the dictionary definition of charity and good works. This was accomplished in my time through limited participation in school organizations devised to emphasize the plight of the less fortunate. The only drawback was that the distinction between the haves and have-nots was difficult to draw when we were young and preoccupied with the deprivations and limits imposed by our own life in the convent.

During my first year at Eden Hall I was a member of a group called the Missions. We spent several hours each month learning to make cord rosaries for Catholics in the Marine Corps and preparing "care" packages for Sacred Heart missionary programs in underdeveloped countries. I remember thinking, when letters were read aloud describing the lives of nuns in faraway places who were trying to make a difference in the lives of the oppressed, that in some ways their duties seemed infinitely preferable to ours. They at least had volunteered for their jobs.

The following year, because it provided an opportunity to leave the school property, I joined the Social Welfare Club. Every Sunday after Mass, we were driven in Eden Hall station wagons, with raincoats covering our uniforms, into the "outside world" to a state-run nursing home. We gathered there in a small, overheated room to pray the rosary with an assembly of ancient, sickly Catholic residents. The building reeked of urine and ammonia, and after visiting the bedridden, who reached out with long, bony fingers to touch us, almost as if we were the Children of Fatima, we waited outside for our ride back to school. When time permitted and someone had managed to smuggle out a package of cigarettes, left over from the most recent vacation, we smoked. This was the main attraction of the Social Welfare Club, but in the hour spent in that depressing, hopeless institutional atmosphere, I began to understand that being old and sick was worse than being young and healthy at Eden Hall.

The Society's past is tucked away in the archives at Villa Duchesne in St. Louis, Missouri. Long gray boxes stacked on metal shelves hold histories of familiar-sounding schools and colleges now closed or no longer owned by the Society. The daybooks inside the boxes record early descriptions of property settlements, remodelings, and daily activities. The oldest entries are almost entirely in French, which until recently was the official language of the Society. Occasionally names of individual nuns appear, and even more occasionally the names of students. In the main the books are impersonal records of inconsequential, routine events that made up a school day and eventually a school year. The most memorable moments of those times, of course, are not recorded but remain in the protective custody of memory. Recollections of more recent times are recounted by journalist Candy Stroud, who completed every stage of her education at the Sacred Heart, starting with kindergarten at the school on Ninety-first Street in New York City and ending at Newton College in Massachusetts in 1963. She credits the nuns with instilling within her a love for learning and "engendering in me a big passion for all things spiritual." Remembering a motto from her days at Ninety-first Street, "A man's head and a woman's heart," she says, "The nuns meant us to be every bit as good as a man intellectually, to develop as a whole person, and I think not competing with boys in the classroom was useful. By the time you got into the world you were accustomed to being a leader in your own right, you were used to responsibility." On the other hand, in observing her classmates today, many of whom remain her friends, she feels the nuns were less successful in addressing some of life's more pragmatic issues. "They were very good spiritually and intellectually, but because so many in my class have had their lives wrecked by the inability to make good choices, I wonder if the thrust was a bit too idealistic, and if, like the nuns themselves, we were too cloistered, too protected, had too many unrealistic expectations."

The inescapable demands those expectations put on students were one of the primary ingredients that made Sacred Heart schools different from other private girls' schools where codes of conduct were similarly strict and rigid — coupled with the fact that in every Sacred Heart institution Catholicism was the axis on which everything else turned. Each class, each meal, each day, began and ended with a prayer. God loomed large in the lives of the Children of the Sacred Heart, whose days were structured to remind them of *His* eternal ways, whose welfare was consigned to the care of *His* spouses, those important women whose vocations were based on the love and glorification of *His* Son's Sacred Heart. There was no question where the emphasis lay, just as there was no doubt that that emphasis aimed to produce women of perfection.

The fact that the narrow precepts of Catholicism were the alpha and omega of Sacred Heart education colored the educative process on every level. In addition to the demanding academic subjects, students of the Sacred Heart were required to participate in a variety of extracurricular activities. Along with the prescribed hour of sports in the afternoon, there were classes in letter writing, music, sewing, diction, and even politeness. Each in its own way reflected the Catholic approach and was designed to balance the moral, physical, and spiritual aspects of student life and ultimately to produce well-integrated feminine personalities. For those whose expectations of education were connected with and defined by the faith they had been born into, the Sacred Heart approach seemed eminently right. For others, like me, the experience of being force-fed religion, not only in doctrine class but in math class as well, was a bit overwhelming.

New Yorker writer Suzannah Lessard recalls her Sacred Heart education at Noroton-on-the-Sound in Connecticut as being strong in some areas and deficient in others. "I don't think the curriculum compared in thoroughness with other private schools'. I had a friend at Milton Academy [a nonsectarian boarding school in Massachusetts] who was reading ten Henry James novels to our one. On the other hand, I feel it was pretty solid in other respects. It was unusual to have this whole curriculum that was very traditional, that went through literature and history sequentially for four years and really gave us a very general sense of Western civilization. Yet I think there was a very deep conflict in the nuns' identity as educators and their identity as propagandists, but there is no doubt that they taught us to write and to think. They could not actively encourage us to truly dig and explore things because they had to stick to the party line [Catholicism], which was a fundamental conflict because many of them had intellectual minds."

Author Mary McCarthy in an essay in *The New Yorker* remembered her student days at Forest Ridge, the Sacred Heart school near Seattle, Washington, as intellectually stifling. "I have only to summon up in memory the hushed study halls of Forest Ridge," she wrote, "with the *surveillante* . . . raised above us at her desk on the dais, I have only to see morning chapel, with the girls in dark-blue serge uniforms and black net veils, like widows, intoning '*Oui, je le crois,*' . . . to admit that an intellectual cannot be the product of an élite education. . . . Chapel and study hall, Church of Rome and P.E. merge. I listen to . . . the soughing of the organ, the creaking of pews, and I could weep for it all, for the waste of it."

But what seemed a waste to McCarthy seemed something quite different to conservative author, spokeswoman, and ERA opponent Phyllis Schlafly. Schlafly graduated from City House in St. Louis, Missouri, in 1941. "The Sacred Heart education — its values and lessons," she wrote shortly before her graduation, "is something that will stay with me always. I never as long as I live shall forget the things I learned there. They are etched indelibly on my soul."

When Grace Schrafft arrived at Eden Hall in the fall of 1958 to join our class for her last two years of high school, she was already remarkably independent and astute. Perhaps it was her public school education and pragmatic, frenetic, ingenuous nature that made her seem a sturdy evergreen in Eden Hall's hothouse of wilting violets. She had grown up in Gloucester, Massachusetts, where her mother's family had lived for generations. Of the hundred or so girls I knew at school, Grace was one of the few I loved. The moment I recognized the puzzled, quizzical expression on her face during her first days as a Child of the Sacred Heart, I knew I had found a friend.

She too was a slave to rock and roll, having decided at age fifteen "that you could only pick your friends by who loved rock and roll." At Eden Hall she found, as I had, that most people didn't.

This common link brought us together one depressing Saturday morning. Because we were not allowed to spend time in our rooms for hair washing, radio listening, or other weekend privileges until after lunch, I joined Grace, who was slumped behind her desk in study hall.

She confessed that she had probably been sent to Eden Hall because during the summer she had stolen her father's brand-new Ford Hydromatic and wrecked it. Her mother had been a Child of the Sacred Heart but had never considered sending her daughter away until the car incident, which topped a long list of offenses. "I guess my mother decided it was time for prison," she said matter-of-factly.

I empathized with her and from that point on we began to trade life histories. As I had a roommate from Argentina my first year, Grace had one from Cuba, who she claimed could barely speak a word of English.

"She says things like 'O sheet, I have to change my shits,'" Grace confided, then admitting that during her first weeks at Eden Hall, because she was so lonely, she adopted a spider, who was weaving a web near her bed, as a pet. Every night before going to sleep, she talked to the spider, attempting to alleviate her sense of isolation. "I was used to having pets at home," she said with a laugh, "and so I took a spider as my confidant." Then one night the spider was discovered by her dormitory mistress, who killed it with a broom. Grace began to cry and Mother Mooney advised her that there was no reason to be afraid of a spider.

Grace informed her that she wasn't crying because she was afraid of the spider but because she loved it. This prompted Mother Mooney to launch into a predictable lecture about "appropriate behavior for a Sacred Heart girl" and resulted in Grace's losing her Très Bien card at *primes* the following Monday.

I tried to console her by telling her that that was nothing compared with what had happened to me during my first year. I recalled the time that Mother Forden snatched me out of my pew in chapel and forced me into Father Becker's office to go to confession. It was during my short-lived prayer boycott, when I was conspicuously absent from the communion rail and all public praying.

Father Becker was getting ready to say Mass, as he did every morning, when Mother Forden knocked at his door and said, to my horror, "I am sorry to bother you, Father, but this child needs to go to confession." He appeared just as shocked as I was. I had to kneel in front of his desk and confess without benefit of the anonymity of the confessional, which was humiliating for me and embarrassing for him. In addition, I suspected that Mother Forden was listening behind the door. During my face-to-face confession I said something about not wanting to pray or receive communion because I was having doubts about the existence of God. Father Becker peered down at me through his wire-rimmed glasses and said, "This is a familiar pattern for children your age. Just say a good Act of Contrition and tell God you are sorry." "But Father," I interjected, "I don't think that makes much sense if I am not sure there is a God."

His beady eyes got smaller and darker. "I have to say Mass in five minutes," he said impatiently. "Perhaps you should take this up with one of the nuns."

Grace smiled and said she wasn't sure it beat the spider incident but admitted it was another good example of the oppression we lived under. "I really envy the day students," she confessed. "At least *they* get to go home at night and eat pizza and watch television." Soon we moved from stories to songs, finding ourselves magically transported from our miseries by a musical tribute to the "fabulous fifties." Grace knew every line of every verse, every doo-waa chorus, and when we moved from the obvious to the obscure without missing a word, a beat, or a doo-waa-waa we looked at each other in amazed delight. It was the beginning of a friendship that would last through our convent days and well beyond.

There were not many opportunities to sing rock and roll songs at Eden Hall or to speak alone, but sometimes, when weather permitted an outdoor recreation, the dubious voices of Schrafft and Harrison could be heard searching for the right notes to harmonize the latest hits.

In the spring of our third academic (junior year) Grace and I discovered a secret retreat behind the nuns' cemetery where wildflowers grew and the grass was very tall. For lack of a better name, we called it the Wide, Wide World because for us it symbolized the freedom and privacy we missed at school. It was a place apart where there was no surveillance or scrutiny, where we could share confidences and imagine our futures. Ten minutes in the Wide, Wide World could seem like hours, and we ran there each night after dinner with swift enthusiasm.

"What do you want to do when you get out of here?" Grace would ask as we sank down on the cool, lumpy ground, the moisture of early springtime seeping through the skirts of our wool uniforms.

"I want to write something beautiful," I'd reply, plucking a blade of grass to use as a substitute cigarette while Grace struck an imaginary match to light it.

"You can't do that," she'd say, dark eyes flashing. "That's what I want to do, but I will probably end up marrying George." It never occurred to either of us that it might be possible to do both.

George was Grace's "steady" boyfriend at home. Every day she received his thick letters from the mail basket chronicling his life in Gloucester without her. These were written in a spidery, unformed hand, which we concluded was the reason they continued to get past the censor.

Sometimes Grace would speculate on what it would be like to be a nun; sometimes she even thought she might have a vocation. I always tried to dissuade her from this notion by telling her I was sure there were two people in our class who would not end up in the novitiate at Kenwood.

"Well, you might be right about yourself," she'd say solemnly, "you barely believe in God, but it's different with me. I do believe in Him and sometimes I think it would be nice to be as happy and as holy as Mother Carmody."

"But it wouldn't be nice to be as dull," I'd respond, knowing this would provoke an immediate defense of her favorite nun.

"You just don't appreciate her," Grace would fire back, her head moving closer to mine, cheeks flushed, hair falling over her forehead. "You don't like her because she makes you pay attention in class. You only like the ones with power and charm, but Mother Carmody is the best person I have ever known. She's so good and so . . ."

"Boring," I'd gleefully add.

Mother Marie Louise Carmody, once a classmate of Grace's mother at Noroton-on-the-Sound and for two years our class mistress, came to her vocation late in life. It happened when she was almost thirty years old, pursuing a career in business in New York. Tall and bespectacled Mother Carmody was intense, articulate, intellectual, and, from my point of view, totally inflexible. She lived by exactitude, perhaps not by choice but certainly in obedience to the strict rule that governed her life. While other nuns made concessions and found ways around the rigidity of the religious regulations that prohibited them from establishing personal relationships with the students, Mother Carmody stuck to a literal interpretation. Only after she was elevated to mistress of studies, a position of authority that permitted more intimate student contact, did some of her reserve fall away.

Years later, when I told her of the high place she held in Grace's heart at Eden Hall, she was astounded, for she could not recall having had more than two or three private conversations with Grace during the two years she was at the school.

At the time of our talks in the Wide, Wide World, Mother Carmody was not yet mistress of studies and thus her connection with our class and, more important, with individual students was more formal than it would be the following year when she felt free to assume a closer, more casual role with her students. Still, there were those who loved her, and Grace was certainly high on that list.

But before we would have the chance to further debate the merits of Mother Carmody's personality or Grace's vocation or the numerous other subjects we saved for discussion in our after-dinner retreats, the bell for study hall would ring out and Grace and I would get up in midsentence and as inconspicuously as possible fall into line with our "sisters in confinement" as they moved slowly from the playgrounds.

"Good-bye until tomorrow," Grace would hiss as we approached the school building, for there would be no more talking until after the next morning's Mass.

I'd look over at her and roll my eyes.

"Offer it up," Grace would advise, "maybe it will help some poor soul out of purgatory."

"Why doesn't it work the other way?" I'd say with a hiss in return. "Why can't some poor soul in purgatory pray me out of here?" At that moment we would see Mother Forden, the surveillant, heading our way.

"V V Harrison and Grace Schrafft, please stop talking. Your recreation is over."

"Sorry, Mother."

*C*hild of the *S*acred *H*eart

7

ALMOST EVERY CHILD of the Sacred Heart had a favorite nun, especially at boarding school — one nun who stood apart from the others, with whom, although the rule did not permit it, a special relationship developed. She was the one you looked for in the communion line each morning at Mass, the one you followed around and tried to find out things about — where she had lived and had gone to school, whether her hair had been curly or straight, if she had ever been in love or kissed a boy. She was the one you confided in when you thought you couldn't survive another day; and when you did something to displease her, your betrayal made you feel loathsome and unworthy. She mended your blazer when it was torn, laughed at your antics — often designed to catch her attention — and when she told you personal, private things you kept them proudly to yourself, savoring each one. For to know a little about a nun was to think you knew a lot, but the thing you were surest of, and the thing you were never allowed to say, was how much you loved her.

The nuns' past lives were closely guarded secrets, and there was much conjecture by the children in the schools as to whether they had been born in the convent or had been forced there by an unspeakable act of treachery or tragedy. For some students it was unimaginable that the nuns had freely chosen to shut themselves off from all forms of pleasure, to wear a habit, to live lives of prayer and mortification, and to forever cut themselves off from the outside world. I was one of these. It was always a challenge to put the nuns through what we thought were subtle inquisitions to cull a few fragmented facts. In most instances our imaginations worked overtime to fill in the missing pieces, injecting drama and intrigue whenever possible. In retrospect, I am not sure which things Mother Daley told me about her past life and which I invented to satisfy my own illusions.

But we did know certain things about any nun's life — or at least about her training. The novitiate, the long journey toward final vows, began with a six-month probationary period, equivalent to convent basic training. During this period the postulant, as the young recruit was called, was instructed in the traditions of the Society and wore her own clothes. Beginning in 1866, American novices lived at Kenwood, also a Sacred Heart secondary school founded by Mother Aloysia Hardey in 1852, in Albany, New York. The young postulants held great fascination for the students in the school, who watched them walking the grounds silently in groups of threes or praying in the chapel and who wondered what had propelled them into convent life, a life that stripped them first of all worldly goods (they could bring nothing personal except their clothes) and then of all their worldly aspirations.

At the end of the six-month probation, with the approval of the Mistress of Novices and acceptance by the community, the postulant was ready to publicly declare her commitment. Wearing a white wedding dress, she walked down Kenwood's chapel aisle with the others who had entered the novitiate with her. As a bride of Christ she knelt at the altar rail, then left the chapel to discard the clothes of the world, to have her hair shorn by a professed nun, and to put on the habit, which had been blessed by the priest. Officially dressed, she returned to the chapel as a religious of the Sacred Heart, in a handmade habit, a basic, black, collarless dress with long sleeves worn under a cape called a *pèlerine*. The buttons down the front of the dress were made in France, as was the lightweight wool fabric. The skirt was gathered at the waist, and a thin veil (white for the first two years in the novitiate, black thereafter) was pinned to the top of the white fluted bonnet. There were slits in the sides of each Sacred Heart habit so the long, deep pockets, separately attached by a belt under the waistband, were accessible. Each nun had two habits, one for weekdays and one for Sundays, with a special number sewn into each piece for identification. These were mended, laundered, and repaired when needed by the nuns themselves.

On returning to the altar in her new habit, the novice received the kiss of peace, the equivalent of a corporate handshake, from each member of the community she was joining and prepared to face the demanding five-year period of religious study and character formation. In the first two years of training, the novice was subjected to intensive classes in spiritual exercises conducted by the Mistress of Novices. Then she received her black veil and became an aspirant. During the next two years an aspirant who had a college degree was often sent to assist or teach in one of the schools while one without a degree continued to pursue academic studies. The Society's constitutions stated that no one could be professed until she was twenty-five, although in the early days exceptions might be made for illness or anticipation of early death. Finally, after a probation of another six months and a month-long retreat, the novice made a trip to Trinità-dei-Monti, in Rome. There the young nun made her final vows, receiving the gold French double wedding ring she wore on the third finger of her right hand and the silver cross she wore around her neck. Each symbolized a lifetime commitment to God, through acts of penance and self-denial, through prayer and contemplation, through the vows of poverty, chastity, and obedience, and through the care and education of the students in her charge, known universally as Children of the Sacred Heart.

She was one of the many nuns we called Mother, who wrote R.S.C.J. (*Religieuse du Sacré Coeur de Jésus*) after her name, who had renounced all worldly pleasures, who because she was cloistered would never go home again, eat in a restaurant, drive a car, or take a vacation, to whom we were instructed to say "Happy Christmas" instead of "Merry" and to close our letters "Your loving child," no matter how old we got.

When I first met Mother Margaret Daley in the fall of 1959, she wore the crisp, traditional Sacred Heart habit with the number 32 stitched inside (according to my best calculations, the number was very close to her age).

In the habit, she exuded a comfortable confidence. Though slightly pigeon-toed, she skimmed the polished corridors gracefully, floating like a hydrofoil on a lake. The long, black gathered skirt fit her trim figure perfectly, and the white fluted bonnet held mischievous hazel eyes and a broad, thin-lipped smile. If the Society of the Sacred

Heart had a recruitment poster, Mother Daley could easily have been the model.

She spoke in a soft, deep, throaty voice, her words tinged with a Boston accent. Transferred from the Sacred Heart school in Greenwich, Connecticut, Mother Daley came to Eden Hall in my senior year, which for many reasons is the year I remember most vividly and with the most affection.

I fell under her spell the first time we talked together in a large linen closet on the top floor of the school, where as captain of the field hockey team I was doling out gym suits to the varsity squad. Mother Daley was supervising the procedure, chatting easily with us, punctuating sharp observations with laughter, good-naturedly joining the confusion of pairing each tunic with matching bloomers and belt. After the team had been properly outfitted and dispersed, I stayed behind with her to tidy up, confiding that my position as varsity goalie was a source of embarrassment because I had replaced the fattest girl in the school. She laughed and then posed a serious question. "What do you plan to do with your senior year?"

I closed the closet door and walked with her down the hall.

"Mother, you don't make any plans at this school," I replied with my usual dramatic flair. "Every hour of every day is mapped out in a book in Mother Tobin's office. The only difference between this place and Holmesburg [a nearby prison] is that we have to pay to go here and the food is worse."

She smiled, shook her head, and picked up speed, leaving me trailing behind. Midway down the corridor she stopped, twirled around on the heels of her black oxfords, and waited.

"You know," she said when I had caught up, "a lot of men in prison work hard to take advantage of the opportunities that come their way. The smart ones even come out with degrees sometimes. Think about it." Then she was off, leaving me to ponder her words and wonder if she had already gotten wind of my dismal academic record.

So it began, Mother Daley countering my flippant, sarcastic remarks, making her point, leaving me with the challenge, forcing me to *think*.

She had entered the Society of the Sacred Heart in September 1951, one year after her graduation from Manhattanville College in

New York City. She had grown up on Long Island and had not attended a Catholic school until her father, an insurance manager, was transferred to Boston. She completed her last two years of high school at Newton Country Day School of the Sacred Heart near Boston, where she met the McGowan sisters, Clare and Jean, who were to become her lifelong friends, college mates and fellow religious of the Sacred Heart.

She told me that, like St. Madeleine Sophie, she had wanted to be a nun even before she knew what a nun did. "I never had a choice about it," she said as we walked together at evening recreation.

"But how were you sure, Mother?" I asked, hoping she would elaborate. Instead she offered only one of her mystery smiles to reconfirm the obvious.

"I just knew, that's all."

That was all for the moment, but it was enough to keep me coming back to dig for more details.

More than other religious orders for women, the Society of the Sacred Heart filled its ranks with daughters of affluent, prominent Catholic families. It was a rare novice at Kenwood who had not completed four years of college. The girls who walked down the King's Highway (the corridor that connected the new novitiate building with the old and that for many became the symbolic passageway from the secular world to the cloister) were for the most part well traveled, well heeled, and gently bred. Many left mink coats, convertible cars, and trust funds behind when they entered the convent. There were some who were rumored to have left a trail of broken hearts as well. Naturally, I assumed Mother Daley was one of these.

The summers of her youth had been spent in the Connecticut town where Katharine Hepburn also summered, and railroad tracks cut the town in two.

"Sometimes I invited friends from the wrong side of the tracks home for dinner," Mother Daley once told me, as I pressed close to her side waiting for her next revelation. "My mother would be furious, but they were my friends, and where they lived had nothing to do with how I felt about them."

Of course, it had everything to do with how I felt about Mother Daley, who seemed to me as close to perfection as God intended any human. She told me she had once gone to a coming-out party and had left when she discovered a group of girls looking at the labels in the guests' coats.

"Tell me about Katharine Hepburn," I'd plead, hoping she would not be called away by Reverend Mother, a ringing bell, or a sudden urge to pray.

"We'd see her on the beach or riding her bicycle," she recalled, "and sometimes she'd stop to chat. She was accepted there just like anybody else, and although she was very famous, no one looked at her as a movie star. Once, after I had become a nun and was teaching at Greenwich [Connecticut], we were being driven somewhere in a Volkswagen bus. Suddenly there was this loud honking sound below us that continued until finally I looked out the window. That was against the rules, as we were meant to keep our eyes straight ahead. When I looked down, there was Katharine Hepburn waving from her convertible."

"But how could she tell you were in the bus when all she could see were a lot of cupcake wimples?"

"I am not sure," Mother Daley answered, "but I guess she knew she'd find out if she kept honking."

The opportunity to talk alone came infrequently during Mother Daley's first and my last year at Eden Hall. Sometimes between classes we'd stand in the hall and spend a few minutes exchanging views on various school activities, and occasionally I'd give her something I had read or written as she glided by on her way to chapel or into the cloister. Almost every night I attempted to sneak past Mother Guerrieri, one of the nuns who patrolled the halls, in order to see Mother Daley in the dormitory down the corridor. I knew I was off limits and that the rule of silence was in effect, but Mother Daley usually smiled when she saw me, knowing that Mother Guerrieri would not be far behind to shoo me out.

"But Mother Guerrieri," I'd protest, "I am here on official business. I need to talk with Mother Daley." But Mother Guerrieri would have none of it and would silently beckon to me with her large index finger as Mother Daley darted behind the white-curtained cubicles where her charges were preparing for bed.

Every Sacred Heart school had dormitories for the younger girls consisting of one large room with a line of iron beds and wooden bureaus curtained off from one another to ensure privacy and prevent conversation. It was from these small quarters of isolation during the early weeks of every school year that sniffles and moans could be heard as the seventh and eighth grade boarders cried themselves to sleep. Mother Daley seemed to have little sympathy for the obvious unhappiness of the dormitory children. I witnessed her casual reaction when she was approached by one of them who confided, "Mary Ann is crying because she is very homesick."

"I know, dear," Mother Daley replied matter-of-factly. "Let her cry, but make sure she is dressed for bed before the bell rings."

"Mother, how can you be so cruel?" I asked, only to hear her whisper, "Go back to your room, dear, and be grateful that you have one."

But even when she appeared to be oblivious to their traumas, her charges loved her. She was the eighth grade class mistress and adviser to the Committee of Games, a traditional Sacred Heart organization made up of the school's best athletes, who sometimes assisted the nuns in taking names of those who talked in the hallways or ignored any of the numerous school rules. Their job was defined in the school handbook as consisting of "the spirit of service that goes with charge, professional secrecy, and loyalty in upholding decisions." Some of us considered them members of the Sacred Heart Gestapo.

Like many of the younger nuns, Mother Daley had multiple duties, and like the children she watched over, she slept in a dormitory cubicle, with a white bedspread covering the iron bed and with a crucifix on the pillow. Often she was awakened in the night and rehabited herself to tend to a sick child or to check on a restless one. She rose at 5:00 A.M. every day to meditate, say her prayers, and prepare for the long day ahead.

Although she was never officially my teacher, Mother Daley taught me many things. She counseled me on what to read, introducing me to existentialism, Kierkegaard, Emily Dickinson, T. S. Eliot, and Antoine de Saint-Exupéry. As for religion, she advised me to "think calmly about God and not try to know Him all at once." When I returned from Christmas vacation with a book by Jean-Paul Sartre, whom she had not recommended, she did not confiscate it, as many others would have done, but left a note in my desk that said, "Please give God the same chance you give Sartre."

I watched her pray at morning Mass and envied her piety, which seemed so sure and constant beside my own religious doubts and proclivity to ridicule unquestioned faith. I could not help being impressed by the strong, visible example she set of uncompromising commitment to the unseen. For three years I remained mystified by, but admiring of, the pact between the nuns and their God, which appeared to produce not only visible tranquillity but a peace of mind and heart that was inspiring to witness and impossible to ignore. Like many of the nuns at Eden Hall, Mother Daley indeed wore, as Thomas Merton wrote, "the mild yoke of Christ's service."

Before her arrival at Eden Hall, my interest in religious vocations and those who fulfilled them had been heightened by my talks with Mother Tobin, the Mistress General, and with Mother Geraldine Hurley, who was for two years my dormitory mistress. Mother Hurley was a young nun who had not yet been to Rome to make her final vows and receive her cross and ring. Artistic, articulate, and amusing, she taught in the school and worked on her master's degree in philosophy. St. Augustine was her hero and I was the thorn in her side. She was constantly pained by my slovenly housekeeping ways, so much so that when I returned for my senior year she had designed a card with a special message beautifully lettered in black italic script. It was perched on top of my bureau and remained there for the entire year. On the card was a quote about *order* being essential to *life*. I pretended to be insulted, but in fact I was pleased that she had gone to such trouble to get her message across.

Mother Hurley was a wonderfully tolerant nun who was in the first stages of her love affair with God. We teased her constantly about *Him,* made up a song with lyrics that began "Oh, Geraldine, you're a little bit like every nun I've ever seen, / When you wandered into my room last night, you tried to give me an awful fright." Such behavior would, in most cases, have been reason for lost Très Bien cards all around, but Mother Hurley only smiled and shook her head. We tested her patience at every turn. We screamed at her when she came through the door of our room with the holy water in the morning, pleaded with her to let us keep our lights on for five more minutes after the bell had rung for lights out, and begged her not to report us when she found us visiting in another room. But when she broke her leg, we all stood in line to push her around in an ancient wheelchair.

When Reverend Mother Agnes Barry (sister of playwright Philip Barry), the Vicar General, visited the school, I left a note inside one of my messy bureau drawers that read, "Dear Reverend Mother, don't judge a book by its cover." To my great disappointment Mother Hurley found it before Reverend Mother Barry did, and she called me out of study hall. "I should be very angry about this," she said, handing me the note, "but I am only disappointed that you were willing to jeopardize the effort this school has made to get ready for Reverend Mother Vicar's visit."

"That's why I did it," I confessed. "Under normal circumstances this place is run like a dictatorship, but when someone important is visiting, it turns into something even worse."

Mother Bush (who had taken Mother Forden's place as surveillant) had spent a half hour the day before making us measure the spaces between our desks so the desks would be exactly four and a half inches apart. Mother Carmody had given us answers to history questions to memorize so that we would all appear brilliant in the event that Reverend Mother dropped by our class. We spent months practicing for an elaborate pageant starring Ruth, who was gleaning in the fields all day without once stopping for food or drink. "Why is everyone going to so much trouble to hide the way we normally live?" I asked. "I think it is very hypocritical, especially when our motto is 'Dare to be true.' "

Mother Hurley smiled at me. "Have you ever thought about taking up the law?" she asked. Then she told me she would not report the note but advised me to try to use better judgment in the future.

"You'll have plenty of time to speak out against things you consider unjust in the world after you graduate," she said. "But Mother. . . ." "Enough now," she said gently, "go back and try to concentrate on your homework." And I went back to study hall, not to study, but to write out a list of the things I thought were inequitable about life at the Sacred Heart.

Sometimes, after the bell for lights out had rung, my roommates speculated in whispers about their futures: "I bet your husband will love you more than you love him, Martine."

"How many children do you want to have, Sheila?"

I would slip out into the corridor and ask Mother Hurley to let me help her wash down the bathroom floor.

"V V, go back to your room."

"But Mother, I can't sleep."

"All right, but only for five minutes."

"How did you know you wanted to be a nun, Mother?"

"How do people know they want to be doctors or nurses or soldiers?"

"Nobody wants to be a soldier, Mother."

"Read the life of General Patton."

"Is being in love with God like being in love with a real person?"

"God is a real person, V V."

"I mean a feeling, touching person."

"Do you ever think about wanting to be a nun, dear?"

"No, Mother. Do you ever think about not wanting to be one?"

"Five minutes is up. Now go to bed before we both get into trouble."

Then I would slink back into my room, silently slip between the cool sheets of my bed, and wonder how it was possible to live like Mothers Hurley, Daley, and Tobin and appear to be so happy.

The night before my graduation, while my roommates packed their suitcases, joyously anticipating the next day's events, I sat on a windowsill outside Mother Daley's dormitory, waiting until she finished passing the holy water.

The outline of her white cap and silver cross was all I could see moving toward me in the darkness. It was then that I felt the surge of sadness I had sought during the previous days of preliminary graduation activities.

"I don't want to leave," I said quietly.

"That's only the way you feel tonight," she assured me. "It's the thing you have talked most about wanting this entire year."

I moved off the windowsill and we walked past the infirmary to the edge of the wide hallway that split into a double corridor.

"I think that you have grown in many ways these last months," she said. "From now on I think you will understand many of the things you have been worried about. Just remember, never be afraid to be the best you can be."

Before she could say any more, I threw my arms around her neck and sobbed. In that moment, all my reserve and the unwritten edict of never touching a nun vanished. I wished I could take her into the world with me, for I did not believe I could be the best I could be without her.

As we stood together, my tears dripping onto her habit, I felt none of the elation I expected to feel on my last night at Eden Hall. All the anger and rebellion had disappeared into some foreign past from which I was momentarily removed. Mother Daley patted my back and I began to regain my composure. When I stepped away from her embrace, she squeezed my hands.

"We'll talk more tomorrow," she said, and for the last time I walked down the Holy Angels side of the split corridor toward my room.

The following morning, when I stood for the final time with my classmates, it was raining. There had been no opportunity for Mother Daley and me to resume our conversation, but what had been said was sufficient to shore me up for the remaining hours.

Clad identically in stiff white piqué dresses, laurel wreaths, and white gloves, we graduates filed into the chapel singing the Sacred Heart hymn: "Jesus be our King and Leader / Grant us in Thy toils a part, / Are we not Thy chosen soldiers / Children of Thy Sacred Heart." By the time we filed out again, clutching red leather folders that held the coveted diplomas, my friend Grace was crying and so was I.

"I don't know why I'm crying," she sobbed. "I hated this miserable place." And the irony of it all made us giggle.

My father was crying too. His dream of seeing me graduate from a Catholic school had finally been realized, and he expressed his gratitude to Mother Tobin, Reverend Mother Ashe, and any other nun he could find. My mother stood nearby trying to inconspicuously put down the glass of red punch that had been pressed upon her.

Back in our rooms upstairs, which had already assumed abandoned, forlorn, impersonal looks in their almost-emptiness, I joined my classmates in stuffing last-minute items into bulging trunks and changed from my graduation dress into "city clothes."

Cars driven by brothers and fathers took turns parking in the circular driveway below the porch of the main building. Trunk tops slammed down in a series of crescendos. The rain had stopped, and beyond the lake there was a rainbow. My father pulled his station wagon up and removed his jacket before hauling my luggage into the back.

The nuns had gathered in clusters on the porch, their white handkerchiefs at the ready. I ran up the stairs for a last round of farewells. Mothers Tobin, Hurley, Carmody, and others who had been such a significant part of my life at the Sacred Heart embraced me and looked surprisingly pleased. When I reached Mother Daley she took my hand.

"I am ready to go now," I said.

"I never doubted it for a minute," she replied, and then she laughed and hugged me.

Opening the Windows

8

WHEN I ARRIVED at the entrance of Villa Duchesne, the castlelike gray stone Sacred Heart school in St. Louis, for a week of archival research, I felt as much an alien as I had during my first weeks as a student at Eden Hall. I was there to seek answers to the question that had started me on my pilgrimage, to determine how the Second Vatican Council had affected the old religious order I had known and loved and believed would never change. As I climbed the winding stairs, laughing students tumbled by me on their way to class. They wore no uniforms, did not march in ranks, and obviously were not required to observe a rule of silence. Shirttails fell out of waistbands, shoes were scuffed and unpolished, hair was arranged in a variety of styles, and fingernails were polished in an array of bright colors. The mix was interestingly contemporary and unorthodox.

I stopped midway up the stairs to ask directions from a woman who appeared to be at home there, although I had no idea whether she was a nun or a lay teacher. Following her instructions, I turned down a corridor with large inside windows that overlooked the silent, empty chapel. At the end of the hall a door was open and when I passed through it, I could hear the voices of Sisters Wheeler and Padberg, with whom I had arranged my visit. The greeting I received was unmistakably Sacred Heart. I carried no special credentials other than my affiliation with Eden Hall, but that was sufficient for the three of us to exchange hugs in greeting instead of handshakes.

Twenty years had passed since their lives had been restrained by the rule of cloister and the monastic traditions of the past. Gone were the habit, the rosary beads, the silver cross, the gold wedding band, and the term "Mother" that had formerly identified them as religious of the Sacred Heart and had given them grace, distinction, and instant recognition. During the post–Vatican II reordering of religious life, the habits had been replaced by secular clothes, the term "Mother" by "Sister," and the gold rings by silver ones. Cloister before Vatican II constituted a life of restriction most people could not have tolerated or even imagined. Sequestered in their convents, the nuns offered their physical and mental energies for the benefit of others and the perfection of their spiritual selves. Religious life was difficult for the best and a struggle for the rest. Yet the enforced daily regimentation offered security and protection from the distractions of the outside world, a balance of structure and spirituality, which for the religious of the Sacred Heart combined the external challenges of education with the internal obligations of their spiritual commitment.

Behind the walls of their convents and in the capacity of teachers and administrators at Sacred Heart institutions of learning, Sisters Wheeler and Padberg, like many before them, had lived lives of simplicity and order, with little opportunity for choice or preference in even the smallest matters.

Today they are liberated women, whose liberation came late, unexpectedly, and required major adjustments. Sister Mary C. Wheeler, a Sacred Heart nun for more than sixty years, entered the Society in 1926 when she was eighteen. As a teacher she was one of the Society's finest, acquiring four master's degrees and a Ph.D. during her long, distinguished academic career.

She admits that the obligations of the past were difficult at times but says that in many ways the old life was a freer and less complex existence than the one she lives today.

"Believe me," she says with a smile, "it is a whole lot harder to live in a small community with no rule of silence. You have to talk at meals and deal with a variety of things that just simply weren't present under the old regime. In those days you could walk into a meal dead tired, sit down, and listen to an interesting book being read, and if you were too tired to listen you didn't and nobody was the wiser. No one could stop you and say, 'Look, I've got to talk to someone.' Now anybody can stop you at any time, and we were not used to that. Certainly our lives appear to be more relaxed now, and they are, but it is very, very demanding to live in religious life today."

She turns the thin silver ring around the third finger of
hand. In January 1965 all Sacred Heart nuns were asked
quish their gold profession rings to the Holy Father's cha
monetary value of that contribution was less than $20,000, but for
many of the nuns the sacrifice was more costly. Sister Wheeler halt-
ingly concurs with the sentiments of some of her sisters that the
giving up of the rings was probably a meaningless gesture, but she
thinks it demonstrated obedience, good will, and the spirit of changing times. "The rings had a special significance for each person,"
Sister Wheeler explains. "They were our wedding rings, engraved
with our initials and the date of our profession."

In 1965, two years after the assassination of President John F.
Kennedy, the people of the United States were immersed in a struggle for peace, equality, and self-realization just as the people of God
in the Catholic Church were beginning to be drawn into a process of
renewal. This process would cause major shifts and changes that
would affect the very visible ceremonial aspects of the Church: elimination of Latin as the universal language and abolishment of rules
and regulations that governed the lives of the faithful (lay and religious) and for centuries defined their religious obligations. The process of renewal called into question the intrinsic value of tradition,
history, and ceremony, which through years of acceptance had
come to be familiar touchstones to the Church's vast constituency.
Many did not understand the mysteries of the faith they practiced
but were devoted to the rituals that represented them.

Like many other Church congregations, the Society of the Sacred
Heart had passed down its own set of traditions, its methods of
education and discipline, its spirit of unity, its ceremonies and symbols to many generations of religious and students. These were the
links that connected one Sacred Heart generation with another and
gave them all a unique common vocabulary that overcame language
barriers and geographic location.

On April 26, 1958, Sabine de Valon succeeded Marie Thérèse de
Lescure as the tenth Mother General of the Society of the Sacred
Heart. Born in Cahors, France, in 1899, Mother de Valon entered
the Society at the convent in Marmoutier and took her final vows in
Rome in 1929. When she summoned the Society's twenty-fifth General Council in 1958 she spoke of coming "face to face with the
reality of today." During the first years of her generalate she trav-

eled through Europe visiting schools and meeting the modern Sacred Heart students, who, she discovered, were better educated, more inquisitive, and more independent than any previous generation. "Just now, when the evolution of all things is so rapid and when, so easily and under the pretext of progress, all things are questioned, it is good to seek together the way that we must follow. Are we going to run blindly after every novelty? Are we going to immobilize ourselves in the possession of a legacy from the past as if, by this effort, we could stop the too rapid movement of our times?" Mother de Valon asked the Society to reflect on these questions as it considered its past, its future, and its continuing worldwide expansion.

At the opening of the Second Vatican Council in 1962, Pope John XXIII said, "We are going to shake off the dust that has collected on the throne of St. Peter since the time of Constantine and let in some fresh air." When the windows were opened, a dusting process began that started with a feather and ended with a hammer.

In its broadest definition, the aim of Vatican II was to force the Catholic Church, for centuries a rock of stability, anchored in absolutes, to become more attuned to the world in which it existed. The word "renewal" was used again and again to assert, explain, and push forward numerous new and experimental ideas regarding clergy, cloister, and Church customs.

Holy Mother Church was about to throw off her cloak of medieval authority, step down from her authoritarian pedestal, and boogie with the people. The Church would no longer be defined as guardian of an ancient set of traditions and rituals, most of which had lost their meaning.

To update and revitalize the old Church and its institutions, to give them a more contemporary connection to their times and more flexibility in meeting the needs of those they served, seemed an appropriate and necessary agenda. Institutions tend to harden and become less pliable as they move through time. This was as true for the Society of the Sacred Heart as it was for the Catholic Church. One reflected the other in its tendency to reject reform and revere traditions that had been formulated at a distant time in history. As the Society began to move away from its foundation roots, as the words and intentions of its foundress were interpreted by those who followed her, reverence for decisions of the past became a significant stumbling block that impeded progress and, paradoxically, often went far afield from many of Mother Barat's original concepts. To follow the old patterns seemed the surest way to preserve a history and ensure a future. This resistance to change kept many monastic communities rooted in antiquity.

Yet the 1960s, a time of social revolution and dramatic upheaval, were also a time when both the Church and the Society flourished in membership. In 1965 the Society's worldwide membership peaked, with 7,074 religious in 205 houses. The American Catholic population was 46,812,178, and 71 percent attended Sunday Mass.

During the 1960s, Sacred Heart schools were opened in San Diego, Houston, Miami, Buffalo, and Princeton, New Jersey. Harlem Preparatory School was started by Mother Ruth Dowd in 1967. Under the sponsorship of Manhattanville College and in conjunction with the Urban League of New York, Harlem Prep was an innovative, nongraded, coeducational school for high school dropouts. It filled a great need and became a great success. Mother de Valon was aware that while the Society was more than adequately fulfilling its mission of educating the upper classes, it was removed from many other segments of the world's population. In 1963, she encouraged and endorsed the Society's movement into a slum area in Barcelona, Spain, which provided the first opportunity for a few religious of the Sacred Heart to live among the very poor. This was followed by schools in Bilbao, Spain, on the Canary Islands, and in Madrid. In France an apartment house–turned–convent on avenue de Lowendal became a study center for student nuns. Experimentation in the Society began cautiously with a view to integrating the lives of its members with those of a broader group of people.

Change must come, even when it threatens survival, and many good Catholics along with many devoted Sacred Heart alumnae who had railed against the anchor of authority when it restricted their lives cried out in anguish when it was pulled up. Before the Second Vatican Council the path to salvation had been narrow and clear. There were certain duties all Catholics were required to perform to remain in good standing with the Church. Membership in the Catholic Church offered a host of opportunities to attain salvation and to lose it.

The preconciliar people of God had a high regard for the authority that was transmitted to the laity through priests and religious and to them through their superiors. When that authority began to be questioned, when priests and nuns began to move away from traditional roles, when the language of the Mass changed from Latin to English, when altars were pulled away from church walls to face the people, when folk songs replaced liturgical music, when the corporate image of the uniformed Church, its institutions, and leadership began to fragment and to be replaced by the formlessness of experimentation, a sense of betrayal and resentment engulfed a large number of traditionalists who, in many cases, had gone to extremes to live by the book. Now the book was being condensed and revised. Everything appeared to be up for grabs. For the first time in modern memory, Church preservationists were being replaced by reformers, and a good number of its most visible and inspiring leaders began to drift away from the world of anchors and absolutes into a sea of swirling change.

On June 3, 1963, when Pope John XXIII died, Vatican Council II had already turned its attention to the updating of religious life. Giovanni Montini became Pope Paul VI, and on November 22 of the same year President John F. Kennedy was assassinated. Thus began a time of turmoil and turbulence for many segments of the world's population, including the Society of the Sacred Heart.

The Society's twenty-sixth General Chapter (the first to be called Chapter instead of Council) met in Rome from October 12 to November 15, 1964, and while the Vatican II documents relating to religious life were still under discussion, the direction in which they pointed was clear.

Mother de Valon addressed the chapter, encouraging its members to deal actively and openly with the problems confronting the Society in the following areas: recruitment of novices, training of young religious, cloister versus apostolic activities, the coadjutrix religious, the boarding schools, and involvement with people in the larger community.

On these issues and many others there was intensive discussion and vigorous debate that resulted in the first major changes within the Society. One of the most important changes was the decision to close the sociological gap between the choir religious and the coadjutrix sisters. After the chapter of 1964 and after a "little probation" (short training period), these women who had entered the Society to serve as domestics and housekeepers were permitted to take the vow of education and receive all rights and privileges due them as choir religious of the Sacred Heart. Until that time they had led separate and unequal lives within the cloister. They wore a different habit, followed a different rule, and lived a different daily routine of recreations, meditations, meals, and spiritual obligations. When the coadjutrix sisters became Mothers, all were one, but soon all would be addressed as "Sister."

Among the most important issues considered by the chapter of 1964 was the question of cloister. Cloister, which prohibited the nuns from leaving the convent except for reasons of health and, later, education, was written into the Society's constitutions: "They will keep cloister whose advantages are so precious to keep the integrity of the Vows; cloister, however, which must be modified and tempered according to the spirit and end of their Institute." There were times in the Society's history, during wars and revolutions, when cloister was "modified and tempered," and in some countries it was even temporarily abolished, but for most of its 164-year history the Society had strictly enforced the "separate life."

Vatican Council II had recommended the elimination of the mixed life, to which the Society subscribed, which combined apostolic works such as teaching with monasticism. St. Madeleine Sophie and her successors had endorsed the cloistered life because it strongly supported and protected the spiritual side of the Society's identity. But the foundress was also aware of the severe limitations it placed on the educative, apostolic side of her Society's mission. Vatican II had proposed that congregations dedicated to apostolic work be exempt from cloister, and Mother de Valon, with certain reservations, agreed. "To go more towards the world, since the Church requests it, yes certainly . . . to go to the world without restriction, no." She cited the words of Pope Paul VI in his remarks to the heads of men's orders at their chapters: "It is necessary," the pope said, "to watch the authentic notion of religious life, such as it has always been received in the Church, which should never be obscured by adaptation of today. . . . It is obvious that a good religious life absolutely needs discipline, certain laws and conditions permitting the observance of them. That is why the first task of the General Chapters must be to keep intact, in the course of time, the rules established by the Founders, for their religious family."

He directed every religious institute to convoke a general chapter within three years to study the Vatican documents relating to renewal alongside the order's constitutions. The purpose was one of rediscovery and reevaluation, a reaffirmation of values, original intent, and authenticity. It would be a search for roots that would bring each institution into a more realistic place in the world while retaining its individual character and spirit.

Mother de Valon knew there would be new needs for new times, and she was determined that the Society act cautiously and prudently as it obeyed the Church's call to relevance. On the issue of cloister she said, "Up to now our cloister protected our vows. Now, our vows are going to safeguard our spirit of cloister." When the chapter of 1964 ended, among the most significant newly adopted practices was the one permitting nuns to go home to visit dying parents. Before this, Sacred Heart nuns saw their families only in the convent parlors. Other changes concerned ceremonial aspects of the nuns' daily routine, including the freedom to kneel in chapel pews instead of in private stalls, to join hands at the waist when going to communion instead of holding them erect, under the nose, in the old-fashioned manner, to sit where they chose at recreations, to rise at 6:00 A.M. instead of 5:30 on Sundays, to have newspapers available to read, and to wear contact lenses. Sacred Heart nuns were now permitted to donate blood to blood banks and drink water between meals, "especially in warm weather." Additionally, it was established that a sick religious could ask what her temperature was after it was taken, which had previously been forbidden. "We had given everything we had to religious life," Sister Mary Elizabeth Tobin later explained, "and that included our bodies. Fact was, we were treated like children."

At the chapter of 1964 consideration was given to "the possibility of talking once a week in the refectory and at goûter," to a twenty-minute (rather than fifteen-minute) breakfast, and to the extension of the time of retirement from 10:00 P.M. to 10:20. These small concessions to modification were only the first of many changes the Society of the Sacred Heart would eventually initiate to create an environment that would allow its members to take responsibility for their own lives. To some the changes represented a long-overdue reordering process, to others they symbolized the beginning of the end.

"It is time to recall the differences between Tradition and traditions," the Mother General said. "Certain traditions should be abandoned if they no longer have the soul that made them meaningful and if the new generation is incapable of discovering this soul; a purely exterior observance would not be an observance; the young, rightly, want to know the significance of things. Where this significance does not exist, things can and ought to change. This is the fate of 'traditions.'"

At the close of the chapter of 1964, five nuns were elected assistants to the Mother General and were given the title "assistant general." One of them was Reverend Mother Mary Elizabeth Tobin, who had influenced my life and the lives of many others as Mistress General in our schools.

Sister Tobin later recalled: "The Church said that faith was in the people of God and not in a hierarchical structure. That was one of the major shifts, for then everyone is expressing that spirit and it becomes fundamental in the whole way you look at religious life. If the religious are supposed to be leading the people, then they have to be with the people. Before, there were three distinctions in religious life — cloistered, mixed, and apostolic. Vatican Council II did away with the mixed category; you were either strictly contemplative or you were apostolic. When we were given the choice, we did not want to be separated from the students we were working with, and cloister by its nature was strictly understood by the Church as a separation, as set apart. St. Madeleine Sophie did not want her Society set apart by walls and grilles; she wanted it set apart by spirit and interior walls. The principle of cloister no longer existed in the Society after 1964, and it was dropped because the Church asked us to drop it. Mother de Valon had some real problems in putting into action the changes the Church asked. She would say, We are going to do this or that, but under these conditions or those conditions. Still, she was going to go with the Church no matter what."

During the three years between the chapter of 1964 and the special chapter called in 1967, the Society began to experiment with a more flexible style of living. Life in the cloister was on its way out, along with many other monastic practices. Nuns were no longer required to participate in the countless archaic, and in many cases meaningless, rituals that had been established hundreds of years before and had passed unchanged from generation to generation.

In 1965, Reverend Mother Helen Fitzgerald, vicar of the New

York vicariate, made her annual visit to Noroton-on-the-Sound in Connecticut and reported, "In general the rule is well kept and the little community seems happy and appreciative of the kindness of Reverend Mother McAgon. The changes indicated by the 26th General Chapter have been received with joy — the fusion of the former sisters with the choir religious has taken place very simply, all are content and grateful. The financial condition is good; regret so few students go to Catholic colleges."

These comments are probably true as far as they go, but according to Sister Anne Dyer, presently headmistress of Stone Ridge in Maryland, the fusion of the Sisters with the Mothers was not received totally with joy and gratitude. "When we were short-handed in Florida," she remembers, "and we needed five people to say the Office, we couldn't get one of the new Mothers to participate. They didn't want anything to do with it. They said, 'You never asked us to say it before and now you are asking only because you need another person.' One former sister balked when she was told to study for a degree so that she could teach. 'For twenty years you never let me read a book,' she said, 'and now you are asking me to study.' " There was bitterness and a sense of too much too late. Inequity still existed between the two levels of nuns that new habits and new opportunities did not wipe away.

In the spring of 1966, for the first time ever, Sacred Heart nuns began to recite their Office in English. Sister Dyer remembers the experience with some amusement: "When the vernacular first came in, we studied the Psalms and lessons, and some did it more carefully than others. We read over those passages from the Church Fathers, and they never sounded strange in Latin, they never sounded anything but solemn and serious. In English they sounded very strange. We would run across things like 'My enemies will be ground into powder under my feet. Glory to God, the Son, and the Holy Ghost.' We would say these horrendous things and then bow down." This was the first crack in the mystery and mystique of the well-ordered, high-level, inspirational life that embodied the Latin chants, the monastic music, and the traditional robes, the self-controlled, self-sacrificing life that was required to tread the ever-demanding road to perfection.

At Christmastime 1966, the beautiful traditional Sacred Heart habit was replaced by a modified version, which according to Sister

Wheeler and many others who wore it left a lot to be desired. "The new version," she said, "was not only ugly and expensive [seventy-five dollars per habit] but had the most uncomfortable headdress imaginable. One of my friends in the Society commented that if twelve thousand ears felt the same way hers did it wouldn't last long, and it didn't." By the following year it was gone.

The year 1966 also marked the first in a series of Sacred Heart school closings that would represent to many the disassembly of the Society. The Sacred Heart finishing school in Manhattan, Duchesne Residence School, closed its doors for lack of applicants, and the seeds were sown at Manhattanville College of the Sacred Heart for its eventual transition to a nondenominational, coeducational institution.

In April 1966 Mother de Valon announced that the Society's special chapter called for by Vatican II would convene in Rome in October 1967. Part of the preparation that followed this announcement was the opportunity for every member of the Society to send suggestions to the motherhouse for changes to be considered. At previous chapters, although all the nuns were free to offer opinions in writing, few had chosen to do so. Now all were encouraged to participate and almost the entire international community replied.

Sister Anne Dyer, then teaching at Eden Hall, remembers the sense of urgency her contemporaries felt to participate in the Society's renewal process. "This was the first step toward real change, and everybody had an opportunity to write in what was called our *desiderata*, the things we desired. I was a young nun at Eden Hall, on verge of being professed. We were four young women in a house full of octogenarians, and they told us we could take part in the process. Now this was easier said than done, because the four of us were never free at the same time, and we still had the rule of silence. We could not speak out of recreation, so it was a sort of joke, but we took it very seriously. There was this rather large linen closet in the cloister, and the four of us would meet there at night, after the children had gone to bed, and speak about the things we thought should be changed. We made our great decisions there and duly wrote them up, signed them, and sent them off."

She is hesitant to be specific about the changes the closet conspirators favored but characterizes them as dealing with "lifestyle and internal discipline": "We thought there should be some changes made in the archaic, monastic traditions we were living at that time, and very obviously we weren't the only ones who thought so."

Sister Anne O'Neil, whose term as American provincial of the Society ends in 1988, told me, "Most of us were taught that change was not possible in the Church, but Vatican II proved that to be untrue. When cloister was abolished in the Society I think it resulted in a lot of people having to sort out what was essential in their dedication and finding a way to personally live it that was very different from the old road to perfection routine."

Sister Mary Elizabeth Tobin, then an assistant to the Mother General, also recalls that some of the strictures to be discussed and eased by the special chapter in 1967 were still very much in evidence: "We knew that at this very important special chapter, at this crucial time in our history, the Church was asking us to make some major shifts. The abolishment of cloister radically changed the way in which we had lived and the way in which we would carry out our mission. Before Vatican II the works we did were confined to the property we owned. For instance, we owned and operated St. Katherine's as a parish school within our complex at Eden Hall, but when the time came for the first communion ceremony, the nuns could not go across the street to the church. When cloister was abolished we were free to be where the people were instead of always having them come to us. We primarily lived according to a monastic rule, which was both a structure and a routine that was followed strictly every day. We were treated like little kids; we had given everything we were to religious life and there was a high power of control."

Permissions for the smallest requests were sought from Rome, but as one former Manhattanville nun recounts, "There came a time when the exceptions to the rules were becoming more numerous than the rules themselves and it seemed crazy to have to continue to cable Rome every time someone wanted to leave the campus." Yet until the chapter of 1964, that practice had continued. Customs and constitutions varied in other orders, and many were updated several times in their history. The Society of the Sacred Heart took pride in the fact that its own constitutions had remained the same document that St. Madeleine Sophie had drafted with Father Varin. Clearly Mother Barat had been a visionary, but it would have been impossibly unrealistic to think her vision of religious life could extend into the twentieth century or remain forever appropriate.

Inside the grand houses of the Sacred Heart, beyond the mysterious cloister doors, life was still being lived in the mid-twentieth century in a truly medieval manner. Rules and regulations that had once appropriately governed religious life no longer applied. Communities of nuns found themselves acting out roles of humility, penance, and deprivation that were silly and obsolete. When I was at school, nuns were still using the discipline, a whiplike device, and a small metal ring with spikes that fit over the arm as methods of self-inflicted pain, although at the time we did not know it. "We did know," my friend Grace Schrafft recalls, "that during Lent things were very bad for them. They ate practically nothing, and I remember most of them were short-tempered and crabby." I used to tease Mother Daley about wearing a hair shirt, never suspecting that she might have been doing so. When a nun menstruated she was required to wear diapers in place of sanitary napkins, and on entering the Society of the Sacred Heart she was required to bring with her an ample supply. Patterns of convent life that had been established in the early centuries were passed down like commandments: Perpetuated by reverence and fear of change, they created a mode of life that not only was outdated but was a real impediment to healthy growth and certainly to individual maturity.

Until the time of the special chapter, when a Sacred Heart nun received permission to attend classes at a university or to travel to an educational conference she was always accompanied by another religious or an appropriate companion. While studying for an advanced degree in an outside institution, she was required to eat unobserved, which in one case forced a young nun to brown-bag it in a ladies' room stall. The rule they were obliged to follow did everything imaginable to protect them from harm's way, but it was equally effective in cutting them off from reality. "If there was a difficult and obscure way to accomplish a task, that is the course we followed," says Sister Dyer. "This was never intended by the foundress, who was a pragmatic and sensible woman."

In her book *The Nuns*, Marcelle Bernstein reports that a Sacred Heart nun who had entered the Society at the turn of the century studied for her college degree inside the convent, as was the practice at that time, but under university rules was required to appear in person for the final examination. Great time and attention were given to the problem, which was compounded by the fact that examination time was from 7:00 to 9:00 P.M., when greater silence was enforced. It was finally decided that the nun should go at the appointed time but should dress in mufti, including a wig to cover her shaved head. She agreed to leave the wig on the top of the hatbox when she returned as a sign that she had done well. There were numerous amusing tales in the Society relating to the extreme measures some nuns were forced to employ in order to obey the rules imposed on them.

In anticipation of the special chapter, vicars and representatives from the United States and Canada had met in Montreal in 1966 to draw up a list of suggestions for consideration at the chapter. When word reached the motherhouse in Rome that a "mini-chapter" had already been held, the tension that was beginning to be felt was exacerbated. Reverend Mother Helen Fitzgerald, vicar of the New York vicariate, hastily wrote to Mother de Valon, "We thought that this would be a good time to exchange ideas, to be more and better informed of one another's thoughts. We never thought of it as a national or international chapter." Among the chief issues discussed at the Canadian meeting were decentralization of the Society's government and the suggestion that reports from the special chapter be sent to the vicariates. The motherhouse assured the delegates that government would be considered an important topic of debate but said that reports from the daily meetings would remain secret. The old ways had always encouraged secrecy and thus enabled the power of decision to remain in the hands of a few. It appeared that this protective modus operandi would not be altered.

On September 7, 1967, when Reverend Mother Fitzgerald left New York for Rome on the SS *United States*, she knew there would be many complex and compelling questions facing the representatives at the special chapter: the need for openness to the directives of Vatican II, the need for change in the governmental structure of the Society, and, the most essential, the need to preserve the spirit of unity. "We are HIS," she wrote from her stateroom, "the Society of His Heart in which His love unites us." She arrived in Rome on her seventy-second birthday. Her presence at the historic special chapter was a significant and informed one. She had carefully studied all the documents addressing changes in religious life and was ready to contribute her talents and insights to the deliberations concerning how a religious of the Sacred Heart would now be defined. She would be one of the moving forces at the chapter of 1967, her last formal participation in the Society's governmental process. She recognized that change was inevitable and could come only out of pain and prayer. As another sister later wrote, "She was happy with the Society as it was. There was a dignity about it that matched her dignity; there was an order to it, there was a clarity — and she felt that it was a very effective group. She knew it would not be able to live if it continued in the old ways, and the life of the Society was more important to her than the things she held dear." There were many in the Society who shared her sense of impending loss — or at least her sense of anxiety about the future.

For those who felt the Society was dragging its feet in implementing the experimentation the Church had asked for, the time of the special chapter was a frustrating period of waiting. For those who were suspicious and fearful of what those experiments might bring, it was a time of high anxiety. Many nuns felt they had no voice in the Society's reevaluation process, especially the young, unprofessed nuns, the Society's next generation of leaders, who had to rely on the agenda of their elders and pray for their wisdom. And for all those who did not participate in the chapter, news of the proceedings was long in coming.

On October 1, 1967, in the Chapter Room of the former residence of Victor Emmanuel II on the Via Nomentana, once the motherhouse of the Society, eighty-six representatives from thirty countries gathered to begin deliberations on the future of the Society of the Sacred Heart. "It was," Sister Margaret Williams later wrote, "the most arduous Chapter ever held — and the longest, October 1 to December 14, 1967."

At all of the Society's previous councils only vicars and assistants general were invited to participate. The special chapter of 1967 included elected delegates from each vicariate. Since some had only recently been elected, some of the older delegates worried that inexperience might cause delays and misunderstandings. This fearfulness was added to the general confusion that was already mounting, another unknown in a sea of unknowns.

The American delegation was second in size only to the Spanish and included the five American Vicars General: Reverend Mother Helen Fitzgerald from the New York vicariate, Reverend Mother Elizabeth Sweeney from the Washington, D.C., vicariate, Reverend Mother Helen Sheahan from Chicago, Reverend Mother Eleanor Mulqueen from St. Louis, and Reverend Mother Elizabeth Nothomb from California. There were six elected American delegates, including Reverend Mother Elizabeth McCormack, president of Manhattanville College of the Sacred Heart, and Reverend Mother Margaret Coakley, Mistress of Novices at Manhattanville. An elaborate translation system was set up so the deliberations could be heard in English, French, and Spanish. Fra Angelico's picture of the Sacred Heart of Jesus hung over the chairman's seat for inspiration and remembrance.

Mother General de Valon, who had suffered a heart attack in 1966, was still fragile and unwell when the meeting began. She opened the first session of the chapter with these words: "Is it not urgent to confirm by our witness — since religious life is a sign — that the spirit of the Gospel is always new, that it can solve all problems and that it will never be out of date? I think that our Chapter must consider the world today through the Heart of Christ, in order to bring to it more faith, more hope, more love."

But the special chapter opened in an atmosphere of tension, apprehension, and expectation. There was fear in some European delegations that the Americans, who were strong advocates for immediate change, would control the deliberations. For as Sister Tobin says, "Never before did the structure of religious life change so rapidly. New thinking began to come into the Church after the Second Vatican Council which changed the whole theology in many, many ways, and it necessarily affected religious life. I think it is very difficult for an international organization to keep pace with world situations because every country moves at a different speed. The United States was very different in many respects and still is. We had the greatest number of young religious except for Spain, and those young religious had, for the most part, been very highly educated. They had been given opportunities for study in theology and had developed much further than the Society as a whole. They saw what was happening in the lay movement as something that was very vital in the Church and naturally they wanted to move with it.

The Society in the United States had changed from a very stable movement to a very flexible one, but you don't change people's attitudes or the history of their lives overnight. We had to be cautious, but on the other hand we had to begin to make the necessary reforms."

Leadership and loyalty were at loggerheads at the special chapter. After the first few weeks, it was apparent to many in attendance that Mother de Valon's health was a question that had to be addressed. For while her devotion to the Society and her commitment to carrying out the requests of the Church were unquestioned, her ability to lead and to put those directives into action was diminishing. The American delegation generally held the opinion that to get beyond internal debate and move the chapter forward, her resignation as Mother General might be necessary. This was unprecedented in the Society's history. St. Madeleine Sophie's eight other successors had served faithfully until death. Differing opinions mounted: accusations of disloyalty versus firm statements of support regardless of Mother de Valon's physical condition. On November 7, Mother de Valon unexpectedly gave her resignation "for the good of you all." This controversial, unanticipated occurrence added another troublesome ingredient to the already problematic chapter. Cardinal Antoniutti, prefect of the Sacred Congregation of Religious, accepted her resignation in the name of the Church, and a few days later Mother de Valon left Rome for Naples.

Elizabeth McCormack recalls the conflict and confusion surrounding the tumultuous chapter: "I went to that chapter in 1967 never having in many, many years a doubt about my vocation in the Society. But when I got there I became very, very disillusioned by the lack of leadership, by the fact that I, who had taken one hundred hours of French immersion to be able to cope with that chapter, found myself in a leadership position from a country that couldn't really have a leadership role. The Society was European-dominated and was never going to elect a Mother General from this country. I was just appalled at the naiveté of most of the people. You see, the real issue was not what the changes were going to be, for the vast majority had already been made at the chapter of 1964, but how they would be implemented and what restrictions, if any, would remain. I felt very strongly that unless they put some safeguards in, they were on a collision course. I remember saying to Mother Bultó [who was to succeed Mother de Valon], 'You must be very careful about the restrictions you remove.' And she said, 'What do you mean? If a superior wants to take her community for a picnic in a park near the convent, she should be able to do it.' I said, 'Unless you put restrictions in, there won't be anyone to take to the picnic — they will all be at the movies.' And she looked at me as if I were crazy. I mean, they were all very naive."

A month after Mother de Valon's resignation, Mother María Josefa Bultó was elected the Society's new superior. Born in Barcelona in 1905 and professed in the Society in 1932, Mother Bultó was elected by more than the two-thirds majority the chapter members had hoped for in their desire to retain a strong and united front. One of the vicars described her own apprehensions and those of Mother Fitzgerald during the balloting: "We were sitting beside each other in the front row of seats in the Chapter Room and we both were very anxious, though fairly sure of the outcome. We feared that the vote might be divided. . . . Mother Fitzgerald said to me, 'I am not going to count the votes.' (We knew there had to be a certain number, something like six hundred, to ensure a two-thirds majority.) I said, 'Well, I *am* going to count them,' and proceeded to do so. I remember that when the number was reached (Mother Fitzgerald was saying her rosary or pretending to do so), I gave her a great dig in the side and said, 'It is all right!' She was, of course, as relieved as I, and the great majority of us."

The Society's special chapter pushed on, directing itself to the pressing issues at hand: revising and updating the method of government and the style of training and teaching novices as well as expanding the Society's commitment to serve all segments of the world's population, not only the elite minority it had previously catered to. Now that its members were beginning to use their new freedoms to live and work in the world beyond the convent walls, the demands on individuals would in many respects be greater. For now a real sense developed that responsibility for the continuation of the Society would be rooted more in individual effort and personal choice than in the motherhouse in Rome. The filtering down of power had been part of the Society's history since the foundation days when Madeleine Sophie invited brave and selfless women to join her in an unknown undertaking that required personal courage as well as personal judgment.

The document *Orientations for a Time of Experimentation*, which emerged from the special chapter in Rome, marked the true beginning of a new and untried life for the religious of the Sacred Heart and served as a guide for three years of experimentation that would ultimately extend to thirteen. The decisions made in the Chapter Room at the motherhouse were geared to a more realistic relationship between the Society and the world at large, specifically to transfer the authority of decision making from Rome to the local level. (Although this form of government was not written in the original constitutions, Madeleine Sophie, on March 28, 1842, urged her superiors "not to do what others can do.") In the spirit of Madeleine Sophie, the members of the special chapter agreed to regional responsibility that would permit decisions to be made by individual communities according to their geographic location and their personal needs. Provinces would replace vicariates, and those elected to office would have limited terms and be assisted by councils and commissions. No one over age sixty-five would be eligible to hold elective office. The Mother General would serve a six-year term with the possibility of reelection. Prayer life for the religious would be designed by individuals for themselves. Time for meditation, adoration, and examination throughout the day would no longer be legislated by a rule book but would be self-determined. Menus would be varied and there would be no more spiritual reading during meals. Every nun was now free to act according to her own time clock. In short, each religious would assume control of her own destiny and would have the opportunity to formulate, along with the advice and consent of her provincial, a ministry that suited her talents. "Community life should make it possible for each religious to be so open that she becomes fully herself," the guiding document stated; "a suitable psychological preparation of the group will help each one to be herself, just as she is, a needed part of the whole and thoroughly at home."

In educational, apostolic works the Society would collaborate with other educational organizations, integrating lay people into its apostolic mission, allowing them to share equally in administrative and educational functions. The question of social security and health insurance would now have to be addressed, for Sacred Heart nuns had never drawn a salary or contributed to a retirement fund. The special chapter also put emphasis on social issues. "In order to go to those less favored with this world's goods, we will have to suppress some works that are no longer fruitful and even sometimes those in full activity. . . . In a world where hunger and ignorance can be overcome only by education, we should ask ourselves if our pupils leave us with a real sense of social justice and the determination to work to change the world, . . . and if we ourselves educate the children who have the greatest need of us. . . . In a world where the Church calls us to new tasks, we must give to education its full present day dimension." It was a call to come to grips with previous failures and present challenges of contemporary conditions.

The special chapter addressed every aspect of the Society's past identity, including the habit, which was itself in a state of transition, having been redesigned in 1966. There was no decision to make another immediate change except to allow individual choice in the length of the skirt and veil. It was at this time, too, that the much beloved title "Mother" was struck from the Sacred Heart vocabulary and replaced by "Sister."

At the closing session of the special chapter on December 14, 1967, Mother Bultó turned back to St. Madeleine Sophie for her final remarks: "She would ask us 'to be always the little Society,' wholly consecrated to the transpierced Heart of Our Lord Jesus Christ and active members of the Church in these postconciliar times. It is for you to bring to your Communities, together with these new orientations, an increased fidelity to the spirit of St. Madeleine Sophie. It is only by deepening our primitive charism that we shall be able, helped by grace, to bring about the spiritual and apostolic renewal of our religious life. . . . At a time when the signs of the times and the needs of the apostolate necessitate a more flexible adaptation of what is accidental, we must seek the means, not only for preserving, but for strengthening and making more authentic our Cor Unum. The basis for this will no longer be uniformity, but confidence, love and the sole desire of working together in the apostolic work which the Church confides to us."

The Society's longest chapter closed on a note of optimism but with many questions still unanswered. For what is written and spoken, discussed and debated, aspired to and planned for is often far more intricate in execution than in conception. As the superiors of the Society returned to their countries and their communities to report on the results of their two-month stay in Rome, they were greeted with varying degrees of enthusiasm. They were entering a time that would test the courage, strength, and commitment of each religious, a time that would require courage and faith, result in a loss of many structures, literally and figuratively, and raise questions in and out of the Society concerning its character, spirit, and ability to survive. During the early days of its foundation, a bishop had once cautioned Mother Barat that it was risky to be contemplatives while doing the work of education. Through the years the Society had discovered the seeds of truth in that observation. But in fact, it would be even riskier to be religious-educators in a world devoid of the safeguards that cloister and monasticism had once provided. What cloister denied was access, and what access provided was unlimited opportunity to pursue a wide range of activities. Whether women who had lived such severely suppressed and restricted lives would be capable of imposing their own measures of restraint and protection now that their old security system was being disconnected was unclear. It was in this struggle for self-realization that the Society faced its greatest challenge.

Leaping over the Wall

9

○ THE YEARS immediately following the special chapter in Rome were chaotic and traumatic for the Society of the Sacred Heart and for those whose expectations of it had been formed by exposure to its uniformity and traditions, high standards of education, and penchant for perfection. For so many years the Society had been a solid, unified foundation with a singleness of purpose that, even with the restrictions of cloister and monasticism, had succeeded in setting a foundation of Catholic education for young women that went far beyond the norm. Now that foundation was being enlarged and broadened, redesigned to conform with a time in the Church's history and the world's that was itself unsure, untested, and unstable. Now it appeared that the well-sewn fabric of the once well-ordered life was beginning to unravel. Many Sacred Heart nuns, anxious to explore their newfound freedom, joined with the children they were teaching in testing the fads, trends, and in some cases the fashions of the soaring sixties.

The nuns said it was because the Church asked them to change and experiment; the alumnae said it was because the nuns were looking for an excuse to let down their hair, throw off their habits, leap over the wall, and cut the ties that once had bound them so closely. The Society said it was time to separate the accidentals from the essentials. The end result was massive confusion and painful misunderstandings.

When I spoke with Sister Mary Elizabeth Tobin in her office at Stone Ridge Country Day School in Maryland, where she counsels lay and religious men and women on the spiritual aspects of their lives, she compared the changes in the Society of the Sacred Heart with the changes in the world at large. "Never before did the structure of religious life change so rapidly," she said. "I don't think you can isolate one thing. If you take it out of the world situation or the Church situation, it throws it all out of gear. Advances in communications caused the world situation to change radically from information localized in various places to information available worldwide. World War II caused a tremendous change in the world situation, which dramatically affected not only the Church but religious life. After World War II, I know that our congregation changed because all during the war, particularly in Europe, we could not keep cloister because we were living with men camped on our grounds. The nuns went out in search of food, they were taking care of sick people and doing a number of things that required them to leave the convent grounds. Then, after the war, the doors were closed again and cloister was enforced, but life had already shown us that cloister was no longer practical, that what had been true in the past would no longer be true in the future."

In the beginning most of the women who entered the Society of the Sacred Heart, including St. Madeleine Sophie herself, had been strongly attracted to the spiritual side of religious life, the one that had been contained and protected by cloister and by the programmed days each member of every community willingly submitted herself to. Now the nuns were being asked to reverse that behavior, to assume responsibility for their own prayer life, to make decisions for their own well-being, to direct their own talents, and to cope with their own feelings.

Sister Mary C. Wheeler, who was sixty years old in 1967, recalls, "We didn't know how to communicate at all, so at first we spent a lot of time just talking, getting to know each other. We were really just feeling our way at that point and of course the changes bothered some religious terribly. We just didn't know a thing about how our own people thought or felt about anything personal because under the old regime that was forbidden, there was no time allotted for personal conversation."

So began the "getting to know you" process within the Society of the Sacred Heart. As one former nun put it, "It was really a great shock to the system because for years we had lived this highly regimented life which was broken into various segments: prayer life; spiritual reading; community recreations, with every conversation directed through the superior; and teaching. Suddenly we were thrown in with this group of women who were yakking their heads off about every subject imaginable. It was then that I began to question whether my vocation would fit the new mold."

The question of what a vocation really meant became ambiguous. Some said if you answered the call, submitted to the training, accepted the opportunity to further your education, and took final vows, your commitment was forever, no matter how circumstances changed, no matter how you "felt." Others believed it was now possible to be called to religious life for a finite amount of time, especially if the order you entered no longer offered the life to which you were initially attracted. For the great majority of Catholics, a religious vocation was viewed as a marriage, a sacred trust that was not entered into lightly or terminated easily.

"The nuns seemed to give up on us and on their prior commitments pretty quickly," my schoolmate Grace Schrafft observes. "No sooner were they released from cloister than they began closing up the schools." And she was right. Between 1968 and 1972 twelve Sacred Heart schools were shut down, and six Sacred Heart colleges were either sold to the Jesuits, as in the case of Newton College in Massachusetts and San Francisco College for Women, or deeded over to their boards of trustees, as was Manhattanville College in Purchase, New York, and Maryville College in St. Louis, Missouri. "It came like lightning," one of the older nuns recollects. "Most of us really had no idea. It seems the order hired a professional consulting firm to evaluate Sacred Heart schools across the country. They looked to the future and saw that there were not going to be very many vocations, that the focus of new vocations was drawing away from teaching, and that many in the order would soon be too old to teach. Anyway, they decided that the best thing to do would be to consolidate some of the schools and close the rest." But the Society sometimes failed to communicate its intentions in the decisions it was forced to make about its schools. Grosse Pointe Academy is a case in point. The Sacred Heart school on Lake Shore Drive in the exclusive Detroit suburb was founded in 1867 when the Society purchased forty-two acres of land for $15,300. The school flourished in the same location for more than one hundred years.

As Mary Kay Tracy Farley, a Grosse Pointe Academy alumna and former president of Manhattanville's Alumnae Association, says, "I think the point had been reached where the Society could not staff all their schools and they felt a great pressure to get out of middle-class education and start relating to the very poor, for which they had not been trained. I think the Grosse Pointe closing embodied a lot of what happened to the Society. The school was very heavily endowed by families like the Fords, the Fishers, the Briggses (former owners of the Detroit Tigers), and other wealthy parents of students. When the decision was made to close the school, the Society never talked to the parents. They just immediately began talking to real estate developers, lawyers, and zoning commissioners privately. When the parents and alumnae got wind of it, all hell broke loose and people were very, very bitter."

Toni Robinson, a Grosse Pointe Academy alumna and parent, concurs. "When we got the letter in January 1969 saying the school was going to close, the reaction was total shock. Disbelief gave way to anger and bitterness on the part of a lot of people."

One of the primary reasons for that anger and bitterness (beyond the fact that the school was debt-free and had a waiting list of prospective students) was the parents' belief that their children were being given a fine academic education as well as values to live by. "It was the only school in the Detroit metropolitan area that provided a fine value-oriented Catholic education in a community where there is a lot of materialism," says one parent.

Sister Anne O'Neil, the treasurer of the New York Province at the time, now admits that the way in which the closings were announced and executed "was done badly to say the least." Before the bulldozers came, a series of explosive meetings were held, attended by Sister O'Neil and a group of parents and alumnae who wished to save the school.

Sister O'Neil recalls, "I had been a member of the Society's school planning commission, and one of the reasons we chose to close Grosse Pointe was that it was debt-free. We couldn't have closed Bloomfield Hills (the other Sacred Heart school in Michigan) because the same situation did not exist there. The Grosse Pointe alumnae wanted to take over the school, and that solved a lot of problems and anguish. The fact that the Society was going to withdraw was clear, and I suppose it could have been done better. It was the beginning of the realization that the rich Madames were not rich enough."

Eventually the Society apologized for the abrupt way it announced the closing, and ultimately the parents and alumnae did buy the school. In August 1969 the religious resigned from the board of trustees, and the following September the school opened as a coeducational day school. Although today the school in Grosse Pointe is not a member of the Sacred Heart network of nineteen schools, it is Catholic by tradition, relying on many of St. Madeleine Sophie's teachings, but with an ecumenical student body of four hundred.

Mary Kay Tracy Farley adds, "As a footnote, when the nuns left Grosse Pointe, they sold off an awful lot of the beautiful things that had been given to the school — paintings, silver, china, furniture — and the patrons said, 'You are not marching out of here with all that stuff.' But they did. Practically the only tangible thing they left behind was a great big trunk filled with their old habits, and to me that said volumes."

The new transition habit the Society had designed and used beginning in 1966, which pinched the ears, allowed some hair to show, and boasted a shorter hemline, had been unsuccessful. By 1969, two years after the special chapter, that habit was beginning to be shed by some American nuns. On September 2, 1969, a letter addressed to the parents and faculty of Noroton-on-the-Sound in Connecticut went out from Sister Mary E. Fisher, a Noroton alumna and faculty member, saying in part that the nuns in the United States and Canada had been granted the option to wear secular dress and that in the coming school year those who desired it would appear out of the habit. It further stated that the "decision to do so is made in full recognition of all that the habit has meant in the past, but with the conviction that radical religious commitment cannot be tied to any single life-style or mode of dress."

There was a growing consensus among the younger nuns, and others as well, that a habit was an impediment to communication with the outside world with whom they wanted to relate. St. Madeleine Sophie had said that the dress for the Society should be "simple and common to all." She chose a widow's dress, which in her time was unremarkable and in keeping with the current fashion. As the years fanned out, the habit became a uniform, a garment of respect, trust, and distinction as well as a source of identification, but it had long ceased to be representative of contemporary times. As Sister Prue Wilson writes in her book *My Father Took Me to the Circus:*

"By the mid-twentieth century no one in their right mind could have called the habit simple, and for anyone entering between 1914 and the 1960's a feeling of putting on fancy dress was both satisfying (here at least was something to prove a different way of life) and tiresome. The number of strings to be tied, petticoats to be worn and underwear to be coped with was astonishing and hilarious. But the end result declared to all, 'I am a member of the Society of the Sacred Heart and proud of it,' and I remember both enjoying and being liberated by that assurance." After the changes of Vatican II began to be implemented in the Society, for many nuns, including Sister Wilson, that feeling of security in their dress was no longer true. "Directly I found myself driving a car, shopping, traveling on public transportation," she says, "dressed up to appear holier than thou, I was uncomfortable. The discomfort was enhanced by those who liked seeing me defined as a nun. I found it touching but wrong that far older people should give up their places to me on a bus, or that conductors should refuse my fare. It was moving to know that the cloth was so valued, at least by some, but it was saying something about my way of life that was untrue." To some degree the question of the habit was illustrative of the Society's debate within itself about what was essential in the order and what was not. Did the habit itself represent the essence of the vocation? Of course not, but it did lend itself to the corporate image, underlining the conformity of the life apart, the special dedication, and the Society's motto, "One heart and one mind."

The alumnae were outraged when the nuns began to leave the habit in the late sixties, just as they were outraged when Sacred Heart schools began closing and the remaining ones began throwing off the traditions and values of old. Here were the women who had been inspirational to students and parents in their aesthetic settings, their habits, their exemplary lives of sacrifice, purity, and all things holy, who willingly set themselves apart from life's external pleasures, suddenly leaving home in droves with a ticket to ride. Sprung from cloister and habit, the Sisters of the Sacred Heart appeared to joyfully jump from their pedestals and hit the ground running, eager to embrace the world and the many choices now available to them. It was as if they had suddenly discovered Disneyland. For the first time there was visible dissension in the ranks. Many older nuns wanted to continue the more traditional way of life, to retain some semblance of the old traditions and attitudes, while many others, particularly the younger ones, were intent on bridging the gap between cloister and contemporary life as quickly as possible. This was clearly demonstrated at Kenwood, the American novitiate, where a younger nun appeared in the midst of the old guard in a sundress, wearing earrings and eye makeup. "You gave your beauty to God," a disapproving sister shouted, "and now you have taken it back."

Sister Wheeler remembers that after the rules were relaxed she was asked repeatedly by some younger members of her community at the Stuart Country Day School in Princeton, New Jersey, to join them at the movies. "I really didn't want to go," she says, "but they finally wore me down and I agreed. When we got there they really put on a terrible show. They laughed too loudly, talked too much, and behaved like adolescents. When it was over I told them I would never do it again. 'Why, didn't you like the movie?' one of them asked, and I said, 'Oh, it wasn't the movie I didn't like, it was you — you acted liked a group of teenagers.' "

The Convent of the Sacred Heart, Noroton-on-the-Sound, was founded by the religious of the Sacred Heart in 1925. Located on a magnificent point of land extending from the southern shore of Connecticut into Long Island Sound, it was one of the Society's most beautiful, and most exclusive, boarding schools. From the day it opened until it closed in 1972, Noroton was the smallest and probably the most elite Sacred Heart boarding school in America. The majority of students were daughters of wealthy and prominent Irish Catholic families: Kennedys, Buckleys, Fords, and Fishers, McDonnells, Coakleys, Farrells, and Bradys. Among the landmarks at the school were the log cabin where part of the senior class lived and where visiting parents and boyfriends were entertained at tea on Sundays, the tree in the middle of the hockey field, the large swimming pool, the pavilion, and the dock. Like many of its Sacred Heart counterparts, Noroton was a contradiction — physically beautiful on the outside, but for many of its residents harsh and austere within. There were as many fond memories as there were sad ones.

Because the school was viewed as somewhat exclusive, the nuns at Noroton made a concerted effort during the post–Vatican II years to institute a change in the sociological makeup of the small student body. They brought in a handful of carefully selected young black girls from Harlem (previously there had been no minority students). As in many Sacred Heart schools there also always were a few girls from Latin America and Europe, children of affluence, many familiar with the Sacred Heart way of life through ties with the Society's schools in their own country. They represented another culture, but certainly not a different economic plateau. With good intentions, and in keeping with the thrust of racial equality that was now a primary consideration in public and private education, but with little or no experience in this sensitive and explosive area, the nuns found themselves in a situation far more complicated and complex than they had anticipated. Many of the students were from broken homes and far more liberal environments than the one they found at Noroton. A generally rebellious attitude prevailed, engendering a lack of discipline, and soon a chaotic clashing of cultures began to emerge within the school. Some of the white students aligned themselves with the minorities, who were lost and unhappy in the strange, evolving Sacred Heart atmosphere. There were rumors of drug and alcohol use, depression, feelings of alienation from all sides, and a general malaise, all stemming not only from the obvious complications of merging poor, inner-city children with the children of privilege but from the nuns' own ongoing identity crisis, which distracted them from the problems at hand.

In 1969 a written survey described a changing Noroton as attempting to "make concrete the American ideal of pluralism by its enrollment and its encouragement of each individual to be herself. Noroton students are admitted on the basis of two considerations: the student's willingness and ability to complete the academic curriculum, the school's preference for a diverse student population, both average as well as outstanding students of different geographic, racial and economic backgrounds." The survey added that religious affiliation was not a factor in the admissions policy, but all students were expected to have a respect for religion. This enraged the Catholic parents, who expected the nuns to continue to enforce the traditions, decorum, and high academic standards they were known for and, at the very least, to offer their students a strong Catholic education, the foundation stone on which the Society of the Sacred Heart had built its reputation.

During the tumultuous time of change in the 1960s, experimentation was a critical part of the reevaluation process in every Sacred Heart school, and Noroton was no exception. The Society was anxious to rid itself of its old image, that of running schools for the rich, but its administrators were unsure and unskilled in the sensitive task of instantly integrating the student body. For those who sent their daughters to Noroton to expose them to the continuing Sacred Heart tradition, the changes were unexpected and shocking. Those who had known the school only in its new incarnation were equally distressed that the level of education was dropping as rapidly as the enrollment was increasing. What was obvious to all who witnessed the complications resulting from the school's opening its doors to a more representative group of students was that Noroton was foundering.

Sister Anne O'Neil, former Mistress General at Noroton-on-the-Sound and former treasurer of the Society in the United States, served the last year of her six-year term as American provincial in 1987. A graduate of the Manhattanville College class of 1950, she went to school with my own Mother Daley (now Peggy Daley) and a dozen other women who entered religious life. Her family founded the General Tire Corporation in Cleveland, Ohio, where she was raised.

I first met Sister O'Neil when she was my sister Lee's Mistress General at Noroton, and twenty-three years later I interviewed her at the provincial house on Pine Street in St. Louis. Dressed casually in denim skirt and plaid short-sleeved shirt, her hair cut short, she appeared comfortably at ease with herself and her surroundings. The last time we had talked was on my sister's graduation day in June 1963. At that time she was wearing the traditional Sacred Heart habit, was addressed as "Mother," and was curtsied to by the students. Now she was Sister O'Neil, an attractive, accomplished woman in her late fifties, with a demanding job. She moved with the same graceful strides I remembered, but now she was bare-legged and her feet were shod in sandals. As we sat across from each other in her small air-conditioned office it was another hot June day, and we spoke first of the past and her days as Mistress General at Noroton.

"I don't think you could say that Noroton was typical in many ways of other Sacred Heart schools," she said. "It was very small and self-contained, there were no day students, and it was very isolated. Noroton was a little island in a much bigger system. My memory is that I was uncomfortable with a lot of the children, but I am sure I was full of affection for a lot of them too. I was young for the position of Mistress General, and because I had never attended a Sacred Heart secondary school, the superior at Noroton was supposed to make sure I understood how Sacred Heart education worked. I think the Society thought it was risky having someone as headmistress who hadn't had that experience. I was told that we didn't call students by nicknames, and I remember thinking the girls wouldn't know who we were talking to if that was true, and the parents certainly wouldn't think we had a very close relationship with their children if we used only their given names. So I went through the files hoping to find one or two Mistresses General before me who had used nicknames, and I found them. Then I went back to the superior and said, 'Here it is on paper and I want to do it this way, I can't do it any other way.' I think that was representative of the kind of formality that was honored in those days. If the individual nun did not make an effort to find ways around that formality it could be very austere, and I think a good deal of life at Noroton was. To be human was not the thing at that time."

Writer Suzannah Lessard has mixed feelings about her years there in the early sixties: "It was certainly not the best preparation for the modern world, and I think perhaps it took us too long to adjust to things as they really were because the nuns had given us such unrealistic expectations. Still, I must say that on the whole my memory of those days is a positive one, although many aspects were quite painful. I did love the early morning Mass and the different kind of privacy achieved when you do something over and over again, but I think there is no question that it took most of us too long to grow up."

Mona Lyons Carr, an alumna now practicing law in Washington, D.C., remembers that "we all used to pretend that we couldn't wait to get out of there for vacation, but I am willing to bet that eighty-five percent of the people were counting the days until they came back and did not have to worry about whether or not they had a date for the Gotham Ball or the Christmas dance or whatever. I think a lot of us were glad to be back in uniform, back on the hockey field, back in protective custody. We were away from the very personal authority of our parents and in the almost impersonal authority of the nuns. It was a very special time, a difficult one, but one that at least for me had tremendous value."

Mav Deegan McCarthy was sentimental about leaving the protective custody of Noroton too, even though she admits she felt it was "cold and remote. . . . It was a safe haven and I was planning to totally implement my life from the things I was taught there. When I got to Georgetown nursing school, much to my dismay, I began structuring my days based on the Noroton routine. I laid my clothes out at night, meditated, blocked out an hour a week to wash my hair and write letters, and generally tried not to waste time. I even went so far as to advise my roommate to lay out her clothes before bedtime in case there was a fire. I am sure she thought I was crazy, but that is what I had been programmed to do. Also, I was very alert to mortal sin, and nearly everything sexual seemed very close to it. In the beginning of my new life I couldn't make the distinction between what was appropriate at school and inappropriate out in the world."

Two hundred years ago St. Madeleine Sophie said, "We must be busy about our children. We must enter into everything that concerns them, listen to them with interest, and comfort and encourage them. To be useful to them, we must be gentle and patient." This was wise and practical advice, and yet as the Society of the Sacred Heart spread out and moved away from its founding mother's counsel, concepts, and country, it seems this philosophy sometimes got lost in the effort to discipline, restrain, and control.

My sister, Lee Harrison Child, a divorced mother of three, recently described her four years at Noroton as "the worst years of my life. I think there were seventeen in our freshman class and seventy-two students in the entire school. I found the work there quite hard. I had come from a small school in South Carolina, had never had French, had never heard the word 'doctrine,' and had never played field hockey. When I look back, which I don't do often, I see a terrible dichotomy. Here I was in this breathtaking setting living like a character in a Charles Dickens novel. The Sacred Heart nuns prided themselves on creating a family atmosphere, on playing the role of mother, but for me there was no evidence of love, motherly or otherwise. I never felt close to any of them, and certainly not well cared for. The nuns were very removed and totally remote. No one ever gave us a pat on the back, literally or figuratively. I just remember a very cold atmosphere, very strict, with a lot of reprimands and few compliments."

She recalled one incident in particular that represents Sacred Heart discipline: "When we were all very new and had never heard the term 'losing your Très Bien,' my roommates and I were sitting on the floor of our room doing exercises after lights in silence. Our dormitory mistress came in and told us we were going to lose our Très Bien cards at *primes* that week. The next day she said that because it was our first offense she had decided to give us a penance to do instead. So we had to take cold showers and pass up *goûter* for a week. I did it faithfully and willingly, and to this day I remember stepping into that shower, which is probably the reason I never lost my Très Bien cards the whole time I was there. In retrospect it seems a poor motivation."

When she was given permission to call home, my sister, who says she "cried in my pillow for four years," began the myth our mother still believes. "I told her I liked it," she said softly. "What else could I do?" Unlike mine, her words never became reality.

"You could have gone and talked with Mother O'Neil," I suggested, and Lee quickly pointed out, "But I was not like you. You have a different nature. You don't mask your feelings and that was part of my problem. To a very large degree I was reacting to what you had gone through. You had been to several boarding schools and I just didn't want to cause our parents any more trouble. I thought you had put them through enough. You were a bit of a devil and I was trying to be an angel. Besides, I really thought or hoped it would get better for me, but it didn't."

When it didn't get better, she never uttered a word, at least not until her third year.

"I had been so stoic for the first two years that everyone thought I was blissfully happy," she recalled, "but on the day of my outburst things seemed particularly grim. I had gotten an English paper back from Mother Cooley that had been mimeographed and distributed to the class as an excellent paper, but on every line she had made corrections. That was somehow humiliating. There was a lot of pressure in the eleventh grade, the classes were tough, and there was a great emphasis on college boards. At lunch I got a letter from a friend who was at a fun boarding school and I just thought I was in the worst place possible. I started to cry and couldn't stop. I guess I was sent to see Mother O'Neil in her office, located in the middle of study hall, which we always curtsied to each time we passed, even when the door was closed. Anyway, I remember that she was quite compassionate and suggested I take the afternoon off and go into town for a cigarette. In those days cigarettes were the elixir for all emotional strife, and I remember thinking, *Wow!* Yet I don't think things really improved very much for me over the long haul.

"The thing that really astonished me was that everyone was treated the same, academically and socially. The nuns made no effort to know us as individuals, and there were no creative courses if we had leanings in that direction, and I think I did. We were looked at as a mass, a class, and I think that can be very damaging.

"I remember once when I was sick they didn't believe me. My friend Maureen Sullivan and I kept telling them we didn't feel well and they just kept telling us to go to class. Finally we just took to our beds. We were lying there in agony and a nun came in and said, 'Don't you know you are not supposed to lie on your bed until bedtime?' They finally sent us to the doctor and Maureen was sent home because she was so sick and I was put into the infirmary. I think that demonstrates what I am trying to say — we never got the feeling they trusted or cared for us. I wouldn't want my mother to treat me that way, and I certainly don't care for my children that way. What made it worse, in my opinion, was that all the while they were proclaiming God's love."

"I don't deny it was tough at that time," says Sister Tobin in response to criticism leveled at the nuns at Noroton for creating such a sterile, hands-off environment. "Yet more than three hundred former students came back recently for a Noroton reunion in New York and many more wanted to come. I believe they came back because they really cared and they really believed in what it was all about. The values that were given them continue in their lives today. So despite the fact that it was strict and had its regime, something of value was intangibly communicated. I do understand the complaints. I remember standing in the study hall at Noroton when I was a young nun and hearing Mother Miller yell at some senior in English class, 'Don't raise your eyebrow at me,' and I was shaking inside. But they all crawl to see Mother Miller today. I have seen many people who come back and say to me, 'I could never have, survived the suffering and difficulties of my life if I hadn't had that training.' Granted sometimes it was achieved at a great price by an individual, yet there was something given there that these women have been able to live out of, and I think that's what brings them back to reunions. . . . What's the cry you read in every psychology book — it's the battle against authority, and so at Eden Hall and Noroton and other places, we had between eighty and one hundred and twenty-five children battling against authority and authority was saying, You might not like this, but this is better for you. So I don't think you can take out the human element and say, Oh, it was rigid, it was strict, it was this or that — sure, for the adolescent at the time, but conversely it was what made the difference in their lives and it just doesn't happen as effectively today. Very frankly, there were people who could take it and some who couldn't. There are some who might say they were injured for life and I believe that is true. I mean, I can go to bed at night — and I have — thinking, 'What did I do wrong for so and so?' I see someone and I think we didn't handle her right. I can't tell you the number of people we agonized over that way."

Sister Tobin admits that the Society's old rule in some respects hindered the kind of communication St. Madeleine Sophie encouraged between nuns and children in the schools.

"It's true," she says, "the rule did not provide for long strolls in the park with Susie Q. We were supposed to speak in a few words and a low tone in a special place, but when we were with the students we were completely with them, and when we were not with them we were about our other duties of religious life. In spite of that, I say that when a nun was required to say to a child, 'I can't do this now, I have to go to spiritual reading or to say Office or to speak to Reverend Mother,' still a communication was there that said, 'What we are all about is you.' That was communicated whether we could speak to a child or not. That is what our lives were about. Now if you want to come away with the fact that Y could not speak to X at a particular time that was vital to her survival, fine, but if you come away with the fact that the only reason the nuns were there was that the only thing they really cared about was you, then you understand the essence of it. Despite the fact that the rules made it difficult at times for the nuns to communicate on a very personal level with the students, it happened over and over again. I think your relationship with [Mother] Peggy Daley is a very good example of that. I just never get the impression when I see the line of people who come back here to Stone Ridge that they thought the nuns were a bunch of cold fish. Maybe that was true for some individuals, but for the vast majority I think there was a great bond of love and respect. They don't come back here because they like the grounds; they come back because they had relationships here, experienced love, compassion, and understanding."

At Eden Hall, among the first schools to close, which it did in 1969, the children were increasingly from broken homes and diverse backgrounds. Sister Anne Dyer, who taught there, remembers Eden Hall as a "Victorian nightmare." Many of the children, she says, "were in need of psychological counseling, and we were not trained to give it to them. There were suicide attempts, there were kids who had no idea of bending to the strict discipline, marching to class in silence or curtsying to the nuns or conforming to the old ways. They were coming out of a much different world, a world of conflict and controversy, and we simply had to gather our strength and do what we could, but given our restricted and limited experience, I am afraid it wasn't enough."

At Noroton the situation went from bad to worse when a nun's veil was torn off by an angry minority student and four girls were expelled for using marijuana. A memo from Sister O'Neil to Sister Margaret Coakley, at the time the New York provincial, about this incident reveals the tension and the level of distress that were present. "There is a growing sense that not all are in support about the way the administration is running the school. It seems inconsistent to have expelled four kids who were first time users of marijuana when the students and some faculty members are aware of regular users and some who may be pushers in the student body (and they are not black students). Madame Pace [a lay faculty member], a member of the admissions committee, does not feel she has a chance to say much about some of the mid-term applicants who slip in — the recent psycho case is a case in point. She feels certain people use the school to place some of their clients. . . . She does not know why the nuns seem somewhat afraid to take a stand and to take more responsibility for the lack of discipline."

Many of the parents did not understand this either, and resentment began to build against the nuns and the manner in which they conducted themselves, dealt with the students, and ran their schools. Disciplinary problems were one thing, alcohol and marijuana another. But Noroton was not alone in its struggle to balance the new, permissive elements in society and retain the standards of decorum and education that had formed its reputation. Almost every boarding school in the United States was experiencing the same conflict, the same dilemma. If they did not begin to reduce the number of rules, the students would rebel; if they became too permissive, the parents would not enroll their children.

On January 6, 1970, the parents of Noroton received another unexpected piece of news that affected the entire Noroton community. The headmistress, Sister Labourdette, had decided to "resume lay status and leave the Society of the Sacred Heart." After that, attempts were made to restructure and save the school. Money was raised for a new addition, a lay headmaster was hired, but two years later Noroton closed down. The property on the Sound was later sold to a developer, and today the old school has been redesigned and converted into condominiums.

The Jewel in the Crown

10

"AH, MANHATTANVILLE," an aging alumna sighed. "Now there's a sad story."

In 1917 the religious of the Sacred Heart applied to the Regents of the state of New York for a charter that would make Manhattanville College eligible to grant college diplomas. Because the Society was unable to come up with the five hundred thousand dollars necessary to obtain an absolute charter, a provisional charter was granted. Although the name of the new college was listed as College of the Sacred Heart, Manhattanville was legally incorporated as an independent liberal arts college with an independent board of trustees. The first board had thirteen members, nine of whom were religious of the Sacred Heart. The nuns on the board of trustees continued to represent a majority until 1959, when for the first time the religious were outnumbered by lay people. But even then, the non-religious board members, with few exceptions, continued to be fathers, brothers, and husbands of Manhattanville alumnae. "They were all fine men," one former nun board member says. "Their loyalty to the nuns was unquestioned, and they were happy to do what Reverend Mother asked."

A familial bond existed at Manhattanville, not only between the nuns and the lay board of trustees but between students and faculty as well. The family spirit of the Sacred Heart was pervasive in almost every aspect of daily life, and Manhattanville was a prime example of how it succeeded. The Manhattanville alumnae, not unlike graduates of other Sacred Heart schools and colleges, looked upon their years at the campus in Harlem and, later, in Purchase, New York, as years of formation and friendship where, as one alumna put it, "I expected everything, and everything is what I got,"

Each class had a nun adviser called the class warden. For four years, in addition to her teaching duties, she offered guidance, advice, and often a willing ear to the cares and confidences of the college girls in her care. Many enduring friendships developed between classes and their wardens, and to this day many former wardens are included in reunion parties and correspond regularly with their old students, who continue to ask for their prayers.

Because the college was small, strict, and parochial, Manhattanville's student body, though economically and geographically diverse, shared an experience that shaped them in a special way. It was often noted that Manhattanville produced not only beautiful women but women with strong convictions and superior organizational abilities. "Whenever I want to get things done," a bishop of New York once observed, "I look for a Manhattanville girl." These were the women of Catholic Action, the feminine minds the nuns carefully molded to lead others down the sacrificial path of marriage, motherhood, and often religious life, whose expectations were limited not by knowledge but by choice. These were the women who attended daily Mass, had their Child of Mary medals dipped in gold at Cartier's, and offered up the disappointments in their lives for the "poor souls in purgatory." Manhattanville also produced its share of career women — doctors, lawyers, writers, and politicians. For many, Manhattanville was a confined, protective continuation of the secure, serene, religious environment they had experienced at Sacred Heart boarding and day schools or in their own families.

The first graduation ceremony took place in 1918, when two young women were granted bachelor of arts degrees. The absolute charter of accreditation was obtained in 1919, and by 1925 the college had grown sufficiently to cause the secondary school on its property (the Female Academy of the Sacred Heart) to relocate in Noroton, Connecticut.

During the first decades of its existence, the College of the Sacred Heart offered only one degree (bachelor of arts), but in 1937 the bachelor of music degree was added when the Pius X School of Liturgical Music, established in 1916 by Mother Georgia Stevens and Justine Bayard Ward, was given accreditation. Students came to the Pius X music school from all parts of the world for classes conducted by internationally recognized scholars of Gregorian chant. After Manhattanville moved to its new campus in Purchase in 1952,

Mother Josephine Morgan, who was unquestionably one of the most popular nuns in the college, took charge, and the Pius X school of music gained international recognition, producing records and the Pius X hymnbook familiar to all Sacred Heart students.

Also in 1937 the college, long known in Sacred Heart parlance as Manhattanville, changed its name officially to Manhattanville College of the Sacred Heart. As the secondary schools of the Sacred Heart in the United States had come to be known as institutions that catered to the well-bred Irish Catholic girl whose family regarded the French influence and the religious emphasis as valued elements of their daughter's education, so too Manhattanville became their college of choice. Although many of the daughters may have had other preferences, for most there was little opportunity for negotiation. The nuns in the secondary schools were often willing coconspirators with the parents, conveniently "forgetting" to mail applications to non-Catholic colleges and thereby narrowing the options of the applicants considerably. This trend continued into the 1960s. Delphine McCosker Shakley, a 1961 Eden Hall graduate, remembers being told at the end of her senior year that her application to Vassar had been "misplaced," leaving Manhattanville as her only alternative. "I was furious about it," she said, "but what could I do?"

Rose Fitzgerald, who would later become matriarch of the Kennedy clan, had wanted to enroll in Wellesley College but succumbed to family pressure and entered Manhattanville instead. She was well versed in the Sacred Heart tradition, having attended the Convent of the Sacred Heart at Blumenthal in Holland, where she had become a member of the prestigious Child of Mary sodality, an international Sacred Heart organization for those who were deemed exceptionally devout within the schools and colleges. After a girl received her Child of Mary medal in a special ceremony, she was permitted to write the letters E. de M. beside her name (for *Enfant de Marie*) and was required to perform a set of spiritual exercises that could easily fill a day. Before going to Blumenthal, Rose had also spent a year at the Convent of the Sacred Heart on Commonwealth Avenue in Boston. It was at Blumenthal, Doris Kearns Goodwin writes in her book *The Fitzgeralds and the Kennedys*, "that Rose let a part of herself go, that part of herself that had originally conceived of independent ambitions and career accomplishments, that part of her that had once wanted so fiercely to go to Wellesley College. The convent had done its work on Rose; the long silences, the immutable routine, and the daily lessons of the Sacred Heart curriculum had readjusted her vision of the world."

It was true that Sacred Heart girls had a different, some would say limited, view of the world and their place in it. The Sacred Heart experience reaffirmed their faith, awakened an active social conscience, and developed a loyalty to God, family, and country that was often envied by those outside the Catholic Church. Women like Rose Kennedy and her daughter-in-law Ethel Skakel Kennedy were prime examples of Sacred Heart girls whose religion was an integral part of their lives. If they had not married, the chances were good they would have become nuns. "Ethel was very devoted to the Lord," Sister Josephine Morgan remembers. "She spent a lot of time in the chapel and I really thought she might have a vocation, but then she met Robert Kennedy and we lost her." The Kennedy women faced unspeakable tragedy in their lives and used their religion, their personal relationship with God, as well as the example set for them by the religious of the Sacred Heart as a primary source of strength in bearing the unbearable with dignity and grace. And there were countless others like them.

Some affluent Irish Catholic and Italian Catholic families in the United States in the early twentieth century attempted to escape the prejudice and discrimination heaped on them by society and attain acceptance by sending their sons and sometimes their daughters to boarding schools in Europe or to elite nonsectarian preparatory schools in New England. But even in their desire to emulate the Protestant families that scorned them, most were unwilling to completely neglect the obligations of their faith, which required Catholic parents to provide their children with a Catholic education. More often than not they chose Catholic schools and colleges over secular ones for their daughters. In the foundation days of the Society of the Sacred Heart in France, and later elsewhere in Europe, prominent Catholic families were counted among the aristocracy, but for many generations in the United States, they were considered anything but. The struggle of Joseph Patrick Kennedy to overcome the stigma of parochialism and break down the educational and social barriers to Catholics, first at Harvard and then in New York, Palm Beach, and Hyannis Port, was indicative of the struggle of other prominent Irish Catholics, who succeeded in business but were denied membership in clubs and participation in an array of social events.

Like other minorities, Catholics were often forced to create their own society. New York's Gotham Ball and the Catholic Big Sisters were organizations established for Catholic women by Catholic women. Rose Kennedy was a member of the Cecilian Club in Boston, the Catholic girls' answer to the Junior League. Because of its affiliation with the Society of the Sacred Heart, Manhattanville was considered the Catholic answer to the Seven Sisters. Although it ranked below colleges like Vassar, Smith, and Radcliffe in prestige and social standing, Manhattanville represented the best the Sacred Heart had to offer, and for many first Irish and Italian families that was good enough. Author Phyllis Theroux wrote that Manhattanville was "almost a breeder station of beautiful, appropriate Catholic women who would presumably lead beautiful, appropriate Catholic lives." It was also called "the nun factory" because of the number of graduates who eventually became Sacred Heart nuns. As the military academies were feeders for the armed forces, so Manhattanville served the Society of the Sacred Heart.

Many of the nuns who taught at Manhattanville were scholars of the first rank who attained recognition as authors, critics, and lecturers in their chosen fields outside Catholic academic circles. Women such as Margaret Williams, Mary Clark, Josephine Morgan, Cora Brady, Kathryn Sullivan, Eileen O'Gorman, Adele Fiske, Ruth Dowd, and Jean McGowan were examples of the Society's best and brightest who taught generations of Manhattanville students and brought honor to the college. Sister Janet Rebardy, herself a Manhattanville alumna, said, "The nuns who taught at Manhattanville were absolutely magnificent women, and a lot of people entered the Society because of what those women were. They were not only well educated but very human and broad-minded. They were serious about their work, but with a wonderful balance and real senses of humor. I think this is what appealed to a lot of people, that balance of mind and heart." The class of 1950 at Manhattanville produced more than half a dozen postulants who persevered, made their final vows, and became religious of the Sacred Heart. Peggy Daley was one of these.

Under one of its most famous presidents, Mother Grace

Cowardin Dammann, whose term lasted from 1930 to 1945, Manhattanville broadened its base by opening its classrooms and lecture halls to a variety of local talent. Mother Dammann's strong sense of social justice led her to encourage her students to work as volunteers in the Barat Settlement House in the Bowery, Casita María in East Harlem, Dorothy Day's Catholic Worker, and Baroness de Hueck's Friendship House. She was particularly struck by the Harlem Renaissance during the 1930s and invited black playwrights, philosophers, and poets such as Langston Hughes, James Weldon Johnson, Countee Cullen, and Walter White to give readings and performances at Manhattanville. A pioneer in the field of racial equality, she attacked the issue with courage and conviction at a time when it was neither fashionable nor fathomable to do so.

Her views on racism were eloquently expressed at a controversial Manhattanville alumnae meeting on May 31, 1938. In her speech, entitled "Principles Versus Prejudice" (later published and used as a guide by many college administrations), she addressed the issue not only in theory but in practice and informed her former students that a young black girl, who was fully qualified, had applied to Manhattanville for admission. Mother Dammann told the startled group that it was her intention to admit her. She refuted the view that St. Madeleine Sophie had founded the Society of the Sacred Heart for the upper classes, although she printed out that "the Negro group as well has upper classes, based on refinement and education." She cited the example of Mother Philippine Duchesne and the small cabin in St. Charles, Missouri, "where the Society made its beginnings" in America and where "there were no countesses or duchesses or princesses to be taught." She continued, "Saint Madeleine Sophie founded the Society to save souls.... Peasant born as she was, she taught the children of the nobility, since they needed her services, not for their social prestige, but for their salvation." She reiterated that the Society's philosophy of education focused on the development of the whole person and that each person was entitled to enrich her potential. "However few the colored girls who can meet the requirements of Catholic colleges, each one of them is a potential leader, each one is infinitely precious to God, and each has a right to a Catholic education as strong and as deep as can be given her.... Your education at the Sacred Heart," she stated, "was planned to develop in you that sense of the value of truth and that spirit of sacrifice which will do the truth, cost what it may. . . . You have failed to grasp the essence of that education if you keep any area of your life outside the control of positive Christian principles or if, in spite of a sort of good will, through culpable ignorance you fail to know these principles."

In "doing the truth" as she saw it, Mother Dammann ran head on into a wave of formidable resentment and resistance. Anonymous letters were sent to Manhattanville by a small but vocal segment of alumnae whose fear, limitation, and ignorance were sad examples of the vicious prejudice Mother Dammann had spoken about. One letter asked why "they can't continue to go to their own colleges." Mother Dammann's answer was quick and to the point: In 1937 the Negro population in the United States was ten percent of the population, and of that number two percent were Catholic. There were no Catholic Negro colleges in the North and not enough eligible students even in the New York area for a single nonsectarian institution. Bryn Mawr College near Philadelphia had admitted Negro girls in 1927 and since that time two had graduated. Since Bryn Mawr was drawing from the entire Negro population and Manhattanville from the much smaller Catholic element, Mother Dammann concluded that it would be "highly unlikely that the college will be over-run with Negro students." And it was not. The young Negro girl who came North to attend Manhattanville in 1938 left after a short stay. Many reasons contributed to her departure, most having to do with the strain and pressure of adjusting to a strange environment and bearing the lonely burden of being the first black in an all-white institution.

But Mother Dammann's courageous, visionary attempt to enlighten and correct a long-standing inequity was not limited to the admission of one black student. Hers was a life commitment to "doing the truth," which marked her years at Manhattanville and her leadership and is evident in her accomplishments and her attempts at change. The first black student to graduate from Manhattanville was Mamie Jenkins in 1946. She became a Sacred Heart nun and teaches today at the Sacred Heart school in Princeton, New Jersey.

One of her former students called Mother Dammann "one of the most cultured women I ever knew. She had a way of attracting these very brilliant professors, some of whom had been driven out of Nazi

Germany. There was Mademoiselle Maria Thérèse Gehin, who arrived in New York with about ten cents in her pocket and a degree in German from the Sorbonne. The Russian teacher was a tiny woman who had been at the court of the czar." Angela Cave, who headed Manhattanville's English department and taught there for more than thirty years, came with an Oxford education and a penchant for perfection that fell well within the boundaries established by the Sacred Heart intelligentsia. Dr. Daniel Walsh, Thomas Merton's friend and later a priest, was a Manhattanville faculty member whose scholarship and personal charisma as a professor of philosophy inspired many Manhattanville students to major in that subject. Although the college was small at the time of Mother Dammann's presidency, with only four hundred students, the lay faculty alone, in keeping with the cosmopolitan spirit of the Society of the Sacred Heart, included representatives from ten European countries. When Mother Dammann died of a sudden heart attack in 1945, Archbishop (later Cardinal) Francis J. Spellman presided at the solemn requiem Mass held in the Manhattanville chapel. A thousand friends and two hundred priests and fellow religious heard Mother Dammann eulogized as a great educator, a fearless champion of racial equality, and a woman of extraordinary vision who was years ahead of her time. Several hundred people accompanied her body on a special train to the depot in Torresdale, Pennsylvania, for burial at Eden Hall, where she had once been the superior.

Mother Dammann's successor at Manhattanville was Mother Eleanor O'Byrne, who from 1945 to 1966 worked tirelessly to enlarge the college and enrich it by bringing its academic standards to a new plateau. During her administration the bachelor of fine arts and the master of arts degrees were added to the program. It was during her second year as president, in 1946, that talk began to circulate about the possibility of moving the college from its home on Convent Avenue in Harlem to a new location in the New York suburbs. The old neighborhood was deteriorating, the old buildings were in need of repair, and the expanding student body was in need of more space. The real impetus for the move was brought about in August 1947 when Cardinal Spellman suggested moving Manhattanville to the 250-acre Whitelaw Reid estate in Westchester County. Known as Ophir Farm when its former owner, Ben Halliday of Overland

Express fame, opened the first museum of the West on its grounds, the estate was purchased in 1887 by Whitelaw Reid, who succeeded Horace Greeley as owner of the *New York Tribune*.

After learning of the cardinal's suggestion, Mother Gertrude Bodkin, vicar of the Society's New York vicariate, wrote him a letter that said in part, "You will easily understand that our sentiments are all against the change, but we cannot let that stand in the way of the work for the Church, and for future generations of students." Shortly afterward arrangements were made for Mother O'Byrne and Mother Agatha Cronin, treasurer of the college, to visit the proposed site. After seeing it, they agreed with the cardinal that it was beautifully suited for a college campus. So began a period of negotiation and debate among the nuns, the Manhattanville board of trustees, and the cardinal that would last for almost two years. Among the problems at hand were the sale of the land in Harlem and the purchase price of the Reid estate. Potential buyers for the buildings on the old campus were a life insurance company and the neighboring City College of New York. Consideration was also given to condemnation of the Harlem property, which would allow the nuns a settlement for the appraised value of the land and the replacement value of the buildings. Whitelaw Reid's widow originally offered the property in Westchester for five hundred thousand dollars, but as negotiations dragged into 1949 the figure fluctuated. Problems arose regarding boundary lines, roads, zoning, and tax exemptions, and there was no assurance that a buyer for the old campus could be found in time for the nuns to attain the cash needed to buy the Westchester property. For a time the Society dropped out of the bidding altogether. Then, in the summer of 1949, Cardinal Spellman informed Mother O'Byrne that "if prompt action is not taken soon, Mrs. Reid will sell to another buyer." The trustees felt it would be unwise to go forward without a firm purchaser for the existing campus, but Cardinal Spellman was intractable in his belief that the nuns would never find a finer or more accessible piece of land. He offered to loan them the money to buy it, "to assure the future of Manhattanville for one hundred years or more." His loan of four hundred fifty thousand dollars eventually made it possible for the Society to consummate the deal with Mrs. Reid on June 17, 1949.

Throughout that summer the nuns from Harlem made visits to

the Reid estate, inspecting the existing buildings, which included the main house, later called the Castle, a garage, two gatehouses, and several small cottages. One of the reasons the nuns were hoping for a good price on the Harlem property was the obvious need for more construction to make the new campus suitable for occupancy. But with a keen eye for symmetry, Mother O'Byrne was determined to save as many of the old trees on the land as possible. "Those nuns had a real eye for the aesthetic setting," one former student observed, "and Manhattanville was going to be beautiful as well as commodious." January 1950 finally brought the good news that the nuns had been praying for. The city of New York, through condemnation procedures, had agreed to purchase the original Manhattanville property for $8,839,510.50. The cardinal's loan was repaid from money the nuns borrowed in Europe, and during the celebration of the Society's one hundred and fiftieth anniversary in 1950, the cardinal addressed the celebrants: "Now for your great affair! It is by now an accomplished fact, and the sooner it is carried out the better. I know what it means to leave this place hallowed by such long traditions, a place which has been the focal point of spiritual power that has gone out and through the Archdiocese of New York, through the Church in the United States, through the universal Church. But the essential thing, the spirit and the vision St. Madeleine Sophie gave to Manhattanville, is what is moving to the new site. As I told Mother Fitzgerald, this is the greatest single project, involving the most factors and the greatest amount of money, that has been undertaken in the history of the Diocese! Period!"

The more than eight million dollars that the Society received for the old college made possible the erection of five new buildings at the new one. Constructed before Manhattanville officially opened at Purchase on October 1, 1952, they included the first dormitory; Founders Hall; the Benziger Building, named for Mother Ursula Benziger; the main academic building; and the music building, which housed the Pius X school of music. Later, through the fundraising efforts of Mother O'Byrne, came the addition of five more buildings, including the Kennedy Gymnasium, erected in 1957 and named in memory of Kathleen Kennedy. It was at the groundbreaking ceremony in 1955 that Edward Kennedy was introduced to Joan Bennett, who would graduate from Manhattanville in 1958 and later become his wife.

Before the move from the city began, every object to be transported was appropriately tagged for its arrival on the new campus.
The Mothers of the Sacred Heart were nothing if not the most organized, imaginative, and practiced packers. Moving was part of
their history, and one has only to look back to Mother Digby's
monumental accomplishment in closing the houses in Paris in the
early 1900s to appreciate their abilities, which even extended to the
movement of coffins. The nuns entombed in the vault at old
Manhattanville were sent ahead to be reburied in the new cemetery
in Purchase. "Manhattanville's past has gone ahead of it into the
future," someone aptly observed. On July 31, the first of two hundred and eighty Morgan Brothers moving vans (Mother Josephine
Morgan's family's business) began to move out, piled high with
laboratory equipment, beds, chairs, and tables, in addition to ninety
thousand books, sixteen thousand phonograph records, thirty-five
pianos, and numerous other movable objects. When Cardinal Spellman pointed to the Manhattanville transaction as the largest financial deal the archdiocese had ever experienced, he well might have
added that it was also the most impressive physical move. Groups of
nuns from the campus in Harlem moved to the nearby Sacred Heart
school in Greenwich, Connecticut, to be on hand to greet the long
line of trucks that arrived promptly at eight o'clock every morning.
The move was completed on September 4, when Mothers Fitzgerald
and Cronin presented the keys of the old college to Dr. Harry N.
Wright of City College, to whom the city of New York had deeded
the land. The following day, Cardinal Spellman celebrated the first
Mass at the new Manhattanville campus. Such was the end of the
beginning and the beginning of the end.

William Cunningham, a former Manhattanville professor and presently dean of students at Catholic University, remembers being "re-
cruited from the CIA by Mother O'Byrne," who he claimed "had
the best Rolodex I had ever seen. She was a cloistered nun, but she
could call anybody, from the governor of New York on down.
When she needed to get something done, nothing stood in her way.
She was a phenomenal person, whose time was mostly taken up by
fund-raising. The nuns had already spent the money they received
from the property sale in Harlem on the move to Purchase and the
new buildings. There was a very serious financial crunch during the

time they were trying to get themselves established in continuing the building program and trying to beef up the endowment. They were in a very competitive area, a small, Catholic liberal arts college that was tuition-dependent with a small student body. But by the early sixties things began to change radically. An acute social sensitivity began to make itself felt. Many Manhattanville girls now had brothers and boyfriends who were going to Harvard, Princeton, and Yale. It was no longer the Manhattanville girl pinned to the Holy Cross boy. Kennedy had been elected president and I think Manhattanville up to that time had essentially looked at the education of women as a training ground for motherhood."

With the beginning of the women's movement, the new emphasis on sexual equality, freedom of choice for women, and the larger numbers of Catholic women attending secular colleges, Manhattanville found itself involved in a serious identity crisis. A very subtle pressure was beginning to be put on the nuns by the girls who, for instance, would go to Yale or Harvard for a visit, sit in on a class, and listen to a professor who specialized in sixteenth-century literature. When they got back to Manhattanville with its unspecialized faculty and compared the education they were getting with what they had seen elsewhere, they began complaining. The nuns, according to Professor Cunningham, "made a very good effort in seeking out some fine lay teachers during the late fifties — in fact, by 1960 the majority of the faculty was lay — but there was increased pressure from Manhattanville's primary constituency, who were judging the education their daughters were receiving as limited and inadequate. It became clear that they were going to have to incorporate aspects of the secular college model into their own."

In Professor Cunningham's view this was unfortunate only because "the models that were impressed on them were the Ivy League colleges, all heavily endowed institutions with major resources and research facilities that would be difficult if not impossible to replicate. An example of the mounting pressure they felt would be a prominent Irish Catholic family who had chosen not to send their daughter to Manhattanville. When the nuns asked why, the inevitable response would be 'We think she is going to get a better education at Smith or Vassar.' But there were other elements that were being factored into this equation, factors over which they had no control. The Catholic upper middle class was beginning to break out of parochialism for the first time. For people of my generation this was never a question. We expected discrimination, we lived with it and survived and succeeded in spite of it. These girls were coming into a different era. Kennedy had been elected president, and that indicated to them and to their families that they could have it all. It was a symbolic breakthrough of a fundamental principle, and from then on the floodgates were opened."

When Manhattanville moved to Purchase in 1952, Mother O'Byrne was quoted as saying that the college should not grow beyond six hundred students. But the student body grew larger every year and so did Manhattanville's need for financial aid to enlarge its campus, broaden its horizons, pay its lay faculty, offer scholarships, and remain competitive.

By 1959, the Manhattanville board of trustees was predominantly made up of lay members, but the college continued to have a heavily Catholic student body. As one nun said later, "It all had to do with perception. Although legally it was not a Catholic college, in almost every other way it was." After the move to Purchase, the Society of the Sacred Heart entered into an agreement with the board of trustees that the Society would run and staff the college and, although the Society would continue to own part of the land, the buildings and the college corporation would be owned by the board. This fact was misunderstood by many, who assumed that the Society was the sole owner.

In 1966, when Mother O'Byrne retired, she was succeeded by Mother Elizabeth J. McCormack, former academic dean at the college, who became the most controversial president and the last religious president of the college. Elizabeth McCormack recalls, "The thing to know about Manhattanville is that it was never legally a Catholic college. It never belonged to the Society or to the archdiocese, but there were a great many nuns who held key positions in the administration, on the faculty, and on the board of trustees. So while officially it was an independent, nonsectarian college, because of the physical presence of all those nuns in governing positions there was dominance by a group that were not only Catholic but were religious of the Sacred Heart."

The fact that Manhattanville was not legally a Catholic college was obscured by the strong sectarian image it conveyed, McCormack points out. The number of statues, crosses, the large and beautiful chapel erected in 1963, and the presence of the many religious figures on campus made it difficult for anyone to assume it was anything but a religious institution.

One of the first moves Mother McCormack made as president, with the concurrence of Reverend Mother Helen Fitzgerald, who had succeeded Mother Bodkin as vicar of the New York vicariate, was to legally shorten the name of the college from Manhattanville College of the Sacred Heart to Manhattanville College. The name change was instituted because Mother McCormack, Mother Fitzgerald, and the board of trustees recognized that the phrase "of the Sacred Heart" was construed to mean that the religious of the Sacred Heart owned the college, and they never did. The name change reflected a reality that many people never understood.

By this time in the Society's evolution, in the late 1960s, Sacred Heart nuns were no longer required to pursue academic careers as they had been in the past. Now there was a practice of "discernment," which translated into a dialogue between individuals and their provincial to determine what ministry would best suit their temperament, specific area of interest, and sometimes their politics. There was now an acceptance of diversity and a freedom to choose, where there had been none before. Traditional education, as it pertained to the Society's secondary schools and colleges, began to suffer losses in religious personnel.

Until 1970, religious of the Sacred Heart who taught in Sacred Heart schools and colleges did so without financial compensation and at the pleasure of their superiors. But as the number of nuns entering the Society decreased and as many of those within the Society began to assume responsibility for their own lives, the Society found itself increasingly unable to provide the services it had agreed to perform at Manhattanville and its other educational institutions.

In 1966 Mother McCormack began to promote the idea of Manhattanville's secularization, a concept that many of the alumnae and many of the nuns bitterly resented and opposed. In restructuring the college to conform to its legal definition as an independent liberal arts institution, to broaden its student body, enlarge its faculty, and assume a secular identity, Mother McCormack was forced to employ a number of innovations that affected the college structurally, philosophically, and economically.

William F. Buckley, Jr. (whose sister Carol and sister-in-law Ann

Cooley Buckley had attended Manhattanville), writing in *The New Yorker* in 1971, raised objections to Manhattanville's use of state funds for construction of two dormitory buildings. In Buckley's view, Manhattanville had reliquished its religious affiliation to comply with the Blaine Amendment, a part of the New York State constitution that prohibited state aid to a religious college. Buckley questioned whether it was possible for a Catholic college to divorce itself from Catholicism and retain its authenticity or its integrity. In a letter printed in the August 21, 1971, issue of the magazine, Sister McCormack responded to Buckley's criticisms: "I strongly believe that a college committed to the expansion of the mind cannot be closed. We must think of it, rather, as a vicinity. A vicinity is not a completed entity; rather it is an openness, it is a process that evolves in an environment of universality. Our colleges must be places where the deep questions of mankind are asked — questions that will not go away. Students no longer come to the liberal-arts college for answers. They come rather, to learn to ask the right questions; they insist on probing the meaning of meaning.

"To maintain church affiliation and the universality of inquiry will probably involve inconsistency. In the 'search for truth,' it is an imperative that every door be opened, every road explored, no path barred. Sectarian education, by definition, does not meet this end. The church-affiliated college, Catholic, fundamentalist, or any other — however much it may succeed in teaching its students to think, will also be tempted, to a greater or lesser degree, to instruct its students in the particular tenets of its religious faith. To teach a student to think about the tenets of several religions is a very different thing from instructing him in the tenets of a religion. . . . Manhattanville, like so many American institutions of higher learning, was associated in its origins with a particular church. Like others, it has changed. The important point — one that Mr. Buckley distorts — is *why* the college has changed. At the time we were first applying for state funds, many people urged me to forget about it, to avoid the bureaucratic difficulties involved. 'Let's go back to where we were,' they would say, meaning back to where Manhattanville was ten or fifteen years ago. My answer to that was (and is) There is no 'back' to go to. The world itself has changed. One may regret the present, some will expend most of their energy upon such regret. But it seems a good deal more fruitful to try to come to terms with the need to see things as they are, not as they were, and thus to construct a realistic base from which to project a better world and seek to bring it into existence. . . . Manhattanville did not change in order to become eligible for state aid. The changes in the college over the last few years have been instituted because Manhattanville had to go in new directions if it was to continue to make a significant contribution to the educational community. The changes that did take place prior to the Bundy legislation [which allowed state funding of schools run by religious orders as long as they removed all signs of sectarian affiliation], as instruments of a larger educational purpose, made it possible in the long run for the college to apply for state aid with perfect legitimacy."

Elizabeth McCormack recalls that she made a very strong point at the time to anyone who asked that the religious of the Sacred Heart who were teaching at the college were teaching there not because they were religious of the Sacred Heart but "because they were qualified to teach there. Had we continued having religious of the Sacred Heart teach when they ceased having the qualifications, then we should have lost the Bundy money [the state aid] but we should also have lost accreditation of the college."

Buckley's rebuttal to *The New Yorker* was brief and in Latin: *Radix omnium malorum est cupiditas* (The love of money is the root of all evil). And he wasn't the only one who thought so.

Among the changes that occurred at Manhattanville during Sister McCormack's presidency were the elimination of religious symbols on the campus, the admittance of men (in 1969), and the enlargement of the board of trustees to include non-Catholics. This eliminated once and for all the "family spirit" that had long characterized Manhattanville's board of trustees, who with few exceptions had endorsed and acted on Reverend Mother's directives with unquestioned loyalty. As had many of the Society's controversial post–Vatican II decisions, these moves by Sister McCormack caused confusion, anger, and bitterness among many elements of the college's constituency, who, as Sister McCormack pointed out, would have preferred to keep things "the way they were."

Sister Josephine Morgan recalls the day the order was handed down to remove the religious statues on the campus. "I remember Sister McCormack coming over and telling me that we had to move the statue of the Sacred Heart, and I said, 'Nothing doing, it's going to stay right where it is.' To this very day that statue is still there." The pull between the old and the new resulted in tension and recriminations.

In a time of academic upheaval, when students throughout the United States were demonstrating against the war in Vietnam and for civil rights, when they were demanding a voice in their own destinies and aligning themselves with organizations such as the Students for a Democratic Society and the Student Nonviolent Coordinating Committee, Manhattanville was not exempt from its own share of campus unrest. On December 8, 1969, when Sister McCormack was attending a meeting in Boston, eighteen of the college's forty-seven black students initiated a sit-in in Brownson Hall, a building that housed classrooms, art and music studios, and laboratory facilities. They secured all entrances to the building and drew up a petition of nine demands. One of these was a plea for the admission of one hundred fifty black students and the addition of seven faculty members to Manhattanville.

Sister McCormack responded by addressing a letter to the "Members of the Manhattanville Family." In it she quoted a statement she had made on her return from Boston, which said in part, "The basic validity of the struggle for racial justice as well as the right of the entire community to pursue its daily life will continue to govern my actions." She went on to say that she thought it improper for the president of an educational institution to negotiate under duress but reiterated her commitment to the recent restatement of policy on integration in schools by the regents of the state of New York, which said, "Since the stability of our social order depends on the understanding and respect which derive from a common educational experience among diverse racial, social and economic groups, that is, integrated education, we are concerned that all means be used effectively to realize integrated education." "This very principle," Sister McCormack wrote, "led Mother Grace Dammann in 1938 to admit Manhattanville's first black student and to publish her pioneering statement Principles versus Prejudice. It led her successor, Mother Eleanor O'Byrne, to inaugurate the LaFarge Scholarship Program for black students in 1964. It led me to sponsor the creation of Project SHARE in 1966, under which fifteen black students from Harlem have come to this college. There can be no question that Manhattanville is committed to the belief that a good society is a radically just society, a society that is responsive to the needs of all its students."

On June 14, 1968, Otto E. Dohrenwend, who had received an honorary degree from Manhattanville in 1966, submitted his resignation as a member of the board of trustees, citing as reasons his "shock and dismay by the recent trends in educational philosophy" and "the brainwashing of educators by the undefined slogan 'Academic Freedom.'. . . . The spectacle of Manhattanville nuns, faculty and students taking part in demonstrations considered subversive and Red inspired by qualified authorities, was something to make strong men weep." He went on to list a number of other complaints against the college, including "a preponderance of left-wing speakers and lecturers, an increased number of Catholic students failing to attend Mass, a deterioration of modesty and manners, and finally, the authorization of a chapter of the Students for a Democratic Society on Manhattanville's campus."

Elizabeth McCormack later characterized Dohrenwend as "a right-wing nut," but there were many, both in and out of the college, that accused her of being a left-wing extremist. They did not understand her motives for wanting to disassociate the college from the religious order that had founded it and had contributed so significantly to its character. To many it appeared that in no time at all, Manhattanville had gone from a highly respected Catholic women's college to a secular one of lesser distinction that had compromised its fundamental integrity in an effort to appeal to the broadest possible range of applicants. Others were outraged by the manner in which the changes were implemented. "She [Sister McCormack] just got enough people on the board of trustees who agreed with her thinking," one disgruntled alumna said, "and proceeded to do exactly what she wanted. It was just another example of the nuns running amuck, joining in the confusion and questioning that was so visibly and vocally being demonstrated by large segments of the American academic community."

Instead of providing leadership for the values they had formerly espoused — discipline, erudition, and order — it appeared that the college, like the Society as a whole, had reoriented its goals to conform to outside pressures, had turned away from old traditions and principles that had worked so well in the past to embrace an untested reformation philosophy that was popular but had not been tested out. The lack of identity and loss of leadership caused the Society, through the individuals who ran its institutions, to summarily dismiss intrinsic aspects of the spirit and the identifiable trademarks that once underscored its existence. The lines of communication between the nuns and their supporters and their "old children" had broken down. Many within the Society, like some of the alumnae, did not themselves clearly understand what was happening at Manhattanville and why. In the minds of those who opposed her, Sister McCormack had led a crusade that resulted in chaos when she should have been closing the castle gates against the onslaught of progress, change, and the dissolution of the Catholic way. "Perhaps," one former student noted, "she should have just let the college die if it couldn't survive the way it was."

Elizabeth McCormack says, "A very good example of what happened at Manhattanville was Sister Judy Garson, who was a graduate of the college and was a brilliant woman and scholar. At my urging she began study for a Ph.D. at Columbia University. My agenda was that she would go on the faculty at Manhattanville and eventually replace me as president. She began her Ph.D. program and was doing extremely well, but then she decided, before writing her dissertation, that she would take a year off. During that time she came to the decision that academia was not a ministry to which she was called and so she stopped her studies and went elsewhere. What happened during those years of change was that we had nobody coming into the pipeline and the people who had been extremely good religious faculty members were retiring. I saw this coming in 1966 and I did two things. One, I began recruiting faculty from the outside; and two, I began talking about Manhattanville as a nonsectarian institution. This admittedly angered many people, but it was the only sensible thing to do. The traditional pool of students was drying up, and the traditional pool of faculty [the nuns] was evaporating even more rapidly."

The dilemma of Manhattanville was one that many parochial institutions grappled with in the post–Vatican II era, which was marked in many cases by a lack of enthusiasm from individual religious to affiliate with private schools and colleges or to continue serving in their previous assignments. No longer required to submit blindly to their superiors, they were unwilling to limit themselves to the narrow precepts their vocations once prescribed. The nuns of the Society of the Sacred Heart, like those in other organizations, were swept up in a search for personal fulfillment: new jobs, new experiences, new identities, and new answers to the call. As the nuns gave up roles as administrators and instructors at Manhattanville and elsewhere, roles that had defined the educational thrust of the Society since 1800, and as they attempted to incorporate any number of ministerial pursuits under the expanding umbrella of education, it was impossible to retain the solidarity of purpose that had once made the Society so perspicacious and effective. The Church, through Vatican II, made it possible for its religious to stray from the narrow and lonely road to perfection onto the more populous highways of experimentation, discovery, and, some would say, temptation. For many it was a green light to depart from the conventional, to prove in no uncertain terms that nuns were human and that they could make mistakes. Many perceived the changes at Manhattanville as grave and unforgivable mistakes. For although Manhattanville was no longer the college Phyllis Theroux described as "devoid of Protestants or Jews," it was also no longer the place where the next generation of students would encounter the dozens of high-minded, high-spirited, habited women who had previously given it form and definition. In 1970, in a final act to disassociate themselves from the college they had founded but no longer had the personnel to run, the religious of the Society of the Sacred Heart asked to be released from their agreement with the board of trustees to staff the college. In return for that release, they deeded ownership of the land they still owned for no compensation. After 1970, until June 1987, when the last teaching nun retired, Manhattanville continued to have a small number of Sacred Heart nuns on its faculty who were there in a paid capacity and at their own choice. But never again would the campus in Purchase be a sanctuary where lives were changed through the powerful image, influence, and wisdom of the women in black, who created the cerebral environment that established it as the finest Catholic women's college in America.

In 1974 Elizabeth McCormack resigned as president of Manhattanville College and later that year from the Society of the Sacred Heart. In her letter notifying the college community of her separation, after thirty years, from the Society, she said, "The world in which we live is dynamic. It is inevitable that both institutions and individuals evolve as they are moved by the forces of life. The commitment I made in 1944 can no longer be fulfilled by me within the Society." Now married, she is an associate of the Rockefeller Brothers Foundation in New York City.

Manhattanville College continues today as an independent liberal arts college with nine hundred undergraduate men and women from diverse religious and ethnic backgrounds. The statue of the Sacred Heart remains on the campus as one of the few visible symbols of Manhattanville's past. Although it was long perceived by a majority of disappointed alumnae that the nuns gave Manhattanville away, in fact it was never theirs to give. The failed communication between the college administration and its constituency, combined with the inevitable hostility that was part of the separation process, made the transition period a painful and trying one for all concerned, as it had every time a Sacred Heart school or college was abandoned by its founders. In the end there was no question that to survive, Manhattanville had to change. That its survival was not solely dependent on the presence of the religious of the Sacred Heart was for many a bitter pill.

The exit of the nuns from the campus in Purchase was a sad occurrence, and in truth Manhattanville, as so many had known and loved it, went with them. For although the physical setting is much the same today, former Sacred Heart students who revisit the campus find it shabby and unkempt compared with its manicured appearance when the nuns were in charge. One alumna says, "It's like going back to see an old house you once lived in and finding that the new occupants have let things deteriorate. Perhaps it was never as beautiful or as grand as you remember, but one thing is certain, the spirit of the place went when they moved out."

Whatever the sentiments, and there are many connected with the fate of Manhattanville, one compelling question remains. If the Society of the Sacred Heart was no longer able to run sizable educational institutions after Vatican II, would there, could there, ever again be a place like Manhattanville where more than a few religious gathered in His name to do the work for which the Society was founded? And would anything they would ever do as individuals be as powerful, as influential, as memorable, or as effective as their accomplishments in the past?

The House on Ninety-first Street

11

◑WHILE SACRED HEART SCHOOLS like Noroton, Grosse Pointe, Eden Hall, and Manhattanville succumbed to the economic and social pressures of changing times, others, like the Academy of the Sacred Heart in Grand Coteau, Louisiana, survived the years of transition. Grand Coteau is still a vital part of the Society's network of schools, and although there are still complaints from alumnae that the surviving nineteen schools bear little resemblance to their former selves in terms of tradition, religious emphasis, and enforced discipline, academically they are better because their scope is broader and their student bodies more diverse. They no longer share a universal Plan of Studies, but there remains a strong connection to the original principles and values on which each was founded: the education of the whole person, respect for intellectual values, and social awareness.

Sister Claire Kondolf, the former headmistress of Grand Coteau, one of the three Sacred Heart schools that still have boarders, provides a bridge between the old and new methods of Sacred Heart education and training. She had submitted her resignation shortly before I interviewed her there because she thought it was time to give a younger nun the responsibility she had carried for the previous seven years. Relaxed, philosophical, and with a broad range of interests, she remains a devoted religious of the Sacred Heart who has consistently given her talents to the education and personal development of youth. An accomplished equestrian, she was gifted with an Arabian stallion by a school parent during her first year at Coteau but admits that the horse gave her more trouble than the children in her care. "I eventually had to give him up," she said regretfully, "because I was spending more time on the ground than in the saddle."

Her philosophy of education remains closely connected to that of St. Madeleine Sophie, and she feels strongly that despite the changes the Society has undergone during the last twenty years the essentials have remained.

"I don't think the basic philosophy has changed at all," she said as we talked in her large, sparsely furnished office. "What I want for these students is the same thing the foundress wanted — to prepare them to live in their world — but their world is not the world of 1800, theirs is the world of 2000. It is much different, more complicated, because the possibilities for women today are limitless, and the future is so close. That is what we must ready them for, those possibilities, those challenges that await them. We don't want them to hang on to the 1980s, we want them to be equipped to live in the future, and we spend a lot of time trying to understand what the future is going to be.

" 'For the sake of a single child' means exactly what it meant when St. Madeleine Sophie said it," she explained. "It is not the soul or the body; it is the whole person. It is a nice turn of phrase and it is still very true — that is what we are all about. When I hear the words 'the Society of the Sacred Heart,' I do not think anything different from what I thought twenty-five years ago, because in essence it's the same. What has changed along the way are the accidentals, changes that were made and developed to meet the ongoing society that this single child lives in today. It would be absurd to educate a child today to live in French aristocratic society. If you don't change with the times, you die. There is no such thing as standing still, although I think many of our alumnae thought that is what we would do. Great attachments were formed to the manner in which things were done. I realize there is bitterness and anger, but it makes *me* angry to hear people imply that we have gone to hell in a handbasket. To me it means those people never really grew up. They want things to be the same, and they can't be. I don't think any of us in the Society felt guilty for the changes in any way. I don't like hurting people's feelings, but that's just the way it is. Those who hold on to bitterness are usually those who cannot accept change on any level in their lives. . . . I want these students to share in the tradition of Sacred Heart education, which is alive and as well as it ever was, but I don't want them to be bogged down with ties to something rigid and inflexible."

In a small Cajun restaurant down the road from the school, we continued our conversation on a rainy November night. Sister Kondolf introduced me to crawfish and continued her reflections on the changes within the Society of the Sacred Heart, to which she has given more than thirty years of her life: "There are many more options for people to choose from now that we are no longer cloistered. I am not saying we are completely free to choose, because Nance O'Neil, the provincial, has a great deal of influence, but now we have a choice of going where we think we can give the greatest service. For instance, if I have two options and one of them is to be headmistress of an academy and one is to work in a social service agency, my training, my background, and my desire would undoubtedly be to be associated with the school. I think any individual might choose one over the other, not because she thought one was better but because not everyone would think she could deal as effectively in the classroom as she might somewhere else. Today there is more appreciation of individual abilities of the nuns and I think the government of the Society has been very careful in trying to match the right people with the right jobs. In the past the theory was that if you were a good religious you could do anything, fit in anywhere, and you went where you were sent. Now it is different, and from my own perspective I can't help but feel it is a much better approach.

"What you got from Eden Hall and what students get now from the nuns are very different. There are fewer religious associated with the academies, of that there is no question, but again I say it is not a choice of disassociation or embarrassment because of the so-called elitism, although I think it was perceived that way by some people. After the cloister was abolished we were free to say, 'I am no good in the classroom. Even though I have a master's degree in English, I would be more effective in an administrative post or working with the elderly,' or whatever.

"In your day religious life was an image of something mysterious and I suppose a bit glamorous in the sense that the nuns were set apart in a very significant way. Today the kids know us as people, as people who share their lives, and I think the lay people have helped us a great deal with that."

Then she smiled and turned the conversation.

"What about you? I am curious to know why you didn't enter the Society, for it is obvious that you loved it."

"I never seriously thought about it as a possibility because even when I was at Eden Hall I was struggling with my faith in God."

"Why, that is no impediment. Many nuns struggle with that," she said, to my surprise. "Do you believe there is a state called Alaska?"

"Of course," I replied.

"I assume you've never been there."

"No."

"But you believe it exists."

"Yes, but if I want to know for sure I can go there."

She chuckled. "Well, maybe you are right, you were probably not cut out to be a nun. Too bad."

"Who is suited for religious life today, and why are there so few vocations?" I asked between bites of crawfish. "Do you view a vocation today as something temporary?"

"I hope not," she answered. "I think religious life today is different and harder than it used to be, but that is a complicated question and has again to do with the world we live in. There are so many options for women today who want to live religious lives, options that simply weren't available in the past. The people we are getting now are for the most part older women who have been in the professional work world for five or ten years or more. Obviously it depends on the person. For some it was harder to live without the restrictions of the past and for others it was easier. What did the world expect of the Society as it was undergoing changes? That's still mixed, the jury's still out. Expectations do complicate things, for when people's expectations are not met, they become very upset. What were yours?" she asked.

"That it would stay basically the same," I admitted. By "it" I meant the Society and the schools it ran. "One of the reasons for that expectation was that our lives in those schools were predicated on the old traditions and the long connection with the past that those traditions represented. The lives of the nuns were great examples, great enforcers of those traditions, now called 'accidentals,' that imparted something of value. I know it sounds unrealistic and sentimental to say so, but it seemed a reasonable expectation to assume it would continue the way we had known it, the way our mothers and grandmothers had known it. Of course one expects the rules to change, plans of study to be updated, and some traditions to die off, but did I expect Mother Tobin to materialize in my living room wearing secular clothes and asking for a glass of Jim Beam, or Mother Daley to leap over the wall? Never."

"No," Sister Kondolf agreed, "and it would have been quite extraordinary if you had. Nevertheless, the expectation that things would not change was unrealistic. Your life hasn't stayed the same for twenty-five years and neither has ours."

The following morning at the school I asked some of the seniors how they felt about their lives as students of the Sacred Heart. "It's like a family," one of them said. "This is my sixth year and it's hard to describe the feelings I have. I guess the best way to say it is to say it is love. I have met girls from other Sacred Heart schools and it was as if we already knew each other because of the things we share. We had the same way of doing things, the same faith, and the same love. It feels very good to have that connection."

Her friend added, "Several members of my family went here to school and they have the same feeling of specialness that I do. The school develops a certain spiritual aspect of your life and gives you a basic way of living. I am glad I go here. I am proud to say this is my school."

They agreed that their Sacred Heart school had taught them things they probably would not have learned at another school, "things beyond academics."

"Social awareness is something very powerful here. Through working with people who are sick or poor or needy we have learned a lot about the world outside of school. Some people think we are too rural here," one student commented, "that we are just southern belles, but we are not fragile, and we are not going to break. We know about the bad things as well as the good, we know about real life, and if for some reason we don't succeed in life, we will know what it is like to be on the other side because we have spent time with people who have really had it rough."

The social justice program is an important part of life at Grand Coteau. As part of the program, the older girls work weekly with organizations for abused children or senior citizens, or they work in soup kitchens.

"It doesn't just stop with the work we do here," one of them was quick to point out. "We know what is happening in other places, like El Salvador and South Africa. We don't go there, of course, but we know what is happening to those people."

As for the nuns and lay teachers, the students said they saw a difference between them: "I would most likely seek out a nun to confide in because I trust them and I know they will give me their honest opinion. If you do something wrong they will really let you know it. The nuns teach us a lot because they have such open minds. I admire the way they live and appreciate what they do for us, but then I admire a lot of the lay teachers too."

They speak of the traditions carried on from the "old days": Ribbons no longer symbolize the student government but are awarded to girls who are chosen by their peers and ratified by the faculty as role models. *Congés*, field days, *goûter*, and feast wishes are still part of the vocabulary at Grand Coteau, as is *Mater Admirabilis*, the Virgin in the pink dress whose picture still hangs in most Sacred Heart schools.

In celebrating Mater's feast, the students have pink *goûter*: doughnuts and cakes with pink icing. In May they still crown a statue of the Blessed Mother in the garden, and even though events such as these are not as integral to school life as they once were, the spirit of the past they represent remains intact.

Asked if they ever think of becoming nuns, the students laughed. The senior class consensus seemed to be reflected in one girl's answer: "I don't think I could see myself as a nun, not unless a really loud voice came out of the sky."

Students at the Convent of the Sacred Heart on Ninety-first Street in New York City reflected the same enthusiasm for their school as their counterparts in Louisiana.

"When I get up in the morning I feel as if I am going from one home to another," one girl said. "I have talked to friends who go to other schools, private and public, and they can't imagine having conversations with teachers outside the classroom. In order to be a real part of the student body you have to participate, you want to participate in every activity. You have to think Sacred Heart, you've got to be Sacred Heart, and that is what makes the school life so special. This is definitely not the kind of school you go to from nine to five."

"We host a lot of alumnae luncheons," another student noted, "and people are always telling us how being at the Sacred Heart was the best and how many gifts they took away from their schools. They are always hugging each other and laughing and we just think, 'Wow, they feel the same way we do.' "

Asked about the difference between the nuns and the lay teachers, one tenth grader remembered her experience at a school run by another religious order. "I don't know if it was because they wore habits, but it was like they were the nuns and we were the students. Here it is like they are our friends. We get to know them and love them as people. The nuns at Ninety-first Street are always there for you. They are willing to give up their time to help on special projects or just to talk after class. They are willing to do anything they can to help you."

Although lay teachers far outnumber nuns in the nineteen Sacred Heart schools in the United States today, and although the majority of nuns no longer wear habits or live in the school buildings (or sometimes even on the school property), there is an unmistakable bond of affection between the students and the religious. There is also still an admiration for religious life, which, while not as mysterious or intriguing as it once was, remains impressive and a bit curious to the young who encounter it.

Like most of the nineteen schools in the Sacred Heart network, the school on Ninety-first Street in New York City has a long and peripatetic history.

It was at 533 Madison Avenue, on September 21, 1881, that the Society opened what is today the oldest independent school for girls in New York City. The location changed many times before the final move in 1930 to the mansion of Otto Kahn on the corner of Fifth Avenue and Ninety-first Street. But the reputation of "the Ladies," as the nuns were dubbed by local newspapers, who traveled from distant shores to found that school was by that time legendary.

The Burden mansion at 7 East Ninety-first Street, known as Duchesne Residence School, was one of two ornate turn-of-the-century town houses owned and operated by the Society of the Sacred Heart in Manhattan. Since Duchesne closed in 1966, that space is now used primarily by the kindergarten and segments of the lower school. The second town house, at number 1, still houses the New York day school (grades one through twelve), the Convent of the Sacred Heart, known then and now as Ninety-first Street.

The only "finishing school" on the roster of the Society's American institutions, Duchesne was a refuge for girls whose academic records made college an impossibility and entrance into the "real world" unrealistic. I was one of a select group in Eden Hall's graduating class who fell into this category. So, while my classmates were receiving accolades in the refectory as letters of college acceptances were read aloud by Mother Tobin, I sat in a solitary slump, somewhere between embarrassment and arrogance, anticipating the time when my letter would come, as it eventually did, announcing my admission to Duchesne.

Run by a buxom, overbearing nun from Boston, Mother Clare Krim, Duchesne was an overtly pretentious building with a rococo interior. It was chock-full of underachievers who for the most part had attended Sacred Heart boarding schools and were thus familiar with the peculiarities of Sacred Heart life and lore. One of the few exceptions was Dixie Burden, who had graduated from Foxcroft School in Middleburg, Virginia, and whose father's family had built the house now named in honor of Philippine Duchesne. Dixie was a small, shy, dark-haired girl with horn-rimmed glasses who had never been to a Catholic school. Her mother, like mine, was not a Catholic but, as a concession to her father who was, had agreed to Dixie's enrollment at Duchesne. We met and became friends through our mutual interests, which included writing and eating. Twice a week we rode the downtown bus to Hunter College and later the subway to the New School for Social Research to take courses in creative writing. We were both greenhorns in the city and often lost our way to and from our destinations. We had friends in common and had shared a similar mixed-religious background. The only real difference between us was that Dixie loved Duchesne and I hated it. Because she had never experienced life at the Sacred Heart, she was attracted by the "family spirit" and by the personal interest Mother Krim took in her welfare, much in the way I had been during my first weeks at Eden Hall. In contrast to her years at Foxcroft, where she felt alienated and unappreciated, the smallness of Duchesne's student population, which was less than fifty girls (forty of whom boarded), the availability of outside courses for those interested in pursuing something other than the social amenities, and the religious aspect of daily life, which included Mass every morning, made Duchesne a special place for Dixie. She was not a boarding student, but she participated enthusiastically in every aspect of the daily routine, arriving early and staying late.

For me it was just the opposite. After three years of repression at Eden Hall, I looked forward to a time when my life would no longer be confined by countless rules and restrained by surveillance. I was ready to assume the independence I had long sought, and I presumed this would come when I entered college. But Duchesne was not a college, and the hope I harbored for privacy and self-reliance was washed away by another list of regulations regarding appropriate behavior and by the domineering intransigence of Mother Krim, whose presence and power enforced the rules to the letter.

This is not to say that life at Duchesne was as rigid or routinely prescribed as it had been at Eden Hall, but for me it left a lot to be desired. We were permitted certain privileges, such as having radios in our rooms, a phone booth in the hall that we were free to use, weekend permissions to leave the premises for lunch and shopping and, with special approval from Mother Krim, to be out from seven to eleven on Saturday nights. These small concessions to maturity were welcome, but they were marred by the constant obligations that attended our daily lives.

"There is no doubt in my mind," Mother Krim observed during my first conference with her in the fall of 1960, "that you are a nonconformist with a hail-fellow-well-met personality. I cannot help but feel that you were spoiled by Mother Tobin at Eden Hall and allowed certain liberties because of your rather unorthodox background, but things will not go well for you here if you insist on exhibiting this penchant for individualism." Then she proceeded to speak about the virtues of the family life as she perceived them and how the atmosphere of Duchesne was determined by the effort each girl made to contribute to that family. She ended by pointing out, "This is my school, I make the rules, and I make no concessions."

From that time forth we were at war. For I was as determined to retain my own independent persona as Mother Krim was to suppress it. In the beginning our differences existed more in theory than in practice. Then Christmas came.

During the weeks leading up to Christmas vacation, each student at Duchesne was requested to prepare a handmade gift for a needy child. These were to be displayed and inspected by the Reverend Mother from Ninety-first Street at a ceremony in her honor the night before we left for home. My skills in the sewing and knitting department were limited at best, partly owing to my "unorthodox background" but more to an intrinsic aversion to needles of any sort. Since the choice of what to make was implied but not specified, I decided to contribute a model airplane, which I painstakingly glued, painted, and decaled, theorizing that the recipient would be better off with a well-made toy than an incompetently made article of clothing. Mother Krim, when she got wind of what was in the offing, sent word through her assistant, Mother Doyle, that airplanes were not appropriate for the occasion, but I persisted. Finally, on the day of the display, Mother Doyle brought word that because she wanted every student to be represented by an individual gift, Mother Krim would permit my jet fighter to stand on Reverend Mother's table among the traditional crocheted hats and knitted scarves and gloves.

On the night she was brought around to view the Christmas presents, Reverend Mother inspected my model airplane first, pronouncing it "a most unusual and touching contribution." It was a bitter pill for Mother Krim to swallow and one of the few victories she allowed me. From then on, our battles were more overt and prolonged.

Because the resident population of Duchesne was small and manageable, Mothers Krim and Doyle were the only religious assigned to oversee it. Other religious taught in the day school and lived in the day school building, Ninety-first Street, where the cloister was located and where all the nuns, including Mothers Krim and Doyle, ate and slept. As Mother Krim's girl Friday, Mother Doyle was reserved and devoted, carrying out Mother Krim's countless directives with conciliatory conscientiousness. She spoke in a soft, birdlike voice. (Years later I heard that voice on a New York bus, but seeing no familiar habit I dismissed it as an aberration until I looked out the window and spotted a tall, gray-haired woman in a pants suit, with a face I knew well, moving with a group of young black girls toward a movie house. It was Mother Doyle.) She was the one who inspected our rooms for neatness, kept track of our whereabouts, and maintained general order in the house. Often she looked pale and exhausted and occasionally downcast after a particularly trying mission had been assigned her by Mother Krim, but she never once uttered a word of complaint; but then the word "complaint" was not in the nuns' dictionary. I suppose, like her fellow sisters who walked the precarious road to perfection, she offered it up.

When I returned from Christmas vacation my illusions of an independent life in New York City had been sufficiently quashed not only by my inability to get along with Mother Krim but by the realization that life at Duchesne more and more resembled life at any Sacred Heart boarding school. I woke every morning feeling as if I were laced into a straitjacket. It was only at night, after the last light in the house had been turned off and rooms were quiet, or at least as quiet as rooms overlooking Ninety-first Street can be, that I was seized by a sense of freedom and a spirit of adventure. By this time I had aligned myself with three other malcontents. One was my roommate, a tiny, lively mouse of a girl; the other two lived in the room next to ours.

After lights out, which was always at ten o'clock on weekdays, Mothers Krim and Doyle retired to the cloister, leaving a monitor on each dormitory floor and the rest of the cavernous five-story building unguarded. At Eden Hall there had never been a possibility of prowling the house at night, for there were nuns posted everywhere. They slept in dormitories, in closets — it was even rumored that one slept dressed and standing up, at the ready to attend to any nighttime emergency. But the relative lack of nocturnal surveillance was one of Duchesne's few redeeming features, presenting an irresistible opportunity for exploration, an occupation to which my friends and I were naturally drawn. So began our midnight search-and-destroy brigades.

When the house was asleep, we crept in silence, flashlights in hand, down dark corridors in search of food, mystery, and adventure. Before long we discovered where the key to the student kitchen hung and had several duplicates made. This enabled us to dip generously into the double-doored silver refrigerator and indulge our appetites. We would sit on a broad windowsill in the dining room stuffing our faces by moonlight, whispering, laughing, acting more like children than children, and feeling invincible.

As the days at Duchesne dragged by, classes continued uneventfully, the Beatles took control of the airwaves, the Cuban invasion was pronounced a fiasco, and several tea dances were held with skinny, acned boys imported from Fordham University. My friends and I began adding extra pounds to already generous figures as a result of our midnight kitchen excursions, and Mother Krim, who proudly wore a Nixon button on election night, extolled the virtues of conservatism in all things, pointing to the evil and wrong-thinking in liberal literature, politics, and social mores.

I tried to avoid her, for I knew that she had all but made up her mind that I was not finishing-school material, but absolute avoidance was almost impossible in the goldfish bowl we lived in. My worst suspicions were confirmed when I was summoned to her office for the obligatory midyear conference, when she told me that as a Duchesne resident I was "going downhill like a roller coaster." She inquired what plans I had for my future, indicating that I was not likely to be "invited" back to Duchesne for a second year.

In reassessing my time at Duchesne, I can now identify the problem between Mother Krim and me as a conflict more of conviction than of personality. For certainly we had many personality traits in common. I was as stubborn as she was and just as determined to seek my own destiny. The difference in age and experience accounted for part of my contentious nature, which was defined by a youthful arrogance that I have no doubt was frustrating to encounter, but clearly it was an unfortunate pairing for us both. I was convinced that the numerous rules at Duchesne were too strict, too narrow, and too puerile even for a finishing school masquerading as a junior college. I felt I was long overdue for an encounter with the real world, and I am not sure anyone, nun or otherwise, could have converted me. I had been bent, humbled, disciplined, and instructed during my years at Eden Hall and at the other two boarding schools I had attended, but that was behind me and I was determined to keep it there. Mother Krim, like so many of her sisters in religious life at that time, had been living in an ivory tower for years, and the house on Ninety-first Street reflected a past life and time that had ceased to be relevant.

During my year at Duchesne I wrote long letters to Mother Daley at Eden Hall, describing my run-ins with Mother Krim, and as always she responded with insight and frankness.

"To be fair," she wrote, "it is not unkind to tell a child what her faults are when she has developed enough self-confidence to accept that knowledge without being depressed and crushed by it. It is with maturity and objectivity that one realizes everyone has these faults and a true knowledge of oneself is gain, not loss, and the Church calls this Christian humility."

There was no doubt I lacked maturity and, it is reasonable to assume, Christian humility as well. Mother Daley cautioned, "You must stop blaming others for what you find lacking in yourself," but at that point I was neither able nor willing to blame my unhappiness on myself when there were so many obvious altars on which to lay it.

So the days passed, as the days of one's youth tend to do, hooked on to one another like a long chain of paper clips with no particular beginning or end. I gave little thought to the future or the fantasies of my classmates, which were wrapped around projections of themselves as good Catholic wives and mothers. I listened with vague fascination to the Catholic woman doctor who instructed us once a week on the subject of marriage, spending half her time speaking of the pleasures of procreation and the other half drawing charts and calendars on the blackboard depicting the rhythm method of birth control. During one of my few amusing visits with Mother Krim, she asked how it was possible to do so poorly in a class as untaxing as Marriage. "The entire class received high marks and you got seventy-five percent."

"Well, Mother," I replied glibly, "I guess if I know seventy-five percent, the other twenty-five will come naturally."

She looked at me across her desk with a mixture of concern and consternation. "We do not grade on nature," she retorted, "but on knowledge. Perhaps you should give more thought to the area between your ears, and less to the one . . ." Her eyes avoided mine as the words stopped and silence hung between us. I wanted to laugh and she probably did too. Instead we sat mute until the moment passed.

When spring came and the weather began to warm, the city sounds outside the Duchesne windows were more pronounced and varied. Many of the classes were winding down, so there was more free time to roam the streets of New York and, at night, the halls and rooms of the convent mansion.

There was no premeditation. Armed with a single flashlight, two boxes of Tootsie Roll Pops culled from the Duchesne kitchen, and a brazen spirit of adventure that had evolved from previous explorations, my coconspirators and I departed from our usual routine one spring night for no particular reason. After sufficiently filling our bellies in the kitchen, we varied our route and detoured into the corridor that connected Duchesne with the convent day school known as Ninety-first Street. Given the proximity of the two Sacred Heart edifices it seemed odd that the contact between the day school and Duchesne, the finishing school, was so limited, but we rarely saw the Ninety-first Street students or nuns, whose numbers were much larger than ours. There were no boarders at Ninety-first Street, and the nuns slept in the cloister, safely tucked away in a part of the house removed from the connecting corridor.

Our flashlight reflected off the cool marble walls as we moved down the corridor in single file like a line of silent mice. The first door we encountered as we stepped across the line of demarcation that divided the two buildings was a heavy iron one with a large brass handle. As first in line I pressed my ear against the door's hard surface; hearing nothing, I turned the handle. The others followed close behind me into the room. Although the room was cloaked in darkness there was no mistaking where we were. Two long, narrow wooden tables formed a perfect T, and straight-backed wooden chairs stood solemnly behind each place, carefully set for breakfast. It was the nuns' refectory, which in all probability had never been viewed by a lay person. Part of the cloister, the nuns' dining room was off limits to everyone save the religious community who ate there. Of all sins that could be committed in a convent, invading the cloister was among the worst. Each of us was acutely aware of the grave situation in which we found ourselves. After the initial shock had worn off, we backed into the hall to consider our options. Inches away from the open door we gazed in wonder into the silent, empty room, with its veil of secrecy and mysterious rituals, and it was then that we decided we could not depart without leaving something behind, something anonymous that would attest to our being there, like a flag left on top of a conquered mountain. The only thing readily available were the two boxes of Tootsie Pops we were carrying. They seemed just the thing. We would deposit a single lollipop in each of the white linen napkins that were rolled and ringed at each place and then retreat. We took great care in the installation, making certain there would be no telltale signs before the next morning's unfurling. When the deed had been accomplished to our satisfaction and every napkin held a hidden treasure, I felt a surge of great relief coupled with a mischievous delight. Half of me wanted to remain and be an unseen spectator when the morning's unfoldings began. The other, more pragmatic side wanted to flee.

Safely back in bed, I remained awake for hours contemplating the nuns' reaction when after years of the predictable, ritualistic refectory routine they should suddenly find it altered. Would they assume it was a heavenly caper? Probably not, I imagined. And although I suspected that the rule of silence and fierce self-control would keep them from laughing, I hoped our prank would, at the very least, produce a few smiles. Of one thing I was certain: Mother Krim would order an immediate investigation, and I didn't fool myself by thinking she would start the questioning with anyone but me.

That night only four people knew about the Tootsie Pop incident; by midafternoon of the following day, more than half of Duchesne knew. It was then only a matter of hours until I received word that Mother Krim wanted to see me in her office.

The Duchesne Tootsie Pop caper of 1961 was one of those events that took on a significance and aura beyond any that could have been foreseen. In reality it was a harmless, childish prank, but it was viewed by Mother Krim as a vendetta against two things she deeply valued, her reputation and her authority.

The face inside the rippled bonnet was pale and serious, the voice husky and controlled, when she asked me to take a chair near her desk.

"It should come as no surprise to you," she began slowly, eyes avoiding mine, hands folded in her ample lap, "that last night at an unknown hour, some body or bodies entered the nuns' refectory in the Ninety-first Street house and performed what I would characterize as a willful act of invasion of privacy."

I could feel a surge of heat rising up my neck and spreading into my face. Moisture began to pepper the palms of my hands. I looked into her face with its coarse features, engraved with lines and creases, for a sign of amusement or compassion and found none. She was white with rage.

"I already have a good idea of who was involved in this little episode," she continued, "but before I make any accusations I would like to hear what you might know about it."

When she stopped speaking I found I was unprepared for the

moment of truth. I felt paralyzed, unable to speak or move, and for an instant, like Little Black Sambo, I thought I might melt. All the cool confidence I had brought to my previous meetings with Mother Krim vanished, leaving me empty and scared. It was not that I ever considered not telling her the truth — in fact, I had looked forward to it — but now, in her presence, all I could think of was expulsion, of calling my parents, of leaving in disgrace. Finally I managed to nod my head and utter one word: "Yes."

"Yes what?" Mother Krim asked.

"Yes, Mother, I know about the incident in the refectory." Her eyes narrowed, and she said, "Thank you," and then went on.

"It seems that trespassing was not the only activity you and your friends have been involved in during this term. In checking over a recent group of examination papers it has come to my attention that three out of four of you managed to obtain extremely high and identical marks. I have already questioned them and they have admitted taking the answers to those examinations from my desk last week. Their parents have been notified and at this very moment they are packing their trunks." She paused to let the facts sink in and then continued.

"I am sure you would say that cheating is a crime far more serious than raiding kitchens and refectories, but I am afraid I don't agree. You see, I believe that those girls with whom you roamed these halls at night were good students and fine residents. I think there is no doubt that you were the instigator in these misdeeds, you were the one who encouraged and urged them on. I blame you for their fall from grace," she said, and then, "I don't quite know where to place the blame for your own." My first reaction was disbelief, my second anger. I had never been aware of the stolen examination answers — my partners in crime had obviously made at least one midnight raid without me — and while I was attempting to sort it all out, Mother Krim kept going.

"As far as I am concerned I would like to have you leave these premises at once, but because your papers indicated that you were not involved in the answer-taking affair, it has been decided that you will remain at Duchesne over the next ten days but will forfeit participation in the final week of closing activities. Is that understood?"

I nodded my head while my insides churned. Mother Krim had

made it clear from the outset that no apology would be sufficient, so I offered none. I was furious that she had allocated all the blame to me, but I was not surprised. Her last words formed a curious question. "What," she asked, "am I going to tell Mother Cavanaugh [dean of students at Manhattanville] when she hears about this?" I watched her rise from her chair and answered her in the only way I knew how. "I guess you will just have to tell her the truth."

That was the last conversation I ever had with Mother Krim, for during my remaining days at Duchesne she assiduously avoided me. As for the other students, I was a hero to some and a heel to others.

The Tootsie Pop caper was to remain a part of my life for many years after I left the house on Ninety-first Street. Mother Krim used it frequently in talks on discipline and obedience as an example of where small misdeeds could lead. I used it often at cocktail parties to entertain my friends. In both cases it seemed to produce the desired reaction and kept my name alive in Sacred Heart lore.

My brief stay at Duchesne was a disappointment. It was, as I would learn later, a situation that is not uncommon when impetuous youth meets intractable age. Now with more than four decades of life behind me and Mother Krim at peace in her final resting place, the whole episode seems only to serve as a reminder of the innocence and simplicity of the time in which it occurred.

On a dreary January afternoon during a lunch break at the Sacred Heart day school on Ninety-first Street, where I was interviewing students and faculty, I met a lively, diminutive nun, Sister Mary Ranney. As we sat around a table eating sandwiches and exchanging Sacred Heart reminiscences, I mentioned my year at Duchesne and the main reason it had not been extended to two — the Tootsie Pops.

Sister Ranney's face lit up. "I know all about it," she said. "I was one of the recipients."

"I don't believe it," I shouted in disbelief, and then, "Tell me everything you remember."

An impish grin enveloped her face.

"At first I thought it was a gift from Reverend Mother," she said with a laugh. "After all, the refectory was cloistered and there was no thought that anyone else could have put the candy in our napkins. We ate in silence in those days, so obviously nothing was said."

"Well, a lot was said to me," I informed her and then reported the conversation with Mother Krim and the scandal that ensued.

"I must say," Sister Ranney recollected, "although invading the cloister was taken very seriously, I never knew that people were expelled for it. I think eventually we did hear that the lollipops had come, shall we say, in a roundabout way, but no, they were not recalled. I think I ate mine." Then she reached out and shook my hand, saying, "I never knew who to thank." We both laughed until tears filled our eyes. Twenty-five years later I had finally gotten the reaction I had initially sought. I had always known it was funny, and now I had proof.

Mothers and Daughters

12

COMMON MEMORY is an enduring bond, and what was common to the Children of the Sacred Heart cannot be boxed, erased by changing times, or eliminated by wrecking balls. An old Sacred Heart joke goes like this: On reaching the pearly gates a new arrival would be asked by St. Peter, "Where did you go to school?" If the answer was "Sacred Heart," he would say, "Go straight to heaven, you have already been through hell." What was hell to some was heaven to others, but in the broad range of reaction to those unforgettable days of white gloves, May processions, blue ribbons, Très Bien cards, and chapel knees, the experience was singularly personal. Often, the most difficult times in our lives are the ones that touch us most deeply and stay with us the longest. They are our war stories, and we speak of them with the pride of survival. "It was like going through the Crusades together," Grace Schrafft says, remembering her days at Eden Hall, "but after it was over you knew you had something of worth under your belt."

When I learned that Grace was coming to Washington on business, I anticipated our reunion with a certain reservation. It had been ten years since we had seen each other and the prospect of renewing the old friendship was filled with the predictable fears and anxieties. But they instantly fell away when she opened the door of her hotel room. We looked at each other and laughed. Grace jumped up and down and shook her hands from her wrists in a gesture I knew well.

"You are still a preppie," she shouted.

"Don't say any more," I pleaded. "It's too depressing. Neither of us has changed; we haven't even grown up."

"But Virg," Grace said sympathetically, "that's only a myth. Nobody ever really grows up, other people just think they do."

Then I hugged her.

In a Georgetown café we shared a bottle of wine and countless stories about our school days at Eden Hall. "Old Eden was a trip all right," Grace said, using her California lingo, and the stories she told made me laugh so hard I cried.

Later at my house Grace suggested we call Mother Carmody. I tried to dissuade her, pointing out that it was almost ten o'clock, but Grace was determined. "You don't have to speak if you are too afraid," she chided. Although they had not been in touch for several years, Grace knew Mother Carmody's whereabouts and within a few minutes had her on the phone. I picked up the extension phone in the kitchen, not sure if I would reveal myself but suddenly overcome with curiosity.

Twenty-two years had passed since I had last heard Mother Carmody's voice, but it was one I was not likely to forget. "How are you, Grace dear?" she asked, and Grace responded by saying, "I am just fine, Mother, and V V is on the phone too."

After we had gotten past the polite preliminaries, after Mother Carmody had told us that we were her favorite class and she would never forget that wonderful production of *Our Town*, it was time to ask questions regarding the whereabouts of some of the other nuns we had known at Eden Hall.

"Mother Tobin is at Stone Ridge in Maryland, and I know she would love to hear from you, V V," Mother Carmody said.

"Yes," Grace injected, "because we all know how much Mother Tobin loved V V, but unfortunately V V didn't prove worthy."

"Now, now, Grace dear," Mother Carmody began with a chortle. "I am sure V V is very grateful for Mother Tobin's support." But before she could get in another word, Grace began asking more questions. Mother Carmody talked easily and openly, responding to each name as it was mentioned. Mother Geraldine Hurley had left the Society and was living in a New York commune. Mother Forden had left and was a paralegal in San Francisco. "Oh good," Grace exclaimed. "If she's just a regular person, I can get her for all the rotten things she did to me."

The phrase "regular person" struck me as a peculiarly accurate one, for as Sacred Heart nuns, the women we had known at school seemed either too perfect or too eccentric to be regular people. In their habits and in their convent confinement they appeared to live on an elevated plane where "regular people" never roosted.

As the conversation stretched out, I began to realize that Mother Carmody was no longer the stiff, pedantic teacher of my past, but a wise, perceptive woman who appeared to have evolved intact from the cloister into the world, unlike so many other nuns we had known. Both Grace and I were vaguely aware of the changes that had taken place in the Society since our graduation in 1960. We knew that Eden Hall had closed in 1969, that the nuns no longer wore habits or were prohibited from leaving the convent property. We had also heard that many had elected to leave the Society of the Sacred Heart. Still, there were things we did not know.

Five years after we left school, Mother Carmody was transferred to Stuart Country Day School, the Sacred Heart school in Princeton, New Jersey. In 1980 she was asked to leave Princeton and move to Kenwood in Albany, the former novitiate, to raise funds for the elderly and infirm religious now residing there.

In 1971 Grace had moved from Gloucester, Massachusetts, to Santa Barbara, California. After two failed marriages she had taken her daughter Katie west to attempt a new beginning.

I migrated from New York City to the nation's capital in 1965 following the election of Senator Robert F. Kennedy, for whom I had campaigned and hoped to work. The variances of our lives had split us like tributaries in a river, but now we found ourselves together again, riding the currents of time that F. Scott Fitzgerald described as "ceaselessly carrying us into the past."

At the end of our conversation with Mother Carmody, all our questions had been asked save one. Unsure if I wanted to know the answer, I asked anyway.

"Where is Mother Daley?"

"Oh dear," came Mother Carmody's soft reply. "I am sorry to say that she left the Society about a year ago." Then after a pause, "We were very sorry to lose her."

"Do you know where she is living?" I inquired, and again Mother Carmody hesitated before answering. "We have heard that she is living in Miami," she said, then hastened to add, "I am truly sorry, dear," as if she had been forced to go too far.

"Some of the changes we have gone through in the last years have been painful ones," she offered, "but I am sure you know that." As Mother Carmody's voice continued, I found my thoughts frozen on Mother Daley, my wise and wonderful mentor, the young nun whose smiling face radiated with the love of God and the sureness of her vocation. For although I had seen her out of the habit and had shared the awkwardness of her reentry process, there was shock and sadness in the knowledge that she no longer was a member of the Society of the Sacred Heart.

During the time we were students at Eden Hall it would have been unthinkable for a nun to leave the Society or for that matter to alter her religious life in any way. Now it appeared that alterations not only were occurring with some regularity but were commonplace. The stage was no longer set with medieval props nor the cast clothed in nineteenth-century robes. I wondered, in the process of change, in setting the scene for a different time and place, what beyond a significant defection in its ranks the Society of the Sacred Heart had lost.

Throughout the first decade of my life away from Eden Hall I had kept in constant touch with Mother Daley. Through letters, phone calls, and visits I detailed my year at Duchesne and later my time as a salesperson at Tiffany's, receptionist at an investment firm, and political campaigner. I confided in her and sought her counsel on a wide variety of subjects, from my continuing doubts about the existence of God to a chance encounter with Peter Fonda.

Her letters, written in real ink on the official Sacred Heart stationery, with the Society's seal in the corner and the initials S.C.J.M. below it (*Sacré Coeur de Jésus et Marie*), were wonderful examples of her wit and wisdom. About Peter Fonda she wrote, "You forgot to mention whether he is Catholic, Christian, or . . . ?" About God: "An interesting piece of information relating to the concept of penance and reparation: hundreds (maybe thousands by now) of truck drivers who go through New York have requested and received hair shirts from Carmel in the Bronx so that their hours of night driving will be hours of prayer and reparation for the sins of the world. (Just thought you would like to know where you can order one.)" No wonder I loved her.

After she was moved from Eden Hall to the new Sacred Heart school in Miami, Florida, in 1964, I saw her in the summers at Manhattanville College, where she came to take courses. We would sit on lawn chairs on the beautiful emerald campus, the sun beating into her eight pounds of black serge, her inquisitive, smiling eyes following my rapidly moving lips as I chronicled my life in the city. We would talk and laugh for uninterrupted hours, until the coolness of late afternoon settled over us.

Each time we parted, I experienced the same sense of regret I felt on my last night at Eden Hall. The beauty of Manhattanville's campus, coupled with the joy of being with Mother Daley, by that time my only remaining connection with the Catholic Church, whose life seemed so perfectly in sync with that aesthetic setting, was always difficult to leave.

She would kiss my cheek and impart the same message: "Be good and happy and holy." Then laughingly she would point out, "Two out of three is not good enough." I'd watch her move across the lawn, black veil blowing behind her, a confidence in her lilting gait that made me hope there was a God who would recognize and reward all the goodness in her.

My relationship with Mother Daley was neither unique nor exclusive. Delphine McCosker Shakley, who graduated from Eden Hall in 1961 and is now marketing director for a tablecloth manufacturer, the mother of three and the stepmother of two, also remembers Mother Daley with vivid affection. "I thought she was a remarkable woman, and I still do. When I arrived at Eden Hall I had two goals, to get around as many rules as I could and to align myself with the people in power. My first three weeks were hell, but gradually I got used to the routine and things began to seem better. I liken it to an internship as a psychiatric aide. For the first time in my life I had a role model or models, and Mother Daley was certainly one of them. She seemed to be more human than most of the nuns and she was a bit of a renegade. One of my favorite stories about her is this one. I was sitting in the front row of her class in Algebra II and she said, 'I can't stand that stupid look on your face one more minute. You are excused permanently. Get your homework assignments from someone else and do your work in the study hall.'

"I said, 'Thank you, you just did me a tremendous favor,' and it turned out just great. I got better grades and learned a lot more because I was required to think on my own. She knew this, and rather than have me disrupt the entire class she solved the problem by forcing me to accept responsibility for my own actions. I really loved her and spent much of my time trying to test her good nature.

Under those bonnets were some really intelligent, creative women who were leading these terribly restrictive lives.

"We were all in the same boat, really. The big difference was that they had chosen it and we hadn't. Although every case was different, it always seemed a terrible waste to me that they were hidden away and their options were so limited."

Many nuns at many Sacred Heart schools and colleges gave individual time and support to those who sought it. Mother Elizabeth Cavanaugh, former dean of students at Manhattanville College, had a long list of admiring young friends during her tenure there. One of them, author Phyllis Theroux, thinks it was due to the squeaky wheel theory.

"I had a personal relationship with Mother Cavanaugh because I needed her," Phyllis recalls. "I was always banging at her door, and I think that was true for a lot of other people as well. Of course, it was easier to get to know a nun in college than it was in high school."

In the main this was true, but in the secondary schools, especially the boarding schools, while a great effort was made to discourage close relationships of any kind, remarkable friendships developed between the nuns and students.

"Maybe it was sharing the adversity that made friendships possible," one Sacred Heart graduate observed. "Maybe it is just impossible for people to remain apart when they live so close together, or maybe it was just an overwhelming need for recognition in a place where we felt such incredible loneliness."

Whatever the reason, there is no doubt that many Children of the Sacred Heart were drawn to the women they called Mother and found consolation in their affectionate caring and a fine example of unselfish dedication in their lives. Many of the friendships formed at school and college endured long afterward. Sacred Heart alumnae were famous for dragging their friends and fiancés to convent parlors for the inspection and approval of a favorite nun, and many named their daughters after them.

Today, Peggy Daley lives in Miami, where she teaches in the Dade County public school system. In 1982, when I was visiting a Sacred Heart classmate in the area, I called her and asked her out to dinner. Only recently released from her religious vows, she was making a new life for herself in the place where she had once been a nun. She had been a member of the Sacred Heart community for twenty-nine years. We struggled to reestablish the ties that had once bound us so tightly and floundered in the awkwardness inherent in that process. As we talked in a Coconut Grove restaurant, she smoked Virginia Slims and asked the waiter for a Dewar's on the rocks.

The last time we had seen each other was the winter of 1971, when she called to say she had been transferred from Miami to Stone Ridge, the Sacred Heart school in Bethesda, Maryland. I was thrilled at the prospect of having her nearby. It was then that she informed me that some dramatic changes had occurred in the Society. She said she was no longer cloistered and had come into the real world, with real hair, real clothes, and a freedom of existence that allowed her to live almost like a real person. She seemed enthusiastic about her new status and eager to see me. So I invited her to my apartment for dinner. This would be the first time we shared a meal and the first time I would see her without a habit. I was to pick her up at the school.

When we met in the front hall at Stone Ridge, she no longer skimmed the corridor with the graceful folds of her habit trailing behind her. There were no rosary beads clinking at her side and no white fluting around her face. She walked self-consciously in multicolored, suede high-heeled shoes. She wore a plaid wool dress and her hair was streaked with gray and swept up in bouffant style. She had gained weight since I had seen her last and she looked older. Everything about her seemed distorted and wrong.

On the drive back to my apartment, because her voice was still the same, I could pretend that Mother Daley was sitting beside me, not the woman in powder and lipstick who had asked me to call her Peggy, but that illusion did not last long.

I was unprepared for the change in her. I felt she was unconvincing as a liberated nun, but then I had known her only in a very limited way. Without the familiar trappings she appeared more human and less divine, and I was disappointed. My high school dream had come true. Mother Daley was now in the world with me, but I didn't like it one bit. I could not see beyond the way she inhaled cigarette smoke or casually asked for a Scotch or talked about her close friendships with priests. Her worldly pursuits and conversation seemed less interesting, far less intriguing and inspiring than they had been when she lived in the cloister. Now the Society was experimenting with many new and freer styles of living and Peggy was participating in them all. She said she was going to paint one wall of her room at Stone Ridge (once a cloistered cell) orange, and she seemed inordinately interested in things material. Also there was a certain lack of charity in her assessment of some of the members of her community, whom she referred to as "busybodies." She told me that many of her friends had left the Society to pursue secular lives. When I asked if she was considering following them, she looked at me incredulously and said, "Never." I wanted to believe her, but I didn't. It was that suspicion, coupled with the terrible guilt I felt in the realization that I was unprepared to pursue a new relationship, that prevented us from getting to know each other, as Peggy put it, "on a more realistic basis."

When Christmas came I invited her back to my apartment for another dinner and gave her a stocking I had filled and a dress from Lord & Taylor that looked appropriate for a nun who attended cocktail parties. After that, although she remained in Washington for four more years, I did not see her again.

Our encounter in Miami eleven years later presented many of the old impediments and some new ones. As we drove to the restaurant in her navy blue Chevrolet, I looked at a face I hardly recognized. Her hair was short, dyed, and cut in a Dutch boy bob. She wore slacks, sandals, and a brightly striped shirt. A gold necklace held a disc with the letter *D* engraved in the middle. I wondered what she had done with her profession cross and assumed it had been left behind with the other symbols of her religious life. We talked about her new life. She commented that she had never been happier. She loved living near the water, did a lot of sailing, and had taken up painting again. She had friends, a job she liked, and, yes, she still believed in God. She was having a good time, although she had little money. The Society had given her six thousand dollars when she left, which had helped her make a new start. She had not seen many people from the old days; in fact, I was probably the first former student to contact her. Clare McGowan, still associated with the Sacred Heart school in Miami that she helped found and that Peggy had worked in, remained a nun, although her sister Jean had left the Society and later married. Clare and Peggy continued to be good friends, although Peggy had not returned to the school to revisit her past.

I wondered if she ever dreamed of herself in the habit or of the days at Eden Hall and if it had really been so easy to separate from a community that had been her family for twenty-nine years. What had happened to her vocation; did it just dry up when the rules changed? Would she have stayed if things had remained the same? There are many questions I wanted to ask, but I asked only one. "When I saw you in Washington you said you would never leave," I said. "Why did you change your mind?"

Peggy looked over at me and replied, "You are not going to lay that trip on me, are you, V V?" And I said, "No, of course not." I felt I had a right to ask the question and to hear an answer, but in truth I understood her reluctance to reply, for I remembered something she had told me at Eden Hall when I had expressed disappointment in someone. "When you expect too much of people," she had said, "you set yourself up to be let down. God is the only one you can always count on." We finished dinner in fragmented conversation straddling the chasm between memory and reality.

The next day I visited Sister Clare McGowan at the pink stucco mansion on Biscayne Bay that is now the Sacred Heart school called Carrollton. She was wearing khaki pants, a white short-sleeved shirt, and aviator glasses. With a large weight gain since her days at Eden Hall, she hardly fit the image of a nun, even a liberated one. She greeted me with a hug and asked how my visit with Peggy had gone. I told her it was awkward and strangely sad. We sat in her office and as we talked she played with a key chain with a plastic picture frame attached. One one side was a color photograph of herself flanked by her parents and on the other side a picture of her sister holding a cat. The thing that caught my attention was that in both instances Clare and Jean McGowan were wearing the old, familiar Sacred Heart habit. "Yes," she said, "if you think it was hard for you meeting Peggy after all that time, just think how difficult it must have been for her. You are the first person she has seen from that time in her life. She knew how you felt about her, how much you loved and admired her. That's a lot of pressure, but you must understand that she has a new life now, just as you do." She talked on about change and how things had been unsettled during the experimental years for those within the Society and those who were attached to it, but now she felt the dust had settled.

"That's all over now," she said, "and I can tell you, no matter how you might view the changes from the outside and how painful it might have been for some of the alumnae, I am forever grateful the changes came when they did. It has given me a chance to go to Boston and spend time with my mother and an opportunity to experience things which otherwise would have been impossible." I looked across from her and nodded my head. "It just feels like someone died, can you understand that?" I asked. "Not just Mother Daley but the whole Sacred Heart system." And she looked down at her desk and impatiently thumped it with her fingers. I told her I was considering writing a book about it.

Her expression tightened, and then she said, "If you say anything rotten about the Society of the Sacred Heart, I'll never forgive you." I knew it was no idle threat.

After our meeting in Miami, Peggy wrote me a letter in which she said, "In seeing you again I was not quite sure what to expect — as the basis of our past relationship is nonexistent and we have both changed in ten years. However, it was a joy to see you and hear you talk about what you do and want to do." I found it difficult to think of our past relationship as "nonexistent," but she was right. She was no longer Mother Daley and I was no longer a child.

Changing Habits

13

WHAT WAS ONCE the Kenwood novitiate for the very newest Sacred Heart members has by necessity been turned into an infirmary and old-age home for the very oldest and is now referred to as Pax Christi. In the recesses of the main building is a modern cafeteria where the residents and staff of the Pax Christi community take their meals. The large room has recently been freshly painted to brighten its dungeonlike walls. A long counter with the traditional slide-along-tray apparatus occupies the back of the room. There are automatic dispensers for lemonade and iced tea and a selection of meats, vegetables, salads, and desserts behind a glass partition. The line forms three times a day and those who participate do so with childlike delight. They come in wheelchairs and on walkers, bent and crippled by age, shuffling, smiling, speaking softly, in some cases to themselves, bobbing their heads in acknowledgment as they pass occupied tables.

These nuns were once the young novices who walked down the chapel aisle in white wedding dresses. Now some are dressed in civilian clothes but wear a symbol of their religious life in the form of a cross around their neck or a pin on their dress. Others are draped in do-it-yourself habits: black, blue, gray, pinstriped. Because there is no longer an official Sacred Heart habit, those who have chosen not to wear secular clothes are forced to create a habit for themselves. Some wear headdresses that slip down and nearly cover their small, smooth, worn faces and carry old shopping bags on their arms. They bring to mind a group of ancient pranksters prepared for a night of trick-or-treating. Others appear strong, energetic, and upright. They walk briskly and bend to help those who look hesitant and unsteady. Some of their names are as familiar to me as my own: Sister Morgan, Sister Farrell, Sister Cronin, Sister Benziger, Sister Guerrieri, and the three Sisters Kent. They smile and wave as if I am a visiting celebrity as I walk with Mother Carmody toward the tall pile of trays. One elderly nun gets up from her table and calls my name. It is Sister Julia Hurley, the librarian from Eden Hall who was infamous for collecting fines for overdue books. "You owe me five cents, dear." She says she recognized my voice the minute she heard it, and I certainly recognize hers.

The nuns at Kenwood sit where they choose at square wooden tables that fill the center of the room, some in groups, some alone. Each says her own grace and crosses herself before beginning to eat her personally selected meal. Although they don't appear to be unhappy, there is something touchingly tragic about them that speaks of displaced, dislocated persons, unplugged from a former identity and too old to form a new one. Which, of course, they are. These are the women who suffered the changes most intensely, whose lives were suddenly disrupted and dislodged by the innovations that followed Vatican II and were implemented by the special chapter of 1967.

"There was no one more shocked than I," Mother Carmody confesses, "when I stood at the back of the community room and heard the news that we would no longer be cloistered or required to wear habits. Of course, it was easier for me to adjust to what was coming than for many of these dear people. They were just too old to begin again. The cloistered life was all they knew, and you just couldn't expect them to go out to a department store, buy a new wardrobe, or start a new life."

Mother Carmody talks openly about her life at Kenwood as she eats lunch. I observe her carefully, amazed at her physical stamina, her wise understanding, and her ability to assimilate. As a teacher under the old regime, she appeared intractable and inflexible, but the years of change, coupled with her devotion to the God in whom she firmly believes, have enabled her to bend and redefine her vocational responsibilities, and she has done so with grace and good humor. She, my old class mistress, now wears a striped shirtwaist dress, glasses with modern frames, and crepe-soled shoes. Her old profession cross hangs around her neck on a chain. Tall and thin with hardly a hint of gray in her straight, bobbed hair, after twenty-five years she still represents authority and the old continuity to me.

She holds herself stiffly erect like a soldier at attention and walks with the same purposeful gait I remember from our days at Eden Hall.

She addresses me as "V V dear"; I call her "Mother." "I love it that you still call me that," she admits. "You do understand why we changed the title from 'Mother' to 'Sister.' It just wasn't practical anymore. Once we went out into the world we found that most other orders referred only to their mother superior as 'Mother.' It was confusing and just another thing we had to explain, another thing that made us appear to be, if you'll excuse the expression, snobs." I tell her I do understand but I don't like it. "Mother" was such an endearing and meaningful title, I say, and she nods her head modestly, then adds, "But after all, it was only a title and the things that that name represented are right here in this very room, and that will never change."

In the spring of 1852, four months after the death of Mother Rose Philippine Duchesne, the bishop of Albany, New York, wrote to Mother Madeleine Sophie in France and in a now familiar pattern requested that the religious of the Sacred Heart make a foundation in his diocese. In 1859 the Joel Rathbone estate, which included fifty-three acres of prime real estate overlooking the Hudson River near Albany, was purchased by the Society for its new school, called Kenwood. Architectural plans were brought from Manhattanville and extensive renovations were begun. In 1865 the novitiate was moved from Manhattanville to Kenwood. The Society's eastern vicariate had been blessed with many vocations during the preceding three years, when more than fifty women took the habit. The first group of novices arrived in September 1866 and from that time until the novitiate moved to Boston in 1969, Kenwood was the place where generations of Sacred Heart nuns were formed. The original school, Academy of the Sacred Heart, grew as both a boarding and a day school, and the nuns erected a second building on the property, which became a free parish school called St. Anne's. For more than sixty years, in keeping with St. Madeleine Sophie's original intent, the Society of the Sacred Heart served the poor in providing educational opportunities for children in the surrounding area to experience the gifted teaching of the Mothers of the Sacred Heart. Eventually the school outgrew its quarters, and St. Anne's moved nearer the parish church. Because the Sacred Heart nuns were cloistered, they could not move with it.

As the years rolled on, Kenwood, because of its dual role as school and novitiate, assumed a special place in Sacred Heart history, becoming the center of the eastern vicariate (which included schools in New York, Philadelphia, Massachusetts, Detroit, and Rhode Island). Its special spirit and character were imprinted on those who walked its wide, polished corridors, studied in its classrooms, prayed in its large Gothic chapel, and were formed in its novitiate by the likes of Mother Gertrude Bodkin, Kenwood's Irish-born Mistress of Novices from 1909 to 1932, who held a doctorate in philosophy and a reputation for giving those under her stern guidance "the courage to be real people." This definition described most Sacred Heart nuns, who despite the severe restrictions placed on their lives emerged from the novitiate as originals. One former Sacred Heart nun reflected that "St. Madeleine Sophie showed her greatest wisdom in incorporating into those most difficult but rewarding years of the novitiate three rules. You could not talk about your family, your health, or the children in the school. This served two purposes: The nuns couldn't say to each other, 'Wait until next year when you get Susie Jones,' but more than that, when we took on the same clothes, the same lifestyle, and could not talk about our past, our families, or our health we were forced to look at one another as human beings. We really were stripped of all pretensions, we had no false security, status, or reputation."

Kenwood was the place where white veils knelt in stalls below those occupied by black veils in the chapel at Mass, where Ann Cooley Buckley, whose twin sister, Kay, became a Sacred Heart nun, and her classmates watched the new postulants walk in the beautiful formal gardens and speculated about what brought them there and how long they would stay. It was the place where a cemetery on the hill, filled with white crosses, marked the end of religious life for many who had begun it only yards away. The list of Kenwood's Mistresses of Novices was filled with prominent names in the Society: Gertrude Bodkin, Agnes Barry, Ursula Benziger, and Margaret Coakley, whom Ann Buckley remembers as "the most beautiful nun I have ever seen." Mother Coakley, from a large, prominent Catholic family in Cleveland, Ohio, had been a bridesmaid in the wedding of Henry Ford II and Ann McDonnell (herself a Child of the Sacred Heart) before entering the Society. Al Smith's daughter was a day student at Kenwood in the twenties, and Sister Mary C. Wheeler remembers her more for the car she drove to school each day than for being the governor's daughter.

The novices who came to Kenwood to pledge their lives to Christ were the women who would eventually fan out to populate the faculty of Sacred Heart schools and colleges throughout the United States and sometimes abroad. As Reverend Mothers, Mistresses General, surveillants, mistresses of studies, and in many other capacities, they did the work of education both academically and administratively. There were jobs for the young and the old, each with an educative end and each with a special mission of love. If the nuns did not teach, they helped run the school and the religious community, assuming active roles in every part of household management, helping create the distinctive family spirit that was evident to all who visited and even more apparent to those who lived there. The silver was always polished to a high shine, the flowers were always fresh, the corridors sparkled, and the students were impeccable in their uniforms of the day. There was a military crispness and pride in the performance of even the smallest chore. Ceremonies and *congés*, feast wishes, and lily processions, even games of *cache-cache* and field hockey, were executed with a learned precision. Nothing was done to excess. Every aspect of Sacred Heart life was carefully practiced and beautifully orchestrated.

The year 1949 saw the establishment of a graduate division of Manhattanville College of the Sacred Heart at Kenwood, where young religious in the Society came to pursue their master of arts degree. During the sixteen years the program was in place, Sacred Heart nuns came from Japan, South America, Canada, and the Antilles to study at Kenwood. During the 1950s the school took in refugees from Korea, China, Hungary, and Lithuania, who gave Kenwood an authentic international flavor for which schools of the Sacred Heart were famous. When the Sacred Heart school in Cuba was forced to close during the revolution of 1959, Cuban novices came to Kenwood to complete their training. The children in the day and boarding schools played hockey, participated in literary essay contests, studied art and music along with doctrine, English, and mathematics, joined clubs, put on plays, and generally participated in every tradition of the Sacred Heart routine. At the same time, novices were being formed to the traditions of monastic life.

In the early sixties the nuns at Kenwood joined an interfaith group to assist families in locating low-income housing in the Albany area. The school donated two acres of its land to a project that constructed 164 garden units to house low-income families. A day camp for children was established at Kenwood during the summer, and a day care center in the east wing, added in 1966, is an example of Kenwood's current participation in outside community activities.

After Vatican II, when the nuns were able to participate in life beyond the convent walls, to involve themselves in a variety of educative and administrative occupations, individuals in the Kenwood community began to work in hospitals, social service programs, retreat houses, parish schools, and language centers. Some even moved away from the school property to live in smaller communities in the inner city. Another result of the post–Vatican II changes was the opportunity for novices to pursue their studies at secular colleges and universities. As the old structures were loosened, it was possible for young aspirants to choose vocational pursuits previously unavailable, and for the first time in its history Sacred Heart nuns were choosing not to teach.

By 1969, because fewer women were applying to enter the order, the novitiate at Kenwood was transferred to a house in Newton Center, Massachusetts. This created space at Kenwood for the foundation of the Pax Christi Infirmary to provide care and housing for the growing population of aged and infirm religious who were swelling the ranks of the now dwindling Society.

After 103 years as the training ground for young nuns, Kenwood became home to a large retirement community from the New York, Washington, and Chicago provinces. Here the Society created a protective haven for those whose official duties had ended but to whom it owed a continuing debt of gratitude. In the pre–Vatican II days, because each Sacred Heart school and college had a community of older nuns and because there was no mandatory retirement age and no salary requirement, many nuns continued to teach into their seventies while others were available for counseling, hand patting, and other unofficial but valuable occupations. But as many of the secondary schools were forced to close, the Pax Christi community was established at Kenwood to replace the infirmaries in the schools that had been closed, and to bring together in one place those who no longer had a house to grow old in.

When I visited my former teacher Mother Carmody at Kenwood in the fall of 1986, she was deeply involved in a successful fund-raising effort to supplement the support of the sixty religious residents who now occupied the old building in Albany. Her first appeal began with a letter written in 1983 to the alumnae of Manhattanville and Newton colleges. A three-page fold-out pictured twenty-five retired religious of the Sacred Heart with the words "Some dear old friends live here. Do you remember . . . ?" The response to that question had been overwhelming. Letters and money poured in from all over the world, each letter reflecting the sentiment of the writer who said, "Do I remember? How could I ever forget?" This was the first time since the changes had begun, twenty years before, that the nuns had reached out to their former Children and asked for help — asked for anything. Many Sacred Heart alumnae felt bitter about the closing of their schools and colleges. The evolution of Manhattanville from a small Catholic women's college to a coeducational, nonsectarian one, the sale of Newton College to the Jesuits of Boston College, the closing of Eden Hall, Elmhurst, Clifton, Grosse Pointe, Noroton, and so many other beloved institutions, coupled with the liberation of their dear Mothers, gravely affected the alumnae, who felt angry and abandoned. They also felt a sense of outrage that the nuns they had known, loved, and so admired had failed to communicate with them during the years of experimentation and transition. There were no newsletters, no alumnae meetings, no effort at all on the Society's part to explain or to share the process of reevaluation it was undergoing. "We didn't understand it very well ourselves," one of the nuns said later, "so how could we explain it to others?" Communication was limited in many cases to defensive responses from the religious and bewildered resentment on the part of the alumnae, who watched in sorrow, and sometimes horror, as their heroines threw up the skirts of their newly acquired civilian clothes and displayed their feet of clay. It was a traumatic time for all concerned, but especially for those who had shared in the Society's legacy and tradition and witnessed the historical aspects of its identity begin to fade away.

As Mav Deegan McCarthy, an alumna of Noroton, said, "In 1968 when the changes were beginning, I had two babies, and I was bathing them in the sink and offering it up. I was still pretty serious about going to church, still saying my rosary and meditating, living like a true Child of the Sacred Heart. Then I got wind of nuns going out to exercise class and to the movies, and I thought, 'Dear God, there they are in miniskirts and sequined dungarees, leaping over the wall to marry divorced men and have children (which some of them did), and they never even sent me a memo saying you can get rid of your Child of Mary medal and your white-glove attitude because it's all over now, girls.' I felt I had kept rumbling on, living their life, or something very close, and now they weren't living it anymore — and no one told me to stop. For me the Sacred Heart experience was a lot more than four years of boarding school. By the time I got out of Noroton, it had become a way of life."

Mother Carmody's letter to the alumnae did much to repair the rupture between the old Mothers and their devoted daughters, who for many years had felt like stepchildren. Many of the nuns were participating in encounter groups, getting involved with social justice, working in Harlem, in housing projects and many other organizations relating to the poor and the Third World, and they seemed to have no desire or inclination to involve themselves with those who for so long had defined their original vocation, the girls of privilege whom St. Madeleine Sophie wanted to teach so they in turn could make contributions to those less fortunate. There still were nineteen existing Sacred Heart schools, but the religious population in each had dwindled to a precious few. The letters Mother Carmody received in response to her appeal spoke of past memories and universal affection. She reads a sample of them out loud, eyes glistening with appreciation: "My debt to the Sacred Heart can never be repaid." "You dear Mothers taught me to deal with the realities of life." "The very special love given me by the religious of the Sacred Heart remains as the one true constant in my life." And finally, "This contribution most closely touches my heart. My Sacred Heart years prepared me to receive in giving, to think, and to live. These are hefty gifts."

Afterward she hands me an itinerary she has typed up with the names of the nuns I will interview. The first is Sister Ursula McAgon, formerly Reverend Mother McAgon, who was the superior at Noroton when my sister was there in the early 1960s. Now she is head of the Pax Christi community. A small, sprightly woman in her late sixties, she wears a well-tailored skirt and a cable-stitched sweater. The first question I ask is about the abolishment of cloister, and she quotes Janet Stuart, the gifted Mother General from England, who said, "We will never be the first to move, but we will never be the last." "I think," says Sister McAgon, "that cloister was a safeguard in many respects and as an order we were rather slow to move compared with many other American congregations. But when the Church ordered it we had no choice, and it was on that basis that we began to move forward."

But move forward in such a seemingly confused way, I suggest.

"If you are saying that we really didn't plan our changes, from my experience I would agree," she says. "Before Vatican II we certainly had a reputation for an excellent education system and plan of studies. To my way of thinking we haven't found the counterpart of that yet, but I think it is coming." She admits that there was mass confusion in the beginning and that mistakes were made all along during the years of experimentation. "I think we regressed as a congregation and as individuals," she continues. "When the structures were eliminated, we went through an adolescent phase, we behaved like adolescents, and as far as the closing of the schools went, we made a bloody mess of it. Whether we are spreading ourselves too thin now, only time will tell. Maybe we are really being called to a far greater diversity of ministries than we already have."

Sister Margaret Williams, one of the Society's acknowledged intellectuals, studied at Oxford University and, in addition to being an English professor at Manhattanville, wrote many books on the Society's history and founding mothers. Now retired, she continues to offer classes in Old English, to give lectures, and to write books. "I think St. Madeleine Sophie would be with us all the way," she says, referring to the Society's new life, "bringing her usual wisdom, perhaps helping to prevent some of our mistakes. But in principle I think she would have continued moving right along with the times. I think the young people in the Society today find the present in the past, and the old people find the past in the present." About the change of habit she explains, "It says somewhere in our constitutions that the habit shall be simple and removed from singularity. Now I ask you, how can a two-hundred-year-old dress remain removed from singularity? To associate the dress with the times becomes impossible; to associate it with the deeper things is natural, and that is what our nuns did."

Sister Josephine Morgan, a jovial, charming, gifted member of the Kenwood community, typifies the spirit, character, and dedication of the religious of the Sacred Heart. She has been a nun for well over fifty years, forty of them spent teaching music at Manhattanville's Pius X school of music. At Kenwood she is like a wonderful grandmother, smiling, joking, lovingly concerned with everyone and everything around her. She sits on a chair in Sister Agatha Cronin's room in the Kenwood infirmary. Sister Cronin was for many years the treasurer of Manhattanville College, and she and Sister Morgan are good friends of long standing.

Mother Carmody reclines on Sister Cronin's bed while Sister Cronin herself sits in an easy chair with her walker in front of her. Sister Cronin is very feeble but still alert and feisty. The room is small, white, and sterile, the floor is linoleum, the bed is iron, but the afternoon sun warms it, and Sister Morgan's stories fill it with laughter. The nuns call each other by their first names. Sisters Morgan and Cronin are dressed in habits, Sister Cronin in the more traditional black, Sister Morgan in a simple gray pinstriped cotton dress with matching short veil. "I tried getting out of the habit once," Sister Morgan says, "but I didn't like it at all. I just looked awful, like a big fat slob. I like beautiful clothes and I knew if I was going to wear beautiful clothes I had to pay for them, and I couldn't take money from the Society to buy the kind of clothes I wanted, so I just went back to the habit and I have been in it ever since. Besides, I like people to know that I am a nun. A lot of people say they don't want that kind of identification. They say when the driver on the bus sees a habit he puts his hand over the fare box so you don't have to pay, and they say how disgraceful, but I say nonsense. I've accepted that many times. After all, we are poor; why wouldn't we accept it?"

The scene in Sister Cronin's bedroom could not have taken place twenty-five years ago, when the nuns slept in cells in the cloister. Now there is music from stereos and television sounds emanating from some parts of the infirmary, where incapacitated nuns are no longer exiled, forced to spend their last days alone, fingering rosary beads and whispering prayers.

"Tell her about the time you got the phone call from Richard Halliday, Jo," Mother Carmody urges Sister Morgan, who throws back her head and chuckles.

"Can you bear to hear it again?" she asks. "Well, it was on a Tuesday at Manhattanville, and it was just about four o'clock in the afternoon. I got a phone call and a man's voice on the other end asked, 'Is this Mother Morgan?' 'Yes,' I said. 'Do you teach Gregerian music?' he asked. 'Yes, yes,' I said, 'we do teach that.'

" 'Well, my wife is going to be in a Broadway play this fall called *The Sound of Music*, which is based on the life of the Von Trapp family, particularly about Maria. You know Maria?' 'Yes,' I said, 'of course.' 'Well, my wife will be the lead in this play and she will play a nun and Mr. Rodgers is very concerned about the first three and half minutes, when this Gregerian music' — he called it *Gregerian*, when he meant *Gregorian* — anyway, he told me that Mr. Rodgers didn't want to use a tape recording or anything like that, he wanted our choir to sing the real thing so that when the curtain opened there would be sisters in habits singing. 'We need some help with the music and the style of dress,' he said, 'for above all Mr. Rodgers does not want to offend the Catholic Church.' 'Well,' I said — and I finally had to correct him about the Gregorian music — 'I have an idea that your wife played in *South Pacific*.' 'Oh yes,' he said. 'Then you must be Mr. Halliday and your wife must be Mary Martin.' 'That's right,' he said. I told him that we would be very happy to help him out. 'We have rehearsal every day at the music school at eleven o'clock, dead or alive,' I said. 'Why don't you come up here and hear us?' He thought that was wonderful and so they came, Richard Rodgers, his wife, Dorothy, the cast, dressmakers, designers, directors — everybody, even a photographer from *Life* magazine. So we sang for them, starting with the oldest Mass in the book and going on from there. In the middle of it all Richard Rodgers beckoned me over and said, 'Will you be the abbess?' I laughed and then I said, 'You are a scream. No, I am cloistered, I have to stay here all the time.' He said, 'Oh God,' and that was the end of that. But many of them stayed at the college because it was during the summer and we had plenty of room. They wanted to observe us, how we walked, how we knelt, how we stood. At the end we wrote a piece of music for them that they used in the opening scene of the play, and I think from what I heard they did a grand job of it. They were a wonderful group and we became great friends. Later when I was in the hospital with a bum knee Richard Rodgers sent me enough flowers to fill the chapel. He also sent us the first cast recording of the play, and I was just listening to it today. He was a darling man."

So it was the Sacred Heart nuns that gave *The Sound of Music* its authenticity, I observe.

"Well, in that first scene, although I never saw it," Sister Morgan concedes, "I think we really did."

Mother Carmody and Sister Cronin smile their appreciation. "That's just a great, great story, Jo," Mother Carmody says, and then as an aside to me, "You can tell why all the students loved her so much. They just wouldn't leave her alone." And I could.

The following morning before meeting Mother Carmody for Mass, I plan to return to the cafeteria for a cup of coffee. Mother Carmody will be eating breakfast at the house she shares with three other nuns on the school property. "Will you be all right?" she asks with Motherly concern, and I assure her that I can find my way and will not be shy about eating in the cafeteria without her. Several nuns I know are sitting over bowls of cereal and cups of coffee, but an unfamiliar, kind face beckons me over. "And who are you?"she asks softly, and I explain briefly, pointing out that I am a graduate of Eden Hall, which gives me instant acceptance. I sit down beside her and ask how she spends her days at Kenwood. She tells me there are many planned activities, trips to places of interest, classes, concerts, lectures on a variety of subjects, but she confides that the thing she likes best is "a new contraption called a VCR that allows you to see movies on television." I ask if she has any favorites, and with a straight face she replies, "For forty years I didn't see anything at all in the way of movies, so I like them all, especially *The Sound of Music*." She speaks about the trips she has taken to visit her relatives and tells me about her immediate family, her nieces and nephews whom she is now able to see with some regularity, but she is quick to add, lest I misunderstand, "The Society is my real family. We have a good life here."

I meet Mother Carmody in the chapel and watch as the nonambulatory nuns are brought down from the infirmary strapped into wheelchairs, which are placed along the chapel wall next to the stalls the novices used to occupy. Their heads droop, their habits, clean but ill fitting, fall about their small bodies. Bedroom slippers seem to be the uniform footwear, and this touching incongruity confirms the obvious struggle between the old and the new. This is the same chapel where as brides of Christ most of them began their religious life. Now they await the final call that will complete the cycle of their lifelong dedication and take them to the cemetery on the hill to rest beside past generations of the Society's American history. The priest enters and the Mass begins as it does every morning. When communion is passed, those nuns who are eucharistic ministers take the wafers to those who are unable to walk. In some cases it is necessary to physically pry open their mouths.

"Margaret, this is the Body of Christ," and the old nun makes a feeble attempt to lift her head to indicate that she is ready to receive it. Soft murmurs of thanksgiving begin to fill the chapel. Others in attendance, besides the old and older nuns and a few lay people, are three young religious associated with the Doane-Stuart School.

A new approach to education was begun by the Society in 1975 when Kenwood Academy and St. Agnes Episcopal School merged. Inspired by the Church's ecumenical movement and Kenwood's need to enlarge its student body, the Doane-Stuart School became a bridge between Protestantism and Catholicism. It offers coeducational classes in grades kindergarten through twelve as well as a girls' boarding department for grades nine through twelve. The school has a nun headmistress, retains membership in the Sacred Heart network of schools, and has an equally distributed Catholic-Protestant board of governors. The handful of young nuns who teach there live in houses off campus. At Mass one wears work pants and a denim shirt. Her casual attire contrasted with the ancient group in habits seems a perfect example of the differences in lifestyles that now permeate the Society.

I think of the chapel at Eden Hall, which in many ways resembled this one — the white veils, the liturgical music, the spit and polish, the Latin Mass and its rote responses, the regimentation, the respect and love that abounded there. I think of the long, black line, the familiar faces in fluted bonnets, the uplifted hands, the downcast eyes, the graceful, studied walk. That image now lives only in the hearts of those who experienced it.

A New Mission

14

❶FORTY-FIVE MILES north of Palm Beach, Florida, people live like animals, in trailers, cars, shacks, and buildings made of crumbling cement blocks. In many cases they live without electricity or running water, without anything. Families share dark, stinking hovels, sleep on mattresses crawling with rats and roaches, and pay rent to do so. Babies are carried in sheets wrapped around their mothers' bodies, clinging to the only constant in their lives. Faces are scorched by sun, creased from exposure, and seared with expressions of pain and oppression that the people have come to expect and accept as part of their uncharted, migratory lives.

This place, this pocket of poverty called Indiantown, is home to a group of migrant workers who spend their days harvesting crops for leading American corporations and spend their lives at the deep end of the socioeconomic pool, eking out subhuman existences. This is the Harvest of Shame that Edward R. Murrow put on film over twenty years ago to shock a nation. It still goes on.

This is where, for eight years of her life as a religious of the Sacred Heart, Sister Joan Gannon worked and lived. "I wanted to work with the poor," Sister Gannon said as she sat on the edge of one of the twin beds in my room at the Seminole Inn, Indiantown's only motel. Dressed in denim skirt, cotton shirt, and sandals, Joan Gannon is pretty, petite, and feminine, without a trace of vanity or self-consciousness. The graying of her short, cropped hair is the only evidence of her recent fiftieth birthday. Described by Patricia Avery, a Manhattanville classmate, as a real beauty pursued by a handsome West Point cadet, she left college and romance behind to enter the convent the year before her class graduated. "The only report we heard," says Patricia, "was that she was so happy in the novitiate that she was afraid she wasn't suffering enough."

At eight o'clock in the morning Sister Gannon sits across from me at breakfast, which is interrupted several times by people coming by to extend greetings and offer condolences on the recent death of her mother. They reach out to touch her, calling her Sister Joan, speaking warmly, smiling appreciatively at her easy, informal manner. It is evident that they hold her in high esteem and that she easily fits into the place she has created in their lives. Her voice is low, her words thoughtful, and her blue eyes intense as she describes her work. "We did not come here to be Lady Bountiful. We came here to live the Gospel, to share our lives with the poor, to help them help themselves. I knew very little Spanish when I arrived," she says after I comment on her fluency, "but I knew it was essential and the people were very helpful and patient with me. Many Sacred Heart nuns were unprepared for the work they undertook when the changes first occurred in the early seventies. It is one thing to do good work, but quite another to know how to make it productive. There was a nun from another order here before we came, and she knew the people and how to respond to them. I think in many instances we acted too quickly in terms of making ourselves known. It takes time to get to know people and build up trust."

After breakfast we pile into her brown Datsun, with a statue of Donald Duck on the dashboard and eighty thousand miles on the odometer. A four-lane highway cuts Indiantown in half. The post office, laundry, and the Holy Cross Service Center, which Sister Gannon runs, are all located in a small commercial complex several blocks south of the motel. The service center, known as El Centro, consists of one room filled with five desks, a small computer, three telephones, several typewriters, and a copying machine. It is here that people come, asking for Sister Joan, seeking her assistance in solving a variety of problems.

Every Tuesday morning there is a prayer meeting at the center, attended by local shopkeepers and any others who care to attend. The morning of my visit the number of participants is small: two Mexican women, one with a baby in her arms, and a man with jagged teeth who sits silently on a folding chair. Sister Gannon reads a passage from the Bible and then comments on the value of sharing one's time and possessions. A moment of silence follows and then the Lord's Prayer. When the prayer service ends, the door swings open and a Chicano couple enter asking for a notary public, the phones begin to ring, and another day in Indiantown commences.

At the local day care center and Head Start school we are greeted by the administrator, a cheerful black woman named Thelma. In the hallway of the modern one-story building a young woman rocks a small, stiff brown baby. The baby is blind, and her mother, who has four other children at home, is looking for a place to live. Thelma asks Sister Gannon if she knows of a place where they might go. "They are living with another family now," she explains, "in an area no bigger than this room. The situation is very bad." Sister Gannon shakes her head. She has heard this request often and is familiar with the lack of adequate housing and the number of people who seek it. "I know a place for three hundred dollars a month," she says, and Thelma sighs.

On the playground a large silver jungle gym equipped with tire swing, ladders, and chinning bars shines in the bright sunlight. Thelma's husband put it together, and she points with distress to parts of it that have been vandalized. There is a basketball court nearby, but the backboards have no hoops. "We had to take them down," Thelma says matter-of-factly. "The games got too rough and boisterous." She speaks openly and expressively about the problems she encounters daily. She understands the things poverty denies and the vicious response it sometimes engenders. "The parents have been beaten down for so long they no longer have the willingness or the initiative to try and make things better," she says. "There is a great acceptance of the status quo, but we do our best to give these children some of the tools they will need to compete on the outside, some sense that there is a better world." Both programs provide the children with two nutritious meals a day and lots of individual attention. Thelma expresses hope that the love and caring they experience will strengthen their sense of self-worth. "We can only start it here," she says on parting. "You tell them in Washington that we need more money."

A few blocks from the migrant day care and Head Start facilities is the Hope Rural School. This is the school that Joan Gannon and Sister Carol Putnam, another Sacred Heart nun, were asked to start when they came to Indiantown in 1978. The eighty-plus children who now attend the preschool and four academic grades are an enthusiastic mixture of boys and girls from a variety of Latino backgrounds.

"We have the great privilege of having children who are not bored," Sister Putnam says. "Primary children usually want to go to school, and to prove my point just the other day someone overheard one little boy saying to his friend, 'Hey, Luis, want to stay in for recess so we can get smarter quicker?' "

The large yellow school bus that stands in the curve of the road was a gift from the proceeds of Paul Newman's salad dressing business, for according to Sister Putnam, "the economics of running a school like this are very tenuous and make it dependent on private gifts and funding. We have great difficulties in raising funds because the resources are simply not in this town."

The parents pay twenty dollars a month when they can afford it, but when they cannot they bring in fruit that they have picked or do odd jobs at the school like washing windows and helping in the kitchen.

Sister Putnam tells of one family that broke out of the migrant cycle. The mother is now the school bus driver and the father has a maintenance job with a new housing project. "They were both picking tomatoes when we came, they were moving around constantly, but now that has all changed. The mother studied bookkeeping, learned to drive, and even to swim with the children in the school. Their quality of life has improved immeasurably and I know we are helping to change their lives. Education is the only way out, but it is a constant struggle. When we started we tried to motivate these people, to help them feel proud of themselves. They have always been at the bottom of the barrel. Our board wanted to give the children in the school everything new: new furniture, new textbooks, real china, because everything they had was secondhand. Now it doesn't matter so much, because the spirit is there, but in the beginning we wanted them to have the best."

The best has been transmitted beyond books, furniture, and china. The children at the Hope Rural School, the men and women who come to El Centro, and the babies in the day care center are represented in the actions of the young Mexican girl who called Sister Putnam from the bus station in mid-August several years ago to say she had come back to Indiantown from North Carolina, where her parents were picking tobacco, to join her class at the local public school. In touching one, the nuns help the hopelessness turn to hope.

At dinner Sister Gannon smokes a cigarette and muses on the changes that have taken place in the Society of the Sacred Heart since she entered it thirty years ago, the call of the Catholic Church to serve the needy and the oppressed, the broadened scope of the Society's view of education. "For me, the Gospel is so filled with those calls to strength, and it isn't just a call to the Children of the Sacred Heart, it is a call to all women to be women of the Gospel. I think that is what our schools should be about, be they traditional or otherwise: a call to strength and a call to faith. We must give our students something with which to face their lives, we must continue to instill conviction. I mind very much when I encounter kids from our schools and have the sense that the fiber has gone out of their training, the starch has wilted, something is missing. There must be a way to go back to a tradition of strong training that underlines those values."

In the twenty-fifth anniversary report published in May 1982, the members of the Manhattanville class of 1957 were asked to sum up their last twenty-five years in twenty-five words or less. Joan Gannon wrote: "What seems most accurate is simply that the last twenty-five years have represented, in my life, a process of heart-widening, simplification, and truth-seeking that have put me where I am right now and that promises to go until the day I die. The process has led me (or through the process God has led me) to want to stand with the poor and the marginalized in our world, to spend my time and my energy serving them and, as much as possible, to share my life with them. Our parish is in a small rural town surrounded by citrus groves, where migrant and seasonal farm workers eke out a living for themselves and their families. Their faith, their generosity, their courage are a constant challenge to me. We run a service center, encourage the growth of the United Farm Workers, worship with them, teach their children, teach them to teach themselves, and watch with awe as little by little they begin to take charge of their own lives. That's what I'd most like to do, what I am learning to do — empower these people with a belief in themselves and show them their gifts. I rejoice in the direction my religious family has taken, enjoy life more with each passing year. One of my greatest hopes would be that all of us Manhattanvillians would be women who work for peace and justice in this world."

Yet nothing stays the same forever, and being a religious in the Society of the Sacred Heart still means movement. In August 1986 Sister Gannon left Indiantown by request of her provincial, Sister Anne O'Neil. "It was a real test of my vocation," she says. "Certainly there was a lot of discussion about it because I felt very deeply committed to those people," but after much soul-searching and prayer she agreed to move on to another ministry in New York City, where she is continuing her commitment of service as a chaplain to the Hispanic community. She believes the Society, to be a contributing force in the world, must align itself with people in every economic stratum and in so doing meet the challenges of faith, instill the virtues of moral courage, and combat the inertia of timidity. "How else," she asks, "can we expect to survive?"

The Society's survival is indeed in question today. Although the majority of its members feel confident it will continue to have a role and voice in the Church and in the world for years to come, its worldwide population has been on the decline for the last twenty years. In 1967 there were 6,882 nuns and 223 novices in the Society, 1,039 of whom were American. In 1987 the worldwide figures had dropped to 4,900, with less than 700 Americans and only 5 in the Boston novitiate. These numbers reflect the loss experienced by many religious orders in the Catholic Church, both male and female, during the two decades that followed the Second Vatican Council. A few, such as the Immaculate Heart of Mary congregation to which Corita Kent, the artist, once belonged, lost more than two-thirds of their membership. Others ceased to exist altogether.

After the Vatican II changes were implemented, when lay people were permitted significant roles in the Church and religious women were given opportunities to participate in a variety of options within their vocations that were formerly unavailable to them, the draw of religious life, once the only choice for Catholic women who sought to spend their lives in religious service, was now only one choice among many. And there weren't many takers. Because many post–Vatican II religious orders were less rigid than they had been in the past and less inclined to be labeled as strictly dedicated to a specific task, they projected a sense of ambiguity and fragmentation that made them less desirable. "Why would a young woman want to throw in with an order that was in process of 'redefining itself'?" a Catholic priest asked recently. "Originally women's orders were founded to do specific things — to teach, nurse in hospitals, or be missionaries — but after Vatican II, when these vocations appeared to have run their course, many nuns felt they were free to find new identities, and as a result many orders suffered a significant loss of personnel and lost sight of their original missions." He went on to say, "There is a crisis in Catholic education today because of the vast exodus from religious life. Some women left because they no longer wanted to be a part of what their orders had become; others stayed but for all intents and purposes were removed both physically and spiritually from their communities."

This was true in the Society of the Sacred Heart, where many whose lives in the past had been compelling examples of dedication, strength, and resolve suddenly began pursuing selective, personal missions outside the institution. It seemed that when the going got easier in terms of structure and form, the tough got going, but in many cases in opposite directions. There was a sense of rejection mixed with rejuvenation that was off-putting to many and tragic to some. It was at this time that many Sacred Heart nuns began to demonstrate a sense of personal vanity, self-indulgence, and vulnerability that had not been evident in their lives before. Individuals were now discerning for themselves personal ministries relating to social justice, reform, and liberation. This did much to support the theory that they had all "gone to hell in a handbasket," as Sister Claire Kondolf put it. "Not," said a former student, "because they had taken up other causes and abandoned their work in the schools which they had run so beautifully, but because they embraced those causes so haphazardly. Their good intentions often got lost in their inability to make reasonable judgments during the reformation period." This was not entirely true, of course, for there were many who remained firmly committed to traditional education or who, like Joan Gannon, fought off worldliness and materialism and self-indulgence and went to places where the need was great and poverty was real. There was no denying the trauma and disappointment that resulted from the severing of old ties, the leveling or selling off of the old schools, and the rather cavalier attitude of many nuns who seemed so anxious to move away from the places and people of the

Two nuns in the transition habit that pinched the ears.

V V Harrison, captain of Eden Hall's field hockey team in 1960, sporting the blond streak she created to assert her individuality.

ABOVE *Goûter, the Sacred Heart snack.*

RIGHT *A typical Sacred Heart dormitory with white-curtained cubicles.*

BELOW *Students let off steam during a run at afternoon sports. Notice the gym suits and the coach.*

ABOVE *Eden Hall's graduating class of 1960. The author is fifth from the left in the top row.*

INSET *The infamous bell ringer wearing her blue ribbon.*

ABOVE *Stone Ridge Country Day School of the Sacret Heart, Bethesda, Maryland, one of the remaining nineteen Sacred Heart schools.*

RIGHT *Convent of the Sacred Heart, Noroton-on-the-Sound, Connecticut, the Society's most exclusive and smallest boarding school, where Buckley, Kennedy, and Ford women were educated.*

The Convent of the Sacred Heart on Ninety-first Street, New York City, where the author entered the cloister armed with Tootsie Roll Pops.

Convent of the Sacred Heart, Eden Hall, in Torresdale, Pennsylvania, where crosses rose from the roof and a tower clock struck off the hours in a doleful tone.

ABOVE *The chapel at Kenwood, the American novitiate, where the bride of Christ ceremony took place.*

INSET *Mother Mary Elizabeth Tobin visits with three white-veiled novices at Kenwood. Sister Anne Dyer, now headmistress at Stone Ridge Country Day School, is on her immediate left.*

TOP *Ann Morgan, left, the author's classmate, being greeted on her entrance to the Society by Mother Margaret Coakley, Mistress of Novices.*

CENTER *Novices praying in the chapel at Kenwood where they had received their white veils in the bride of Christ ceremony.*

BOTTOM *Novices studying at the Kenwood novitiate.*

A group of retired religious in their "do-it-yourself" habits.

Sister Anne O'Neil, whose six-year term as American provincial ended in 1987 and who was once Mistress General at Norton-on-the-Sound in Connecticut.

Students at Hope Rural School in Indiantown, Florida, which Sister Joan Gannon and Sister Carol Putnam founded in 1978 to educate children of migrant workers.

past that had once defined their vocation so explicitly. "The past is no longer relevant to us," one of them said recently. "That was then and this is now." The problem was twofold: a lack of communication on the part of the nuns, who assumed that their new life would automatically be accepted, and a judgmental nonacceptance of many of the changes by the alumnae. It was a family polarized, with tensions and emotions running high and deep.

When it was reported, through the Sacred Heart grapevine, that Mother So-and-So had left the Society and gotten married or left the Society and joined a commune or left the Society and become a salesperson in a department store, there was a sense of outrage, disbelief, and disillusionment among the alumnae, whose perception was that the Society of the Sacred Heart, the order Philippine Duchesne described as many heads in one bonnet, the order that had so effectively exemplified the virtues of moderation in all things and the value of discipline and renunciation, was now advocating radical reappraisal of that whole philosophy. Those who had looked to the Society as a model of orthodoxy and restraint watched its rejection of its historical character with anger and sadness. "But," says an outside observer, "most of that reaction was coming from a group of rich little boarding school girls who felt let down because their *noblesse oblige* training grounds were being liberated by reality."

"Liberated or eliminated," a Noroton graduate said recently, "I'll tell you one thing, it's still a real shock to run into one of your old nun teachers selling cosmetics at Lord and Taylor!"

Carol Neri Lembo, Manhattanville class of 1957, sits in the well-appointed living room of her Park Avenue duplex. She has a husband, two children, a maid, a weekend house in New Jersey, and a career as an educational counselor. Once she was Mistress of Novices at Kenwood, following in the footsteps of many prominent Sacred Heart nuns in the job that was one of the most influential the Society had to offer.

"When I entered the convent," she says, twisting a large diamond ring on her finger, "I believe there were one hundred novices. I think that the Society appealed to an intellectual Catholic woman, to someone who was seeking a union with God in a structured environment. When I was made Mistress of Novices in 1966, I was in my late twenties, and for me it was the perfect position because it allowed me to share the contemplative dimension of my vocation with the novices. I was also trained in psychological counseling, so I could help them balance their lives. As time went on I could see that the girls who were opting for religious life were primarily interested in the apostolic commitment, for it was during that time that the Society was redefining itself. The way the rule had formerly been lived out gave great emphasis to communal prayer three times a day, chanted in common. The religious planned their time to incorporate the spiritual aspect of their lives into their daily schedules, and I think that was essential in bringing each person back to the core of her vocation. As the evolution into the world began, when the habit was discarded, and people were beginning to have a variety of choices about the way they lived, when most of the communal and prayer life was being phased out, I could see the handwriting on the wall. I knew this would breed disaster, partly because of my own character and partly because it really was not the way I saw my commitment to the Society. I think the people who identify with the new life say, 'Life is your prayer and prayer is your life,' but I don't believe that. I believe your life can be prayerful, but prayer is prayer and the human being, being who she is, needs time to distance herself, to be alone and seek her God. I think that once you release the structure, once the discipline is dropped, so too goes the definition of what you are and who you are. You just can't release the structure and expect to keep an institution like the Society of the Sacred Heart intact."

As she continues to speak, her hands, now still, rest resolutely in her lap. Her legs are crossed at the ankles, and her sitting posture is perfect. As one of her former classmates at Manhattanville observed, "There are many things about Carol that still reflect her former life. In many ways she is still Mistress of Novices."

"Leaving the Society was the most painful, the most awful decision I have ever had to make in my life," she says softly, "but the one thing that kept me going was that I knew I had to be true to God and I knew I could not live the new life the Society was beginning to advocate. I simply don't think you can maintain an institution that was basically founded for the education of youth and allow those who enter it to become lawyers, doctors, social workers, secretaries, or whatever. I think those are all wonderful occupations in and of themselves, but if you allow too many choices, the institution begins to splinter and I fear that is what has happened. I just could not live the life of the Society as it moved away from the things I thought were essential to its definition. And yes, it was extremely difficult to leave from the position I held because I knew I was responsible for all these young religious who looked to me, who shared the commitment and the dedication, but on the other hand I also knew, in my heart of hearts, that if my leaving would shake anyone else to the point of leaving, that person should have left anyway."

Here perhaps is the most difficult and complex question of all. When is a vocation to religious life no longer a vocation? When it ceases to be personally fulfilling, meaningful, or fit a former perception? It was the question I asked most frequently as I interviewed countless Sacred Heart nuns and ex-nuns. Each time the answer was different. In the old days when one received the call, there was no question that after the period of training and indoctrination had been completed, after the unsuitable or unfit had washed out, after the vows of profession had been made, those who survived would stay forever, not because it was comfortable, convenient, or personally satisfying but because it was not. Those who had witnessed the life of a religious knew the price it exacted, knew it was a difficult, demanding, sacrificial life that did not come easily or cheaply. In many ways it was the ultimate example of living sacrifice. Not "I lay down my life for my fellow man" but I give my life, daily, freely, thoughtfully, and without reservation, for the benefit of others. It was a life inspirational to some and mysterious to others, but until the reforms of Vatican II it continued to attract women who were willing and in many cases eager to set themselves apart from the temptations and distractions of the world to devote themselves to a special role, one that was not popular, glamorous, or financially rewarding.

"Why would an attractive, intelligent, well-educated woman choose to lock herself away in a convent?" was the sixty-four-thousand-dollar question, and before 1967 the answer was simple: because she was called by God, because she was willing to replace the superficial with the supernatural, and because she desired to put her personal appetites aside to more closely align herself with a greater good. After the Second Vatican Council, that answer was no longer popular or even true. James Hitchcock, in his book *Catholicism and*

Modernity, wrote: "The possibility that God might will certain people to assume tasks they would rather shirk was implicitly denied." He describes a "therapeutic attitude," the precedence of "the desire to be fulfilled" over "the desire to serve," citing a 1975 survey in which "a majority of former nuns, asked why they had left the convent, gave 'inability to be me' as a major reason. It was the therapeutic attitude, also, which virtually destroyed certain religious communities," Hitchcock says, "by robbing them of whatever communal and transcendent purpose they may have had and turning them into mere collections of vaguely like-minded individualists." It seemed, in addition, to turn them away from God and onto themselves. The self that had so long been suppressed came out of the habit, out of the cloister, and out of the self-sacrificing mold, in many instances without the starch of conviction that had previously seemed so impervious to the therapeutic mentality that now threatened it. Perhaps because that self had not grown or matured, had been dependent and subservient for so long, it embraced all aspects of its new liberties with a self-indulgence that appeared self-serving, selfish, and uncontrolled.

The idea of a vocation to the religious life, in the way it had been lived by most women's orders, was viewed by outsiders as impractical, selfish, wasteful, and unnatural. After Vatican II it appeared that many women who had enthusiastically embraced, endorsed, and lived that type of vocation, who were impressive spokespeople for its values and precepts, now agreed with their critics. It was the "How Ya Gonna Keep 'Em Down on the Farm, After They've Seen Paree" phenomenon. As Ann Morgan, a former Sacred Heart nun and my classmate at Eden Hall, said, "Suddenly there was nobody in charge anymore, at least not in this country. There were no more superiors, there was no leadership, no being called forward, no being called back, there was really no one you were accountable to except yourself, and that was, in my opinion, a big mistake."

Within the Society of the Sacred Heart, as the exodus from the convent escalated, many and varied excuses were employed to explain the inexplicable. Many divorced women in particular were furious when they learned that nuns who had taken final vows, had received wedding rings, and were married to God could be released from those vows and could marry.

"Yes, I was a bit resentful," Mary Mooney, a Sacred Heart divor-

cée who raised two children alone, says. "After all, they were supposed to be married to God. I was only married to a mere mortal,
but under the rules of the Church I could not remarry. I thought, 'If
they can leave and get married, then I should be able to get an
annulment,' and I still think it is unfair that they can be released
from their vows and I can't. But what else is new? When the changes
first came in, I said, 'Well, there it goes, it's finished,' but then I
thought, 'I just don't care.' I am too old. I have been a Sacred Heart
girl too long, and I wouldn't care if they wore bikinis — it's still an
order filled with the Holy Spirit. Sacred Heart of Jesus, I put my
trust in you. I certainly couldn't put my trust in another guy."

"I think," says Sister Mary Bush, sitting in her bedroom in the
house she shares in Washington, D.C., with four other older nuns,
"that many of the people who left the Society did not have vocations
in the first place." Sister Elizabeth White, who at ninety-five is one
of the Society's most active and astute members, believes now that it
is possible to be called to religious life for a finite amount of time
and then leave to pursue other vocations. "A religious vocation is a
very special thing," Sister Bush explains. "It combines the human
with the divine, and I think there will always be vocations to religious life. Perhaps they will be a different sort, but certainly there
will always be women who want to give themselves to God and to
the Society of the Sacred Heart." She admits that figures for admissions are dismal in this country, at approximately five a year, but
points out that the women who are signing up today are older,
better qualified and better educated in the ways of the world than
ever before. "Most have followed a profession, have had to reflect
on the sacrifices still required, and have a far better idea of what
they want to do with the rest of their lives and why."

Sister Bush and her housemates live on a tree-lined street in a
working-class district of northeast Washington. Each has a firm
idea of what she wants and why. They are involved in separate
ministries and draw salaries. One works for the National Gallery of
Art, another is involved in a shopping program for the elderly, and
all do work at the local parish school and church. Sister Bush is
affiliated with an institute for the aging. Before joining the Society
of the Sacred Heart she was a social worker and now finds she is
able to do the work she was trained for and loved. Her salary, like
those of all Sacred Heart nuns who earn money (the vast majority

are self-supporting), is sent back to the provincial house in St. Louis. Those who teach in the schools are paid on a par with other private school teachers. Expense money is allotted to each member of the community for self-maintenance and incidentals. The rest goes to support places like Kenwood, where those who can no longer fend for themselves are cared for.

Sister Anne Dyer, headmistress at Stone Ridge Country Day School in Maryland, says, "I don't see the salary I get or negotiate for it. I am hired by the board of trustees and I can be fired by them. The money makes absolutely no more difference in my life than it did fifteen years ago. A check goes out every month from Stone Ridge to the province and an allowance comes back which is essentially less than five thousand dollars a year."

Still there are conflicts and inconsistencies. The vows of poverty, chastity, and obedience are far more ambiguous than they once were, as the ways of the world have crept into community life and the edges that once so crisply defined it have been blurred. Some Sacred Heart nuns who come from wealthy families or have benefactors are gifted with clothes, cars, tickets to travel, and other extras that make their lives seem more worldly and less equal than others'. Friendships have developed between the sexes (mainly between nuns and priests) that have all the hallmarks of romance, though few admit to sexual intimacy, and there are rumors, too, of close relationships between members of the same sex in some communities.

"Certainly there are nuns," said one Sacred Heart religious, who asked not to be identified, "who go out dancing, wear makeup and jewelry, have their hair done, buy expensive clothes, even smoke and drink too much. But I think they are the exceptions to the rule. It only takes a couple of rotten apples to make the barrel smell, but to my mind most are extremely dedicated and committed women who hold strongly to their vows and to the principles of commitment to religious life. They have reached out to involve themselves in a number of worthy causes."

These are the ones who have successfully made the transition from the cloister to the active life, who work in housing projects and day care centers, parish schools and prisons, who are advocates for change, who speak out against inequity and oppression, who share their knowledge and experience and offer their lives for a single soul, no longer in isolation but in partnership with a host of other like-minded individuals. Some are militant and await the day the Vatican approves women priests. Sister O'Neil says there are a number of Sacred Heart nuns who would qualify for the priesthood today, but under the present pope the possibility of those qualifications being translated into ordination is slim to none. Others are content with their roles as women of service, who willingly and actively answer the call in a variety of capacities.

In their convents, in their cloistered cocoon, they projected an image, real or imagined, of quality, of grace, of integrity, unity, and dignity that is missing from their image today. They are more than individualistic now; they are individuals, grappling with the rest of the world in the nitty-gritty details of survival, seeking personal worth, fulfillment, and growth. This is more admirably demonstrated by some than by others, but for each it is still an offering of each day for the betterment not just of the Children of the Sacred Heart but of all of God's children.

"We were never perfect," Sister O'Neil reminded me in the provincial house in St. Louis.

"But you seemed more perfect in the old days," I replied, "and I don't think you can say it was all tied up in the nonessentials, in the habits or the setting or the routine."

She smiled tolerantly and shook her head. "Many things are not what they seem, especially those you remember as a child. You saw something you admired, but just because you cannot make the same identification today does not mean the same spirit of love and dedication is not there. There are still great numbers of exceptional women in the Society today offering their lives every day for the sake of people all over the world. You must not discount their efforts just because they no longer fit the pattern you were used to seeing."

In a sense she was right, but I was right too, and the perfection I was speaking about was not all bound up in past images, in the things that were deemed the nonessentials and so easily discarded, although some of it certainly was. It was more a perception of perfection that lived through the people who had committed themselves to the principles and the character of the Society of the Sacred Heart, and when the character of the Society changed, broke away from the fortresses on the hills, so it seemed did many of its members. If it was unrealistic to think it could remain the same, retain its stuff when the patterns began to shift, then it was equally unrealistic to think that those who were part of it could hold to the structure that dictated the lofty standards of perfection when those standards had ceased to be imposed and became questions of choice.

"There was a big problem within the Society in terms of unity. For a time — and I think it continues today — it seemed as if every nun had a different idea about how things should be, both in the schools and in the Society, a different view of what religious life was all about, and a different method of living out her personal vision," a former student from the Rosary Academy of the Sacred Heart in New Orleans points out. "It was bad enough when the former nun headmistress of our school left to marry a student's father and set-tled down in the community, but in a sense that was just the tip of the iceberg. During the time of experimentation the nuns at the Rosary allowed a jukebox to be put in the cafeteria of the school, an icebox and TV in the senior lounge, and they seemed perfectly con-tent to let the girls watch soap operas all day instead of going to class. I really think they went off the deep end. My daughter went to the Rosary from 1968 to 1982 and if there was ever a horrible experience, she had it. Her class was wild. There were sixty-four of them and they got such little education and so little religion it was pitiful. Over the course of fourteen years I would find out incre-mentally that they no longer had devotion to the Sacred Heart, that they no longer said a prayer to the Holy Spirit, that they no longer said the Morning Offering or had *primes*. They never wrote the parents a letter saying, 'We are giving up this or that,' we just got wind of it through our child, who said, 'Oh, Mother, we don't do those things anymore. They are ancient history.' I am telling you," she continued, "what we all went through down here was a lot worse than the French Revolution and I don't think it's over yet. Just this spring I went with two others to the headmistress's house for dinner during Lent and we were the only ones observing the fasting. The nuns were passing around beer, wine, fried chicken, and chocolate cookies, and I kept saying no thank you, but to them it was just another jolly time. If there was one thing they used to represent, it was a disciplined life lived with good taste. They sure seem to have forgotten about that. Now it's anything that tastes good."

Sister Peggy Brown, the present headmistress of the school in New Orleans, thinks the wrinkles, which she acknowledges were present during the years of transition, have mostly been ironed out. She acknowledges the pain and anguish that occurred in many Sacred Heart schools, both here and abroad, during the late sixties and early seventies when the nuns began to acquiesce to student pressure for a more relevant lifestyle, when the Society as well as the Church was attempting to reevaluate its place in the world. But she is quick to point out that much of the Society's uncertainty reflected the changing culture of the times. She hopes there will always be a nun headmistress in each of the remaining Sacred Heart schools in this country, but given the low number of applications to the Society of the Sacred Heart she admits that that might not be a reasonable expectation. "We just have to trust the spirit of St. Madeleine Sophie to do whatever is necessary to help us continue whatever is worth continuing. One hundred eighty-seven years is a very small piece of history, and we are not essential to history. The trappings are different now and the children who come here to school do not live in a closed society like those who came in the past. They don't see religious life like you used to see it in the schools, so we have to make a special effort to give them little views of our lives, like inviting them to one of our communities for supper during Lent, sharing a simple meal, and praying."

What constitutes a simple meal during Lent, like what defines a Sacred Heart nun today, is far more complicated than it was when the children in the schools did not know what the nuns ate during Lent but speculated that it was probably bread and water.

"There is a lot of nontruth in community life today," Ann Morgan, who officially left the Society in 1986 but retained her job as an associate dean of student development at Boston College, told me. "There are a lot of nuns living on money that they don't earn, and there are lot living by themselves, pursuing vocations that are really quite singular. When you do have groups living together, you have all the same problems you would if you were still living at home with your parents. There are older people who have one idea about how the house should be run and younger ones who have different ideas. You can't sit at a dining room table without hearing the most incredible complaints about other people. When the rule of silence was in effect, that precluded a lot of gossip and lack of charity, which I would say has really gone out the window now. I think the spirit of mutuality has evaporated in the Society and been replaced by competitiveness and pettiness. A nun from Miami once confided to me that in the days she was at Eden Hall, under the old regime, she had been a member of an A team, but now she felt she was a member of a B team, and I think that says volumes."

Marcia Whelan, another ex–Sacred Heart nun who lives and works in Miami, felt many of the same inconsistencies and the lack of accountability in her post–Vatican II religious life that Ann Morgan described.

"There was nothing I wanted more than to be a Sacred Heart nun," she recalls, "but I thought the community really did have to hold you accountable for the way you were living, living the Gospel, living community life, and living the essence of the educational mission. But as the changes began to infiltrate various communities, it seemed to me that all those things went by the board. In my last six months at Carrollton [the Sacred Heart school in Miami], we didn't even pray together. I could be off doing whatever I chose and it didn't seem to matter. So it really became a boarding house existence. There I was, living in this beautiful mansion on Biscayne Bay, spending my weekends by the pool and eventually somewhere else, relating more to people on the outside than on the inside. Nobody wanted to call anybody accountable or impose her point of view. There was a very definite live-and-let-live attitude that for me made no sense. I left because that was not my vocation. I remember a Jesuit priest saying to me a few years ago — and his mother had gone to a Sacred Heart school — 'They have lost the sense of being a family,' and that is what it meant to be part of the Sacred Heart."

Mary Ellen Pohl received her Sacred Heart habit on January 6, 1966, just one year before the special chapter in 1967 that implemented the decrees of Vatican II. She remembers the moment when she learned that the Society would no longer be cloistered. "It came as a great shock to me," she says, "because I had entered this order with a great tradition and I liked it the way it was. I thought, for instance, that the habit had a symbolic value that is not replaced by pins or crosses worn on civilian clothes. I said over and again, because I was elected to provincial chapters where these things were being discussed, that I thought something would ultimately be lost in the abandonment of so many of the old traditions, but I might as well have been talking to the wind. In 1968 we fell into an activism that was and still is a problem. It was true that a certain rigidity had crept into the Society after St. Madeleine Sophie's death, and the new attitude seemed to be 'Let's get rid of all that and then reread the foundress's works and restructure our lives accordingly,' but it didn't result in any new traditions coming about, and the changes just continued. The leadership was in a very difficult position, the troops were restless, and in tampering with the structure I don't think much thought was given to what was worth retaining. There was great eagerness to go with the experimentation and see what it would bring. Liberation thinking was beginning to make itself known, and since the schools had a reputation of being elite, that was just another conflict. In general, I would say, it was just not well thought out. When the doors are suddenly opened, there is this great temptation to do and not to think. In many cases they were trying to create a social miracle, like bringing black children from a totally different environment to Noroton. It didn't have a prayer of working; still, it was done with good intentions." In 1984 Mary Ellen Pohl left the Society of the Sacred Heart and two years later married Judge Robert Bork, President Reagan's recently rejected Supreme Court nominee. Their wedding was at St. Matthew's Cathedral in Washington, and Mary Ellen wore a white wedding dress when she walked down the aisle. Several Sacred Heart nuns attended the ceremony and the reception afterward.

For all intents and purposes, the tangible identity of the old Society of the Sacred Heart, dedicated almost exclusively to institutional education, is gone, for running schools is now only one part of the Sacred Heart dedication, which includes working for peace, equality, freedom, and social justice. For women like Ann Morgan, Marcia Whelan, Peggy Daley, Mary Ellen Pohl, Carol Neri, and a host of others who watched the Society they loved disassemble, the experience of leaving it, witnessing the splintering effects the changes wrought, in many ways was analogous to the death of a loved one. There were fond memories of what had been, sadness in separation, and a personal resolve to go forward to seek a future that for each would be different and impossible to have imagined on the day they entered the novitiate at Kenwood. That same sense of loss was felt by the alumnae, who in many instances lost not only their schools and colleges but also important friendships with women to whom they were strongly devoted and who, at a crucial time in their education, had shown them that there was more to life than pleasuring oneself. But where there were disappointment and disillusionment in the struggle to live up to the challenges of the new personal freedom, there was also the need to live down the inevitable criticisms of the perceived incompatibility of religious life without walls. But alongside all that were also rebirth, readjustment, and renewed commitment by the many nuns who recognized that the essence of their vocation to the Society of the Sacred Heart was in the spirit of bearing witness to the same educative dedication that St. Madeleine Sophie began in nineteenth-century France. The difference was that now that commitment was being lived in a variety of ways, in a variety of communities throughout the world, no longer in an institutional setting with a universal Plan of Studies, but in diverse settings, academic, professional, and missionary.

"People disassemble, not orders," says Grace Schrafft, "and as long as the Society of the Sacred Heart has people like Mother Carmody in it, and it has many like her, I think it will continue to make valuable contributions to the world. The fact that the nuns left the convent and the habit and some chose to help the poor or involve themselves in causes beyond the nice little sodalities of Sacred Heart women doesn't mean that the majority who remain are rudderless, self-centered, and unproductive." Today there are Sacred Heart nuns living, teaching, and working in Argentina and Uruguay, Australia and New Zealand, Belgium, Brazil, Canada, Chile, Colombia, Egypt, England and Wales, France, Germany, India, Ireland and Scotland, Italy, Japan, Korea, Malta, Mexico, the Netherlands, Peru, Poland, Puerto Rico, Spain, Uganda, the United States, Venezuela, and Zaire — living in ghettos and barrios, in sophisticated cities and developing countries, participating in the full range of life experiences, linked with lay people in the Catholic Church and outside it, in an ongoing effort to contribute to the education of all people, not just an elite minority, to sow hope, do justice, and combat ignorance.

"The glory of God finds its highest expression," St. Madeleine Sophie once said, "in the salvation of souls." Sacred Heart nuns are still involved in that universal mission, among many, among few, and in some instances alone. They are doctors and lawyers, filmmakers and fund-raisers, secretaries and nurses, counselors and teachers. They are still women of giftedness and women of God who seek to improve the lot of others by dedicating themselves to those who need them most.

Ten years ago, four religious of the Sacred Heart made a new foundation in Cairo, Egypt, in a poor village called Ghanayem. They learned a new language and new customs, confronted illiteracy, poverty, and sickness, spent their days and nights offering themselves and their knowledge to help those who had nothing, following St. Madeleine Sophie's ideal of "working for justice with the heart of an educator." The missionary aspect of the Society of the Sacred Heart continues to be a primary element of the Society's work and a popular ministry. Sister O'Neil thinks the Society will survive through its vocations from Latin America and Spain, where, unlike the United States, religious life is still attracting a substantial number of young women.

As the Society of the Sacred Heart once stood apart from the world, and some would say apart from the common person in its monastic separatism, it has now joined with the Catholic Church in an active, apostolic life of service. It has fewer members, more communities, fewer academies, more reality, less ritual, and more resourcefulness as it continues to search for newer and more appropriate ways of responding to the increasing needs of the people it serves. It remains to be seen whether the manner it has chosen to accomplish those goals will prove as productive, as memorable, as influential, or as long-lived as the manner it used in the past. Whether lay people can impart the same sense of devotion or singular dedication in the surviving Sacred Heart schools that the nuns once did as a unified body, whether the nuns themselves can hold to a personally enforced spiritual life within the secular ones they now enjoy, and whether the Society of the Sacred Heart, in moving away from so many of the structured elements of its previous existence, can create a new form of religious life that will prove equally effective are still evolving questions.

Perhaps the Society will take inspiration from Rose Philippine Duchesne, the Society's first missionary, whose adventuresome spirit and indomitable will so deeply influenced the first American Children of the Sacred Heart and who on July 3, 1988, became the Society's second saint. With her as its model, perhaps the Society will find that the challenge of its future and the value of its past still lie in the loyalty and affection of those it touched and seeks to touch, in the unity of purpose that created an unforgettable and powerful family of the heart that from its foundation derived its strength in love. For, as Robert Nisbet wrote in *The Twilight of Authority*, "the family, not the individual, is the real molecule of society, the key link in the social chain of being."

E·P·I·L·O·G·U·E

◐ IN THE FALL of 1984 I received a phone call. A familiar voice boomed out from the other end, "This is Martine Ward McGuiness and I just wanted you to know that our Eden Hall twenty-fifth reunion is coming up, and we expect you to be there."

"Be where?" I asked, knowing that Eden Hall had closed in 1969 and had been demolished sometime later.

"We are having it at Ninety-first Street and we are starting now because we want a good turnout."

The conversation continued as Martine, who had been one of my roommates in senior year, sketched out plans for the forthcoming event, laughingly reminding me, "Since you are writing a book about the way it was, it will be a perfect opportunity to see what has happened since we left school."

I assured her I would be there, and she assured me she would keep me informed of the particulars. Throughout the following months, Martine, with the help of another former roommate, Barbara Weiss Visser, became a master detective, tracking down the names and addresses of our thirty classmates, who were spread across the country and around the world. Since Eden Hall had closed, there had been no newsletters or updates of people's whereabouts, so it was a formidable task. In January 1985 Barbara wrote to say that they had found ninety percent of the class and most had expressed enthusiasm about coming to New York in the spring.

We were not a particularly close group; we were eclectic, geographically and sociologically diverse, and, as is often true in boarding school, joined forces more out of need than choice.

In our senior yearbook, under the heading "Class History," it is written: "The fourth of June arrives as does the fourth of June of any other year; we leave and become the yesterday of Eden Hall. We were not an outstanding class; however, each one of us carries a precious seed of love, a shared experience, uniquely ours, and a sense of belonging to a special family."

As literary editor I had attempted to convey something of the Sacred Heart experience that may be lost in the hyperbole of youth and in the inexperience of expression. Still, there was a truth in those lines, a truth that, as it turned out, brought two-thirds of a ragtag class back to see each other long after that school had ceased to exist and the nuns who had taught them had changed habits and the paths of their lives had taken them far away from Torresdale, Pennsylvania, far away from each other.

They came from Venezuela, California, Florida, and Texas, with curiosity, cloudy memories, and personal insecurities. Some came in fear and trembling, others cloaked in the symbols of success, but they came because the seed of love had blossomed and etched lines of compassion and understanding in their faces and created an affection for each other that could not have existed without the passage of time.

Ann Morgan, who was president of our class always and president of the school in senior year, signed up to be a Sacred Heart nun three years after graduation. It was rumored at the time of the reunion that after twenty-two years she had taken a leave of absence from the Society. In 1983, in response to a note I had sent her, she had written me a long letter detailing her life as a liberated nun in Boston.

"I am living in a large, white, Victorian mansion, two blocks from my office, with four other nuns. It is a great house and I love entertaining in it and living in it. I love running and hope to do the Boston Marathon [which she did]. I play golf with the Boston College golf league every week. My ski legs are great and I spend as many hours as possible coming down the mountains of New Hampshire in the winter." At the end she said simply, "Religious life has been a strange trip the past twelve years because of all the changes, but I was young enough not to feel the sting some of our older nuns have. Thank God we left the black cloth and the cloister!"

Now I was anxious to see her again and to talk with her, to find out why her perceptions changed and why the life she described so enthusiastically just a few years earlier was no longer appealing.

Grace Schrafft, who flew in from California to attend the weekend event, laughs nervously as we walk across Park Avenue on our way to the apartment of Kathy Morgan Geri (Ann Morgan's sister), where our class is to assemble for dinner.

"I hope someone is fat like me," Grace says, and I tell her not to worry because I have heard that Katy Kennedy Bumgardner is eight months pregnant. Across the street we spot Susie August Abell, who is not fat but whose walk is unmistakable. The three of us amble toward Kathy's apartment building, shaking our heads, laughing, each attempting to disguise her nerves and appear calmly in control. We get into the elevator and are surprised to find that the elevator man knows just what floor and apartment number we want.

"This is it," Grace hisses before Susie pushes the doorbell, and I feel my heart rate speed up.

When the door swings open there is Ann Morgan, who most certainly would not be in attendance if the Second Vatican Council had not intervened. Ann still looks and sounds much as she did in 1960: short, blond, trim, deep-voiced. Instantly Grace envelops her in a giant hug.

Heads turn as we make our entrance. There is Ricky Dollenberg McLaughlin, Jane Priory Gummere, Louise Majewski Dunleavy, all former day students at Eden Hall, and Bonnie Malloy Fitzpatrick and Mary Lou Kelly Geghan, who were boarders. Most of us have not seen each other for twenty-five years and we grab hold of each other and jump for joy. Ann is trying to solicit drink orders but we are all too busy exchanging compliments and asking questions. The doorbell rings out again, signaling the arrival of another group, and the decibel level is deafening as Maggie Maher Dick, Katy Kennedy Bumgardner, and Maita Sanchez come in. Grace rushes to Katy, for whom she named her only child, and although Katy is large with child, they dance around the room like Rogers and Astaire. The next contingent includes Martine and Barbara, then Sheila Haines Sharpe, Clara Triay Moreno, and Clarissa Bullos. Clarissa informs us that on learning of the reunion only two days ago, Aura Boccheciampe has flown up from Caracas to join us tonight. Then Aura too comes through the door and we all applaud. The last to arrive is Nancy Whelan Diaz, which seems appropriate because

Nancy holds the distinction of being the only one in the class to have actually run away from school. She snuck down to the Torresdale train depot one afternoon after sports and was gone long before her absence was discovered. Even though her parents returned her the following day, many of us admired her spunk and courage, and although we were told by the nuns that she had done a wicked thing, she remained a convent cult hero for many weeks.

So here we are, crammed in a room together after so many years, so many bridges crossed, and my mind and my mouth are moving so rapidly there is no time to ponder or assess. It is like being given a huge ice cream cone and a prescribed amount of time in which to consume it. Here are the kids of yesterday with whom I lived for three years, whose faces and personalities were as firmly imprinted in my mind as my own family's, posing as grownups as if for a school pageant. A touch of gray here, a line or two there, and I wonder if they feel as mystified and as delighted as I do.

Grace, locked in a corner with Katy, shouts to me to get my camera and begin shooting pictures. Obedient as always, I wrench myself away from Mary Lou and Jane and begin. Through the lens I get another perspective, freezing moments for posterity, turning the present into the past each time I press the shutter button.

Kathy Geri's refrigerator door swings open and shut as bottles of beer and wine are removed. In the kitchen someone begins to sing the Alma Mater: ". . . a song of love and pledge of loyalty that will never fade away, the spirit thou hast given will triumph over all and now forever be our victor, Alma Mater Eden Hall." Shouts of "Oh no" rebound from the living room, and then more songs until Ann calls a halt.

We speak of tomorrow's official activities. Mass and brunch at the Ninety-first Street school, where we will be joined by four nuns from our school days: Mothers Tobin, Bush, Carmody, and Holmes. Some people move to a table and scoop up plates of lasagna, others stand empty-handed, too engrossed in conversation to notice.

I tell Aurita how impressed I am that she traveled such a long distance to be here, and she says she wouldn't have missed it for the world because "I loved Eden Hall, I loved every minute of it for five years, and I will never understand why so many say they hated it. I learned so much there — how to form an idea, how to think logically, which helps in my law practice — " I interrupt her, and ask her to recall an especially memorable school day, and she replies, "The third day of geometry class when I understood the principles of how it worked."

"Well," I say with a sigh, "it was just the opposite with me. After the twenty-third class I still didn't understand how it worked." And Aurita shakes her perfectly coiffed head and says, "*Ay,* V V."

Martine sits on the couch, a bottle of Molson's in hand, and announces that her husband, John, has instructed her not to come home without asking each person what she viewed as the most valuable thing she learned at Eden Hall. Grace turns on my tape recorder and passes it around. "Survival," says one; "how to curtsy," says another; "tolerance," says Ann Morgan, "because in sophomore year I had to room with V V."

The first to leave are Clara and Clarissa, with whom I have had little time to converse, and then Jane, who says she will not be joining us tomorrow as she must return to children and husband. I feel a sudden surge of sadness in the realization that I might never see her again, a thought that never entered my mind twenty-five years ago when all things seemed possible and the journey had just begun.

Martine is still trying to elicit information for her husband's edification. "He's a real intellectual," she explains, and Grace rolls her eyes and retorts, "Yes, darling, just like you."

The day is cool and overcast in New York. The Sunday sounds of the city are muted, and so are we. Once inside the great marble entrance hall at Ninety-first Street, we pick out our name tags from a multitude of others, for today's celebration is not ours alone but will include several other reunion classes. As people stream in through the heavy double doors, the greeting process begins again. Grace spots Mother Carmody, who is wearing a gray suit and looks slightly schoolmarmish with her short hair and glasses, and embraces her as others push forward to do the same.

"Isn't this wonderful," Mother Carmody observes rhetorically. "Oh, Mother, it is!" Grace exclaims and then looks over at me and whispers, "Just look at her, she's still so holy and sweet." This time I nod my head in agreement.

In the chapel Grace and Katy sit with Mother Carmody (we all still call our old nuns "Mother," which like many of the old traditions we find hard to give up). I join Ann and Sheila near the middle. As the organ begins to play softly, I feel a tap on my shoulder and look behind to discover Mothers Tobin and Bush, who have driven up from Washington for the day. They quickly slip into the pew behind us and Mass begins.

I have attended few Catholic Masses since the liturgy changed and find it strange to witness a ceremony I knew so intimately in Latin and not at all in English. It appears a more abbreviated version of the one we endured every morning of our lives at Eden Hall and, to me, less inspiring. My attention, much like in the old days, is not focused on the altar but, as Mother Carmody put it, on the wonder of the day.

There is a break in the middle of the new Mass when the kiss of peace is exchanged, when like passengers on a cruise ship you turn around and shake hands with or kiss your neighbor. The organ is playing the first notes of Mother Janet Stuart's hymn "Spirit Seeking Light and Beauty" as I turn awkwardly and brush my cheek against Ann's and then to the row behind, where Mother Bush leans forward and kisses me. Barbara and Susie look somewhat uncomfortable in their seats beside the nuns who once ruled their lives. Now dressed in high-heeled shoes and tailored suits, the nuns are but half as stylish as they were in their habits, and since we have only recently encountered them as people of the world it is difficult to keep from staring.

Voices join the music and hardly anyone glances at the paper in her hands with the words printed out. I look over at Grace, who is now wiping her eyes. Ann sticks an elbow in my side and whispers, "There she goes," and Grace slips out of her pew and walks down the chapel aisle hugging people at random, a smile on her face and tears cascading down her cheeks. "There's no one more sentimental than an old rebel," Ann remarks.

After communion the Mass accelerates rapidly to a close. We stand for the final blessing and hear the organ strike up the familiar chords to the song we have all been waiting for, the one sung in almost every Sacred Heart school by generations of students but now packed away with so many of the other cherished traditions of the past. They dusted it off for us and I am glad. No one needs the printed words for this one. "Jesus be our King and Leader / Grant us in Thy toils a part, / Are we not Thy chosen soldiers / Children of Thy Sacred Heart."

The song ends, the moment moves on, and so do we. Aurita must leave to catch a plane back to her country. As she waves good-bye Katy's eyes fill with tears and she shares this story.

"The night before graduation, Aurita said, 'Even if we never see each other again, just look up at the stars and think of me, because I will be looking at them and thinking of you.' " "Have you done it?" I inquire, and Katy answers, "All the time."

We eat our omelets and sip our wine as the afternoon sun drops down onto the parquet floor of the ornate dining room, knowing our time together is drawing to a close. We discover that a third of us are divorced, the vast majority have children, one has cancer, and one has been in prison. We have jobs and hobbies, friends and debts, most of us still consider ourselves Catholics, many of us say we are more liberal and less judgmental than we were in 1960, and all of us would like more time together to get beyond the superficial, to probe the unseen, to experience the strange familiarity that binds us, the memories that are so precious to some and ambivalent to others. Mother Holmes, who is in her eighties and is descended from Oliver Wendell Holmes, remains the wonderful, jolly Santa Claus figure we loved, and although she spent most of her time at Eden Hall teaching at the parish school, she remembers us, more vaguely than we remember her, but it is enough to make her a part of the celebration. We all share a sense of loss that our school is gone, and there are a variety of opinions regarding the changes in the Society. Someone says it was more a spirit than a place anyway, but admits it would be nice to have been there today and to have seen not just four but all the nuns who had once been our Mothers.

When it is time to leave, there are a few tears, a lot of hugs, and vague promises to write and visit. Perhaps another gathering in five years, but in all probability none of these.

We were sent to Eden Hall to grow and learn. We left with varying degrees of knowledge, ambitions, and dreams. Some have succeeded in attaining their youthful goals. I have become a writer, Ann a nun, Aurita a lawyer, and Grace a journalist. There were those whose thoughts had been only of children and family, and their hopes too have been realized. We have been involved in challenging endeavors, have come up against our share of success, failure, and sorrow, yet so much of life has not turned out the way we envisioned it or the way the nuns laid it out for us in their carefully drawn St. Madeleine Sophie blueprints. We have struggled against personal demons, with our faith in God and in other people, have encountered transition, disappointment, and compromise. And when we succeeded in overcoming, or moving away, or beginning again, there have been no blue ribbons, no Très Bien cards, no guard of honor to reward us. For Eden Hall was only a preparation for life, and once outside its protective custody we were fair game for the real thing.

Milan Kundera in his book *The Unbearable Lightness of Being* writes: "In the sunset of dissolution, everything is illuminated by the aura of nostalgia." This is especially true in remembering the places of one's childhood. The houses are bigger there, the days longer, the sun closer and brighter. Events remembered are splashed with color, the contours are hazy, the action quick. For what is memory is part invention, and what is fantasy is part reality. Pulled through a photographic time machine, processed in the darkroom of the subconscious, and stored in the archives of the mind, the mundane is cataloged with the majestic, the mercurial with the mystical, and, like Peter Pan, we sprinkle ourselves with stardust and fly back to the castles of our dreams.

In a red gym suit and navy blue sweater I stand on the hockey field at Eden Hall. Leaves from giant oak trees cover the ground and a cool autumn wind whips my cheeks. The huge brownstone edifice stands behind me. I watch the action of my teammates, hear the cracking of wooden hockey sticks as they flash in the dusk. Nuns in black woolen shawls pulled tightly around their habits silently walk the pathways in prayer. The tower clock strikes four. In the distance I hear the low, mournful whistle of an approaching train. Through dark, spidery tree branches I peer beyond the hockey field to see the silver tops of passenger cars rumbling by on their way south.

I think of my home, warm and comforting, my parents and friends, and of the endless days that must pass before I see them. My eyes fill with tears and for a moment I am sad, but as the train moves away I am drawn back into the fray of competition and my thoughts of home recede as I run out to meet the ball.

Next month, next year, or in a thousand tomorrows I will begin to understand the jumbled emotions which ebb and flow from this time and place and why, when it has vanished, I will value the experience so intensely and cherish the shadows of lightness it casts over all the days of my life.

B·I·B·L·I·O·G·R·A·P·H·Y

Bernstein, Marcelle. *The Nuns*. Philadelphia: J. B. Lippincott, 1976.

Callan, Louise, R.S.C.J. *Philippine Duchesne*. Westminster, Md.: The Newman Press, 1957.

Cunningham, Ruth, R.S.C.J. *Life Through 125 Years*. Privately published by the Society of the Sacred Heart, 1978.

Goodwin, Doris Kearns. *The Fitzgeralds and the Kennedys: An American Saga*. New York: Simon & Schuster, 1987.

Hendrickson, Paul. *Seminary: A Search*. New York: Summit Books, 1983.

Hitchcock, James. *Catholicism and Modernity*. New York: Seabury Press, 1979.

Magraw, Roger. *France 1815–1914*. New York: Oxford Press, 1986.

McCarthy, Mary. *Memories of a Catholic Girlhood*. New York: Harcourt Brace, 1957.

Monahan, Maud, R.S.C.J. *Life and Letters of Janet Stuart*. New York: Longmans, Green, 1957.

———. *Saint Madeleine Sophie*. New York: Longmans, Green, 1936.

O'Leary, Mary. *Education with a Tradition*. New York: Longmans, Green, 1936.

Quinlan, Mary, R.S.C.J. *Mabel Digby — Janet Erskine Stuart*. Privately published by the Society of the Sacred Heart, United States Province, 1984.

Reeves, Sally Kittredge. *Legacy of a Century*. Walsworth Press, 1987.

Spirit and Plan of Studies in the Society of the Sacred Heart. Farnborough, England: St. Michael's Abbey Press, 1958.

Theroux, Phyllis. *California and Other States of Grace*. New York: Fawcett Crest Books, 1980.

Valentine, Christine. *Convent of the Sacred Heart, New York City, 1881–1981*. Privately published by the Alumnae Association of the Sacred Heart, New York, 1981.

White, Antonia. *Frost in May*. New York: Dial Press, 1933.

Wills, Garry. *Bare Ruined Choirs*. Garden City, N.Y.: Doubleday, 1972.

Williams, Margaret. *Saint Madeleine Sophie*. New York: Herder and Herder, 1925.

———. *Second Sowing: Mary Aloysia Hardey*. New York: Sheed and Ward, 1972.

———. *The Society of the Sacred Heart: History of a Spirit*. London: Darton, Longman, Todd, 1978.

Wilson, Prue, R.S.C.J. *My Father Took Me to the Circus*. London: Darton, Longman, Todd, 1984.

I·N·D·E·X

A·B·O·U·T T·H·E A·U·T·H·O·R

V V Harrison grew up in Camden, South Carolina, and was educated at the Convent of the Sacred Heart, Eden Hall, near Philadelphia. She has been a contributor to the *Washington Post Magazine, The Washingtonian, Best of the Post,* and *American Home* and coauthored with Raymond Mason *Confusion to the Enemy.* She lives in Washington, D.C.